Managing InfoTech in School Library Media Centers

Managing

InfoTech

in School Library Media Centers

Laurel A. Clyde

1999
Libraries Unlimited, Inc.
Englewood, Colorado

Dedicated to Patricia Hand,
who has taken the role of proofreader to new heights.

Libraries Unlimited, Inc.
P.O. Box 6633
Englewood, CO 80155-6633
1-800-237-6124
www.lu.com

Library of Congress Cataloging-in-Publication Data

Clyde, Laurel.
    Managing infotech in school library media centers / Laurel A. Clyde.
        p. cm.
    Includes bibliographical references and index.
    ISBN 1-56308-724-3
    1. School libraries--United States--Data processing. 2. Libraries--United
States--Special collections--Electronic information resources. 3. Instructional materials
centers--United States--Data processing. 4. Electronic information resources--United
States. I. Title.

Z675.S3 C623 1999
027.8′0285--dc21   99-033116

Contents

v

List of Illustrations

Figure

Figure

Table

Introduction

The aim of this book is to provide an overview of the management and use of information technology in school library media centers, with emphasis on:

- the possible applications of information technology in the school library program (including its use in school library management, in information services, and in curriculum-related applications) and

- management of the information technology to ensure that it is used effectively to meet the goals of the school.

It is not intended as a basic introduction to information technology; rather, the central concern is managing and using the technology so that it contributes to the efficiency and effectiveness of school library media center programs and services. Topics covered include planning, selection of hardware and applications, budget implications, implications for staffing and facilities, user education, publicity/promotion, and possible future developments. Technologies (hardware/software and systems) discussed throughout the book include automated library systems; CD-ROM; online information services and the Internet; curriculum software; local area networks/intranets; and generic software for applications such as word processing, desktop publishing, database management, and project management.

The book is aimed at three main groups of readers: practicing school librarians or school library media specialists, people who are managing school library programs at the district or regional level, and students in university/college programs in the field of school librarianship. It is not intended to be used by itself but rather in conjunction with other books, articles, documents, and Internet resources, as recommended in the various chapters and in the bibliography and lists of resources at the end of the book.

An additional feature of this book is the Web site accessed through <www.lu.com> or <http://www.hi.is/~anne/managing-infotech.html>, which contains all the links to Web sites or Web pages. The author will update the Web site periodically.

CHAPTER ONE

Managing

in the School Library
Media Center

INTRODUCTION

At the end of one millennium and the beginning of the next, we are surrounded by information technology, whether or not we recognize it. Satellites transmit news stories, financial transactions, and telephone conversations around the world in less than a second. Credit and debit cards enable us to use our bank accounts through automatic teller machines even when we travel to other countries. Supermarket checkouts, airline reservation systems, traffic lights, Tamagotchi "digital pets," programmable video units, digital cameras, and cellular phones all incorporate forms of information technology. Recent news reports have covered the use of remote sensing devices beside rivers in the north of Namibia to measure floodwaters, police use of a computer database in the fight against petty crime, and the use of images taken by satellites to plan land regeneration projects. More obvious indicators of the increasing pervasiveness of information technology include World Wide Web URLs in printed advertisements, barcode labels on just about everything we buy, and the number of books and magazines about the Internet on the shelves of almost any news agency or bookstore.

As organizations that reflect their society, schools and libraries are using information technology in many ways. At the same time, they are dealing with the reality that change is rapid and increasing, a situation that brings with it budget and staffing problems. Schools face demands for changes in both the curriculum and the ways in which instruction is provided, and there is pressure not only to use still more technology but also to incorporate a range of new information and information technology skills into the curriculum. Libraries are virtually reinventing themselves in the face of new information media such as the Internet. It has been said that "without question, the most desirable management skill" for the new era is "the ability to manage radical change" (Harvey-Jones, 1994, 25). This may well mean abandoning the safe and the familiar and the predictable by learning new skills, adjusting to new relationships, and doing things in different ways. It may not be comfortable, but it could be interesting and challenging and exciting. When it is information technology that is being managed, then the challenges are even greater, for this is the area where change is perhaps most obvious now.

The 1998 document, *2000 and Beyond: A School Odyssey*, prepared by the British Computer Society's Working Party on "The School of the Future" notes that the only thing we can be certain about in relation to future developments in the use of information and communications technology in education is that changes already underway now will be more far-reaching than we can predict. The communications revolution, based on technologies such as the microchip, fiber-optic cabling, wireless networks, and satellites, is changing many aspects of business, industry, government, and entertainment, as well as education. Developments over the next few years promise a billion processors on a single silicon chip; transmission rates over a single fiber-optic cable of 100 gigabytes per second (equal to one and a half million simultaneous telephone conversations or 25,000 television channels); and a cellular communications infrastructure that is many times cheaper than what is in place today (British Computer Society, 1998, 19). Over the past decade, the carrying capacity of information transmission channels has doubled each year (British Computer Society, 1998, 19), while hardware costs (relative to speed and storage capacity) are either static or declining. These developments have enormous implications for schools at all levels. However, if that potential is to be realized, the technology has to be used for applications in keeping with the goals and objectives of the schools and for purposes carefully designed to meet the needs of the school community.

If that potential is to be realized, then the technology has to be used for applications in keeping with the goals and objectives of the schools and for purposes carefully designed to meet the needs of the school community.

It is not just the technology (and its carrying capacity) that is changing. We are now surrounded by more information than we can possibly deal with. Terms such as *information overload, information anxiety,* and even *information phobia* have entered the English language. A 1996 Reuters research study, *Dying for Information,* found that 43 percent of senior managers in the United Kingdom and worldwide felt significant levels of anxiety about their ability to cope with the information that confronted them in their work—to the point where they experienced ill health as a direct result of information overload (Reuters, 1997, 5). Where access to information previously was seen as a good thing, it is now sometimes regarded as a mixed blessing. It is one thing to be able to find information on a particular topic; in reality, a great deal of information seems to find us every day. It is another thing to evaluate that information and to establish a personal information system that will enable us to retrieve it again when needed. Much of the "information flood" is delivered by information technology. However, this is not necessarily at the expense of more traditional media. In fact, it has also become clear in recent years that technologies such as the Internet are having a positive impact on print publishing.

> First it was the computer that would lead, we were told, to the "death of the book"; next it was CD-ROM, hailed by some as "the new papyrus," a modern alternative to the book. Both the computer and CD-ROM are still with us, of course, as is the book. More recent predictions of a limited life span for the book have been related to the Internet; it is probable that these will turn out to be as unfounded as the earlier ones. The reality is that the use of information technologies like CD-ROM and the Internet has resulted in an increase in printed book and magazine publishing, at least in specialist fields associated with these technologies. This is despite the enormous growth in CD-ROM and online publishing. In other fields, too, there is no evidence of a decline in the use of print and some evidence for an increase. In an article titled "Bad News for Trees" in the 19 December 1998 issue of *The Economist*, it is predicted that "despite the advent of electronic books, ever more information will go on meaning ever more paper . . . the use of paper for writing and printing has soared in the past ten years—in Britain it is up by 65% per head." The article further points out that the fastest growth this century came in the 1980s, just at the time

when the personal computer was becoming more widely available. In the years since 1994, the years in which "the Internet has bloomed," the production of printing and writing paper in North America has increased by over 13 percent, and by more in some other countries (Clyde, 1999).

As with the technology itself, there are implications here for schools and school library media centers, including implications for the ways in which information is managed for access in a school, and the ways in which information skills are defined and taught.

This chapter provides an overview of the main elements associated with the concept of "managing infotech in school library media centers:" the information technology itself, a rationale for the use of information technology in school library media centers, the potential applications of information technology in school library media centers, and management processes that are appropriate in this setting.

INFORMATION TECHNOLOGY

What do we mean when we talk about information technology? In fact, different people may mean different things by this term; for instance, computer professionals may see it more specifically (particularly in terms of computer systems) than others. It does not help that the term *information technology* is sometimes shortened to *infotech* or *IT* or that terms such as *information and communications technologies* (sometimes abbreviated to ICT) or even just *new technologies* are used as synonyms for "information technology." To help reduce the confusion, a number of definitions of information technology have emerged, most centering on the idea that this technology is based on the computer or computer chips.

In this book, *information technology* or *infotech* will be interpreted very broadly to encompass a range of technologies and systems used in or available to today's school library media centers. Information technology includes hardware, networks, systems, software, information structures, and information in electronic (digital) form. It includes technologies used to create, collect, process, store, transmit, access, retrieve, and manipulate information in text, numeric, audio, visual, and multimedia formats. It ranges from, on the one hand, the supercomputer and the communications satellite to, on the other, the palmtop computer and the cellular phone with a memory bank. The following, far from exhaustive, list gives an idea of the scope of the field covered by the terminology:

- computers, including large mainframe or minicomputers, personal computers or microcomputers, laptop or notebook computers, palmtop computers, and electronic organizers;

- computer peripherals, such as CD-ROM drives, printers, screens, overhead projection units linked to computers, barcode readers, or light pens;

- communications technologies, including the telephone, satellite communications, video and computer communications, facsimile transmission (fax), modems, and the field of fiber optics;

- network technologies, including file servers, systems, CD-ROM tower, cabling, routers and hubs, for both local area networks (LANs) and wide area networks (WANs);

- information and data capture technologies such as digital cameras, digital video recorders, scanners, and remote sensing devices;

- information/data storage media, including floppy disks, hard drives, CD-ROM disks, Zip drives;

- information sources, including the Internet, online information services, electronic bulletin boards, library catalogs, and electronic mail (email);

- software, including operating system software, application development tools, generic software such as word processors and database managers, educational software; and

- other technologies, including those related to robotics, artificial intelligence, voice recognition, artificial vision, and security systems.

One of the most powerful trends has been the convergence of previously separate technologies. At one level, this introduces new functionality to such older technologies as the telephone, with some newer telephones having memory and display screens for Internet access. At another level, it results in completely new systems, such as digital photography, that have more capabilities than the technologies that preceded them. The basis of this convergence is digitization. Text, sounds, graphics or images, moving pictures, and computer programs can now be represented, stored, and manipulated in digital form—the form that is used by computers—as distinct from the analog form used by most earlier technologies. The result has been the development of multimedia systems that combine audio, video, text, motion, and interactivity in one system (Figure 1.1).

Convergence is also operating at another level, the hardware/system level. Replace the television remote control with a keyboard that incorporates a communications system and an infrared link to the television, and the Internet can be used through the television set—this kind of system is now available in many hotel rooms. In the other direction, broadcast television via the Internet has already been trialled. A mobile phone can be used to access email services through some Internet service providers. Computers with modems can be used to send and receive faxes as well as email and to queue telephone calls. Microcomputers can be linked directly to photocopiers, and photocopiers with internal memory can store and retrieve information. A CD-ROM unit on a computer with a modem or network connection can display relevant Internet resources as well as the information on the CD-ROM.

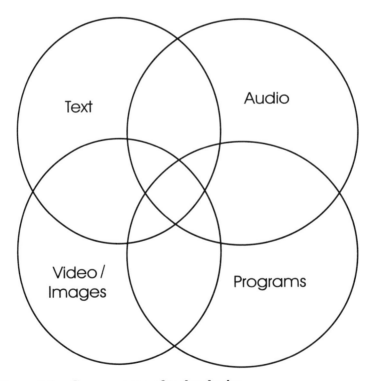

Figure 1.1   Convergence of technologies.

These are just some examples of the convergence of technologies at present. The changes that are under way provide the school library media specialist with many more options in terms of information technology, but they also introduce greater levels of complexity. Consequently it becomes more difficult to make decisions about information technology.

RATIONALE FOR INFORMATION TECHNOLOGY

The school library media specialist is the school information and resource specialist. While this role has many facets, the key responsibilities are related to the educational mission of the school and to information management. The School Library Association of Victoria (Australia) says that the main responsibilities of the school library media specialist are to "initiate and participate in the teaching of information literacy in the context of the total curriculum" and to "manage the school's information resources and services so as to facilitate learning and teaching" (Ferretter & Manning, 1996, 4). If these responsibilities are to be carried out effectively, then information technology is critical. It is now impossible to create a meaningful and relevant information skills program that does not incorporate the use of information technology, since it is increasingly the case that much of the information that is available in our society is available only in electronic form. The provision of information and resources to support the school curriculum is an essential activity for the school library media specialist. As the information needs of teachers, students, and school administrators increase, so the need for powerful information management systems will lead to the use of more sophisticated library automation systems combining access to the school library media center catalog with access to information on CD-ROMs and on the Internet. Further, schools themselves are now complex organizations that create and use vast quantities of information. Therefore, there is a need to ensure that this information—whether curriculum information or records associated with the management of the school—is organized in an efficient and effective way so that school objectives are achieved. In relation to this, the school library media specialist has information management knowledge and skills that are of particular value to the school community. All these aspects of the role of the school library media specialist are reflected in the statement "School Libraries in the Electronic Age," developed by the New South Wales Committee of the Australian Council of Library and Information Services (ACLIS) in 1996 (see Figure 1.2, page 8).

School Libraries in the Electronic Age

School libraries create a learning environment where multiple information sources, including the Internet, and learning can be linked to enable students to connect with information and develop effective information skills in a meaningful way. The Australian Council of Library and Information Services (ACLIS) recommends to all schools the adoption of the following principles relating to the role of the school library:

- The school library should have responsibility for providing and storing electronic information sources. Internet access through the library is essential in fulfilling this function.

- Education for information literacy is a fundamental component for effective integration of electronic information into learning.

- Partnerships between teachers, teacher-librarians and information technology staff are necessary to integrate electronic information resources into the curriculum.

- The library is a major stakeholder in the school information network and should be closely involved in the planning and management of the network.

- Adequate technical support should be given to ensure information access across all platforms.

- The teacher-librarian has an educational role in assisting school staff to identify, access, evaluate, and integrate information resources in their teaching/learning programs.

- Collaborative arrangements with other schools and organisations should be encouraged to extend the range and quality of information resources.

- Funding for school libraries should reflect the need for provision of electronic resources, access to the Internet and document supply from external sources.

Figure 1.2 School Libraries in the Electronic Age. Produced by Neil McLeen and Michelle Ellis for the ACLIS New South Wales Committee.

In a recent ERIC Digest titled "The School Librarian's Role in the Electronic Age," Carol Simpson focuses on changes in the school environment and their influence on current practice:

> As schools change from passive learning environments into active ones, the role of the librarian has to adjust as well. School restructuring requires that the librarian venture from the library to collaborate with teachers and administrators. The addition of technology into the learning environment enhances information retrieval and offers the librarian a new entree into classroom curriculum. New, more student-centered teaching methods demand the support of information resources and training in their use. Library technology reaches beyond the library walls via computer networks to put information resources into the hands of end users at the point of need. With networks linking all areas of the modern school, the best place to access information may no longer be within the walls of the traditional library (Simpson, 1997, 38).

Simpson (1997, 38–39) sees four major changes in the school library media center environment and the role of the school library media specialist as a result. The first is that school library media specialists "must be proficient in the use of the new technologies to promote them and instruct students and teachers in their use" as well as to use them to locate resources; she sees this as being a move away from "warehousing" resources to collaboration and consulting. Secondly, with more information being made available in electronic formats, school library media specialists need to consider issues of access to information through networks, rather than concentrating on development of the school library media center collection—a balance is necessary. Thirdly, the management aspects of the role of the school library media specialist are becoming more complex and more demanding, with, for instance, "designing record-keeping systems" for the school becoming part of the role in addition to the management of the new technologies within the context of library media center services. Fourthly, the role of the school library media specialist in evaluating and providing resources for library patrons now encompasses work with electronic information resources in a range of formats. At the same time, the need for more traditional services such as reading guidance and storytelling has not decreased.

In 1998 an important new document from the American Association of School Librarians and the Association for Educational Communications and Technology was published, *Information Power: Building Partnerships for Learning.* The mission of the school library media program remains "to ensure that students and staff are effective users of ideas and information"— as it was in the previous guidelines of a decade ago—but these new guidelines expand that mission. The role of the school library media specialist incorporates that of teacher, instructional partner, information specialist, and administrator of the school library media program. The aim is to create a student-centered library media program that is based on "collaboration, leadership, and technology."

The guidelines discuss two dimensions of technology, informational and instructional—and indicate that the school library media specialist should have expertise with both (American Association of School Librarians, 1998, 54). Information technology is seen as being electronic equipment and software that can be used to locate, retrieve, and organize information; examples of its use would include locating Internet resources for a curriculum unit or creating a school library media center catalog. Instructional technology is seen as being related to the design and development of instructional units and systems that integrate the technology into the teaching and learning process; an example of its use would be creating a unit collaboratively with a teacher and incorporating the use of the Internet to gather information about current developments related to the topic of the unit.

The ultimate aim is to have students "participate in a global learning community" by exploring resources inside their school library media center and in the world as a whole. They then become actively engaged as information users, information producers, and information communicators. This document envisions the school library media center as "a potentially powerful" service through which students and their teachers are provided with access to information worldwide and to communication systems.

INFOTECH IN THE SCHOOL LIBRARY MEDIA CENTER

The documents discussed previously provide a powerful rationale for the incorporation of information technology into the school library media center's programs and services. This is not to say that technology should be the whole focus of the school library media center program. It is clear that the future of school library media centers will not be "all digital;" even with more information technology, there is no sign that the book will soon disappear. Although some school boards seem to have considered the dangerous idea of doing away with their library media centers in favor of banks of computers with CD-ROMs and Internet access, books and audiovisual materials continue to be heavily used for very good reasons. However, information technology is playing an increasingly important part in today's school library media centers. Information technology combined with print and other resources can be used to develop a media-rich environment to support teaching and learning through improved access to systems and services.

Computers and other forms of information technology can be and are being used in school library media centers in four main ways. Firstly, computers can be used for library administration and management tasks, including the borrowing (circulation) system, cataloging or indexing, acquisitions, periodicals (magazines) management, collection maintenance, budgeting, accounting, record keeping, and statistics collection. When the term *library automation* is used, it is probably these functions that first come to mind. Secondly, computers (often in conjunction with communications technology) are important tools for information retrieval. Information technology can be used to provide access to information within the library or the school or to information sources outside the school (such as online information services and the Internet). Thirdly, information and communications technology can be used for communication, both inside and outside the school; this may include the use of email, listservs, and electronic bulletin boards as well as the creation of Web pages to make information available. Fourthly, computer-based resources are making an impact on the school library media center as part of the collection of educational and recreational resources. Just as the school library media center collection may contain print and audiovisual material to meet the needs of users, so it may also contain computer software and other resources such as CD-ROMs. Some school library media centers even provide computers for the use of teachers and students; occasionally they also lend this equipment for use elsewhere in the school or at home. In addition, resources may be made available to users throughout the school and perhaps outside it via the school network.

These four categories are not mutually exclusive, of course—the creation of an information retrieval tool such as the school library media center catalog is an administrative function, and the catalog can also be used as a teaching resource in information skills instruction. Depending on the software used as the basis of the catalog, it might also be used to provide access to resources on the Internet; for example, some library automation systems allow the school library media specialist to catalog Web sites in the same way that books are cataloged but with an interactive link to the Web site as part of the catalog entry. The library media center catalog, then, may actually fit into all four categories of the model presented in Figure 1.3, page 12. However, the four categories do provide a useful way of looking at the

SCHOOL LIBRARY MEDIA CENTER PROGRAMS

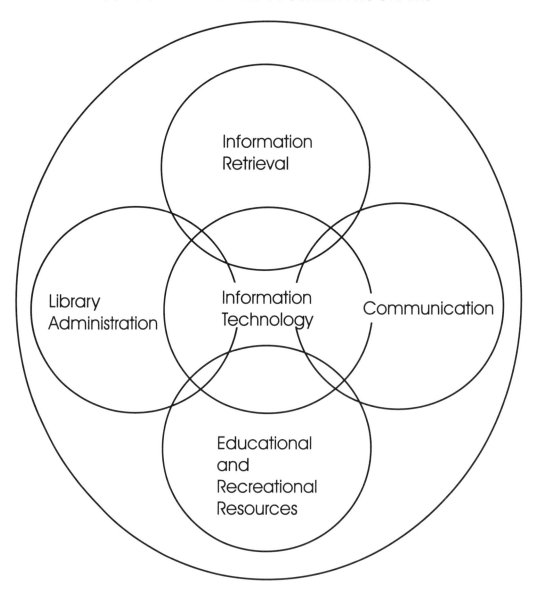

Figure 1.3   Applications of information technology in the school library media center.

applications of information technology in school library media centers. This is despite the following scenario, in which a school network links the applications in such a way that the boundaries are transparent to the users, who may feel that they are using just a single system.

With the development of school networks or intranets that link all or most of the computers throughout the school into one system accessible from all around the school, the distinction among the four categories, and among the various technologies that comprise the system, is becoming more blurred in the eyes of the users who may be using one computer (and one menu system) to access the library catalog, a CD-ROM encyclopedia, the school timetable for the coming week, email, a word processing program, a typing tutorial, or the World Wide Web. For example, a school library media center might be involved in the creation of a school network that is accessible from computers in the school library media center and from a computer in each classroom, a computer lab, the teachers' rooms, and the school office that makes available the library media center catalog, the school district union catalog, the SIRS and Newsbank indexes/databases of current resources, a periodicals database, some local databases, and access to the Internet, as well as a collection of generic software and educational games. While this network has distinct advantages for the users, who work with a small number of interfaces, it may make it more difficult for them to understand just where the information they are using is coming from and, therefore, to evaluate it—an information skills problem.

While some school library media specialists are working with schoolwide networks and information systems, others are just beginning the process of working with information technology, and there are many stages in between. A survey of readers of the Australian school librarianship journal, *Access,* found that school library media center automation was the most popular application of information technology in their school libraries, followed by CD-ROMs, online searching of remote databases, email, and the Internet (Clyde, 1995, *passim*). Since then, use of the Internet for information retrieval and electronic publishing has become more widely accepted, a trend reflected in the 1997 Australian publication *Information Technology in Schools: Implications for Teacher Librarians,* edited by Margaret Butterworth, which emphasizes the use of the Internet for a wide range of information retrieval and information presentation applications and for applications that had become widely accepted in earlier years. This same trend is apparent in other countries—most obviously the United States—where a stream of books in the last two years has drawn attention to new information technologies and their applications in the school library media center. Examples include *The Virtual School Library: Gateway to the Information Superhighway,* edited by Carol Collier Kuhlthau (1996); *Reinvent Your School's Library in the Age of Technology: A Handbook for Principals and Superintendents,* by David V. Loertscher (1997); *Creating a Local Area Network in the School Library Media Center,* by Becky R. Mather (1997); and *The Internet Resource Directory for K-12 Teachers and Librarians, 98/99 Edition,* by Elizabeth B. Miller (1998).

Computers and other information technologies have a range of other possible applications in school library media centers beyond those mentioned. These applications have little in common with one another and either do not fit neatly into one of the four categories already discussed or fit into more than one. They include the use of information technology for library publicity and promotion, for creating library media center and classroom resources (as distinct from providing access to them), for producing lettering and graphics for library displays and signs, for maintaining an electronic gradebook or keeping a record of student progress in educational programs coordinated through the school library media center. Innovative school library media specialists are constantly finding new ways to use information technology to support and enhance their programs and services and to increase the efficiency of their operations.

MANAGEMENT

Management encompasses such processes as planning, organizing, leadership, control (or ongoing supervision), and evaluation of school library resource center facilities and systems. It includes such tasks as forward planning; selecting systems; supervising staff or coordinating the work of others; selecting information technology and organizing for its effective use; budgeting, planning and developing the school library media center facility; publicity and promotion; and decision making at both the long-term and the day-to-day levels. Good management is critical for the effective implementation of information technology.

The strategic planning process (or structured planning or systematic planning) is the approach to management that is taken in this book, with other useful techniques and approaches introduced as appropriate to support the strategic planning process. As Sheila Corrall says, "in general terms," the strategic planning process "fulfils the dual role of relating an organization and its people to the environment and providing unity and direction to its activities" (1994, 3). It is a process that implies decision making; that is, selecting a future course of action from among alternatives. It helps an organization to move from where it is now to where it wants to be in the future. The strategic planning process enables the school library media specialist to define the purpose or direction of the school library media center (in consultation with the school administration and users of the services) and to evaluate its progress; it ensures that changes in the school and in education are monitored and reflected in the collections and services of the school library media center; and it provides a framework that guides new developments, including the introduction of new information technologies as well as ongoing activity and maintenance. Figure 1.4, page 16, shows the strategic planning process as it might apply in a school library media center. While the figure presents the strategic planning process in the classic way, as a sequence of steps, in fact most of the steps in the sequence should be ongoing and constant.

It needs to be emphasized that management and planning are ongoing processes that represent an approach or attitude to running a school library media center. Unlike recalling overdue books, management is not something that can be done once a week or on a slow afternoon; rather, it is behind everything that is done in the effective school library media center. It is a cyclical process: most diagrams of the strategic planning process begin with establishing aims and establishing needs and end with evaluation, and it is the ongoing evaluation of the school library media center services and systems that feeds into the first stages of the planning process to begin the cycle again.

The mission and goals of the school library media center should grow out of and be related to those of the school. They should be adopted through consultation with all stakeholders. Where a school has no statement of mission or goals, and the school district or education authority has none, the process could begin in the school library media center. Apart from the mission and goals giving a sense of purpose and a means for identifying future directions (planning), the consultations necessary to formulate a mission and goals for the school library media center will help to raise the stakeholders' awareness of it and of the possibilities it offers in terms of resources and services. This is also a way of generating support for the school library media center and its programs and of identifying possible new directions. The objectives are specific statements of activity that will help the school library media center and the school to fulfill their mission. This provides a foundation for decision making about information technology in the school library media center.

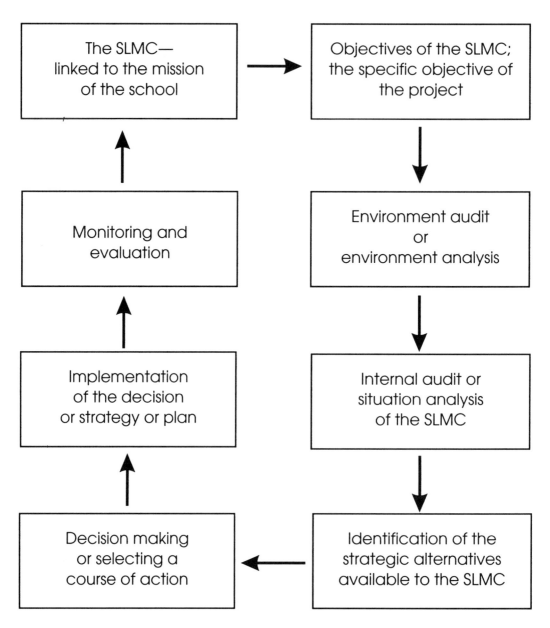

Figure 1.4   The strategic planning process as applied to the school library media center (SLMC).

An *environment audit* or environment analysis provides information about the context within which the school and the school library media center operate. It should cover new developments in education and technology, changes in the educational system of which the school is a part or in the library system of which the school library media center is a part, changes in the population served by the school and the school library media center, changes in the school curriculum and in teaching and learning strategies, and changes in sources of funding outside the school, among other things. In other words, it covers anything in the physical, social, political, legal, cultural, economic, or demographic environment within which the school operates and that is likely to affect the school library media center or its users. In terms of information technology, the strategic planning process may actually begin at this point, with an observation that a new technology with curriculum or school library management implications has emerged. This could be followed by a reference back to the goals and objectives of the school library media center to identify ways in which this new technology might help to achieve them and then could look forward through the steps of the process. The implications of some new technologies (for example, the Internet) have been so far-reaching that they have actually caused libraries to re-think their mission and goals and to go right back to the foundations of the strategic planning process.

The *internal audit* refers to collecting information about all aspects of the school library media center—its collections and services—as a basis for decision making. Who uses the school library media center? Who does not use it? What is it used for? What are the needs of users and nonusers? How does the school library media center contribute to the life of the school? How should it contribute? How effective are the staff, collections, facilities, and services in meeting the needs of people in the school? In terms of information technology, what is available in the school library media center, how is it being used, and how effective is it? What is not available, and what are the implications of this? It is impossible to plan for more efficient and effective school library media center services if details of the current situation are unknown. This process also provides a basis for decision making and for the establishment of priorities for the introduction of new information technology.

The identification of *strategic alternatives* is the process by which the school library media specialist identifies the ways in which changes might be introduced or the possible options for solving a problem or the possible ways to carry out a school library media center function. In terms of information technology, this might mean identifying the ways in which access could be provided to an electronic encyclopedia or the ways in which access could be provided to the library catalog from outside the school library media center. This stage also involves collecting information about the various options and discussing them with all those who will be affected by them, including, perhaps, the person or people responsible for maintaining the school's existing computer equipment.

The *decision-making process* involves selection of a course of action from among the alternatives, using information collected in the previous phases of the planning process. The decision-making process, outlined in Figure 1.5, overlaps the previous phases, emphasizing the importance of the accurate identification of a problem or need or opportunity, followed by the collection of appropriate information on which to base the decision. It is important that constraints or limitations on the decision-making process be identified and that criteria be established for selecting from among alternatives. The possible solutions or alternatives can then be evaluated and the decision made. There are a number of tools or techniques to assist in making decisions. One of these is a process known as SWOT—an analysis of the strengths and weaknesses, opportunities and threats that are inherent in both the current situation and in the possible solutions or innovations. Other techniques include cost-benefit analysis (in which the "costs," not necessarily financial, of undertaking or not undertaking a course of action are shown against the potential benefits from the course of action) and the use of decision trees (through which a problem and potential solutions are represented diagrammatically).

Although the *implementation* phase of the strategic planning process is represented by just one box in the strategic planning process diagram, it is this phase that occupies the longest period of time in any project. This is the period during which the decision or plan is communicated to those involved, implemented (often as a step-by-step process), monitored, and evaluated on a day-to-day basis. To be effective, the implementation must be planned, with realistic time schedules, allocation of staff time and other resources, and ongoing monitoring. Its success depends upon communication, action plans for each phase, regular reviews of progress, the development of contingency plans to cover potential problems or changed circumstances, and a continuing emphasis on organizational needs. Account has to be taken of other activities that will be affected by the implementation—for example, the introduction of new information technology may mean changes to the furniture in the school library media center, and there may be training implications. The implementation phase or process is outlined in Figure 1.6, page 20.

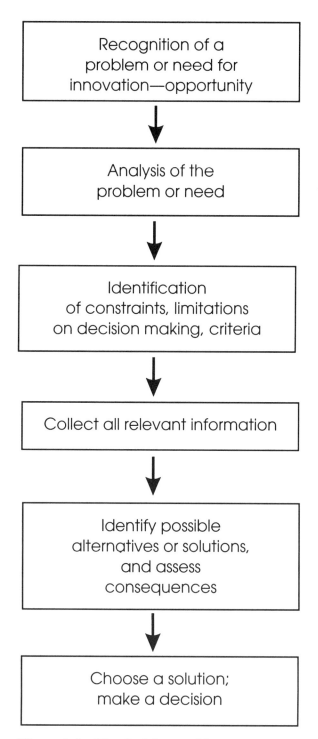

Figure 1.5   The decision-making process.

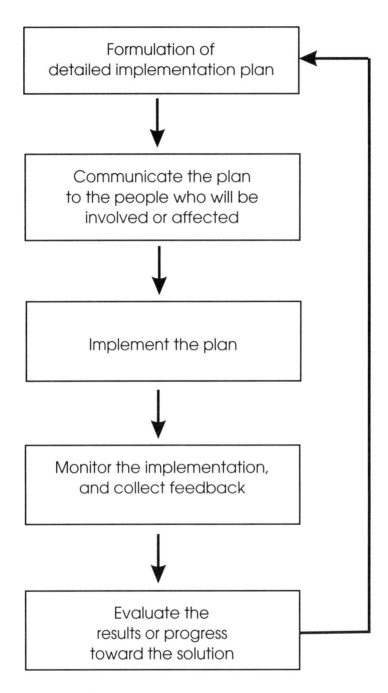

Figure 1.6   The implementation process.

The *evaluation* phase brings together the information collected through ongoing or formative evaluation as the planning and implementation progresses (see Figure 1.5, "The decision-making process," and Figure 1.6, "The implementation process," for examples), along with a summative evaluation of the process as a whole. At both stages, the evaluation may be formal or informal, but if it is to lead to further changes, then it will need to be documented so that it becomes part of the evidence that is presented to decision makers.

In the literature of the field, management is often associated with managing people—management expert Peter Drucker (1987, 18) has even characterized management as the skill or practice that turns "a mob" into an efficient, effective, and productive work group or team—and since most school library media specialists work alone, they have tended to assume that management skills or strategies were not relevant for them. However, managers also work with resources other than people, including money, facilities, technology, equipment, buildings, time, information—all of which are related to the work of the school library media specialist. Even so, school library media specialists are also dealing with people and need to be able to do this effectively, whether those people are administrators, teachers, students, parents, or support staff. When managing information technology in the school library media center, school library media specialists are dealing with the people who provide the budget to introduce the technology, the people whose support is necessary, the people who will use or benefit from the information technology, the people who will supply it or maintain it. The strategic planning process outlined previously helps to ensure that information is available to help convince decision makers that the needs of the people who will use or benefit from the systems are taken into account and that attention will be paid to such essential but often-forgotten aspects of innovation as maintenance.

BRINGING IT TOGETHER

This chapter has provided an initial discussion of the major aspects of the topic of this book: an overview of information technology, a rationale or an argument for the use of information technologies in the school library media center, an outline of the ways in which information technologies can be used in the school library media center, and an approach to management and decision making that could be the basis of the effective use of information technology in the school library media center and the school.

In the next four chapters, the main purposes for which information technology can be used in the school library media center—library media center administration, information retrieval, communication, and as an educational and recreational resource—will be discussed in more detail. Subsequent chapters will deal with developing an information technology plan, selecting and implementing information technology, and managing the technology on an ongoing basis. Finally, issues associated with the use of information technology in school library media centers will be discussed.

A bibliography is provided at the end of each chapter, and there is a list of recommended reading at the end of the book. In addition, lists of resources are provided where relevant. Further information about topics discussed can also be found on the Internet at sites such as "School Libraries Online," the Web site of the International Association of School Librarianship (see Figure 1.7).

International Association
of School Librarianship (IASL)

SCHOOL
LIBRARIES ONLINE

SITE DIRECTORY

Current news
items
from more than 300
print news sources,
related to school
libraries

About the Association
Objectives, activities, officers, history, Policy Statement on School Libraries, Handbook of Organization, International Volunteer Assistance Program, more...

The IASL Noticeboard
Current notices and deadlines ...

The IASL Newsletter
Information for contributors, selected articles, current issues ...

Reviews
Current reviews, review archive, information for publishers ...

The Annual Conferences
The 1999 conference, future conferences, reports of past conferences, published proceedings ...

IASL Publications
List of IASL publications, ordering information ...

Committees and Special Interest Groups
Committees of IASL, special interest groups, how to participate ...

IASL Journal: School Libraries Worldwide
About the journal, the editor, contents pages and abstracts, call for contributions ...

IASL International Awards Programme
Awards and grants, guidelines for application ...

How to Join IASL
How to join, fees, application forms ...

School Library Resources on the Internet
School library associations, resources for school librarians, education resources, more ...

Check out the 1999
IASL/AASL
conference
Website

★ Check out our
collection of links to
School Library
Resources
on the Internet

and resources for the
International Year
of
Older Persons
1999

The International Association of School Librarianship (IASL)
Suite 300, Box 34069, Seattle, WA 98124-1069, USA
Fax: 1-604-925 0566
Email: iasl@rockland.com

★ A Day in My
Life...
by Jennifer Branch
A sample article and

Figure 1.7 **"School Libraries Online," the Web site of the International Association of School Librarianship.**

REFERENCES AND BIBLIOGRAPHY

American Association of School Librarians and the Association for Educational Communications and Technology (1998). *Information power: Building partnerships for learning.* Chicago: American Library Association.

Bad news for trees (1998). *The Economist.* 19 December, 151.

British Computer Society (1998). *2000 and beyond: A school odyssey. BCS Schools Committee Working Party on the School of the Future.* Swindon, Wiltshire: The British Computer Society.

Butterworth, Margaret, ed. (1997). *Information technology in Australian schools: Implications for teacher librarians.* 4th ed. Perth, Western Australia: Australian Library and Information Association, School Libraries Section.

Celente, Gerald (1997). *Towards 2000: How to prepare for and profit from the changes of the 21st century.* New York: Warner Books.

Clyde, Laurel A. (1995). *Information technology in Australian school libraries: A survey of readers of Access.* Reykjavik, Lindin.

———. (1999). The Internet and reading promotion. Paper for the Nordic Conference on Literature for Young People, Stavanger, Norway, 7-10 February.

Cole, G. A. (1990). *Management theory and practice.* 3rd ed. London: DP Publications.

Corrall, Sheila (1994). *Strategic planning for library and information services.* An Aslib Know How Guide. London: Aslib.

Daft, Richard L. (1994). *Management.* 3rd ed. Fort Worth, TX: Dryden Press.

Drucker, Peter F. (1987). A new discipline. *Success.* January-February, 18.

Ferretter, Gerry, and Mary Manning (1996). *Skilling up: Developing a professional portfolio for teacher-librarians.* Richmond, Victoria: School Library Association of Victoria.

Harvey-Jones, John (1994). *Managing to survive.* London: Mandarin.

Kuhlthau, Carol Collier, ed. (1996). *The virtual school library: Gateway to the information superhighway.* Englewood, CO: Libraries Unlimited.

Loertscher, David V. (1997). *Reinvent your school's library in the age of technology: A handbook for principals and superintendents.* San Jose, CA: Hi Willow.

Mabey, Christopher, and Bill Mayon-White, eds. (1993). *Managing change.* 2nd ed. London: Sage in association with the Open University.

Mather, Becky R. (1997*). Creating a local area network in the school library media center.* Westport, CT: Greenwood Press.

Miller, Elizabeth B. (1998*). The Internet resource directory for K-12 teachers and librarians, 98/99 edition.* Englewood, CO: Libraries Unlimited.

Reuters (1997*). The Reuters guide to good information strategy.* London: Reuters.

Simpson, Carol (1997). The school librarian's role in the electronic age. ERIC Digest. Reprinted in *Emergency Librarian.* 25(5): May-June, 38–39.

Weingand, Darlene E. (1987). *Marketing/planning library and information services.* Littleton, CO: Libraries Unlimited.

CHAPTER TWO

for
School Library Media
Center Administration

INTRODUCTION

It is increasingly being recognized that information technology can provide the basis for more effective school library media center organization and administration and for more efficient procedures than can traditional manual systems. Computers can be used for a wide range of administrative, information management, and record-keeping functions in the school library media center. As the processing power and storage capacity of personal computers increases, so does their potential in the school library media center setting, particularly if the computers are networked. If the applications that are to be automated are those that involve routine, repetitive, and time-consuming tasks, then there may be considerable benefits to the library media center and the school as a whole, because of more accurate record keeping, more effective use of staff time, and better access to information. For most school library media centers, to automate or not to automate is not really the question. If the library media center has not been automated, then it has become more a question of when and how.

In an article written more than 40 years ago, Miriam E. Peterson suggested that automation would provide school libraries with greater flexibility to meet changed educational needs in the future (1957, 1–13). By the late 1960s, some American school districts were using large computers or bureau facilities to provide some computer-based cataloging or book ordering services for their school libraries (see, for instance, Reiss, 1969; McCusker, 1968). A few early articles and papers, particularly from the late 1960s, refer to "data processing for school libraries," punched card systems, the need for specialist keypunch operators, and "programming the library shelf list" (Long, 1969). However, with a small number of exceptions, it was not until 1979 that instances were recorded in the literature of individual school library resource centers using minicomputers or microcomputers to automate their own systems.

It was the emergence of the microcomputer (around 1978/1979) that opened up real possibilities for early school library media center automation. In 1980, Betty Costa, library media specialist at Mountain View Elementary School in Broomfield, Colorado, conceived the idea of replacing her poorly used card catalog with "an automated card catalog." Her husband, Larry Costa, a computer consultant, wrote a school library catalog package to her specifications. Known as Computer Cat, it ran on an Apple II+ computer, and provided a public access catalog for student searching. Her prototype system at Mountain View created a great deal of interest; it went into commercial production, and a circulation module was added (Costa, 1981; Costa, 1982). Computer Cat was later purchased by Winnebago, a company that is still involved in supplying automated library systems for school library media centers.

Throughout the 1980s, other school library automated systems entered the market, and some sold very well. By the end of the decade, with the emergence of much larger supermicros and small minicomputers that were within a price range that schools could afford, school library systems had become much more sophisticated, and the distinction between systems for school library media centers and systems for public and college libraries was disappearing. Further developments in hardware and software at that time made for greater portability of systems across a range of hardware from mainframes to microcomputers, which meant that systems originally designed for very large academic libraries could be considered, in their microcomputer versions, by school library media centers. In addition, new features were added to most systems; many were rewritten to run on newer hardware or with newer operating systems; and new systems appeared, developed for a market that was becoming much more demanding. Systems designed for local area networks became the standard.

It is difficult to get accurate figures for the number of school library media centers that have automated library systems today. In her 1995 survey of automated school library systems in Canada (Lighthall, 1996, 39) Lynne Lighthall says that "it seems very likely that more than half of the school libraries in Canada" were automated at that time; many more would be automated today. All the school libraries in some school districts were automated, but there were other school districts where no school libraries had automated systems. Ken Dillon's Australian surveys suggest that by the end of 1995, 69.7 percent of Australia's schools had automated libraries. His analysis did not take into account the number of home-made (noncommercial) systems nor school libraries that were using systems purchased from very small vendors nor, indeed, those school libraries that had automated one or more functions but were not using an integrated multi-function library automation system (Dillon, 1997).This means that the true figure for automated school libraries in Australia might be higher. Certainly it is higher in some states: By the end of 1996 all libraries in New South Wales' almost 10,000 public (state) schools were automated with the integrated library system OASIS Library (12 were not). In the United States, the pattern of school library media center automation varies a great deal from state to state, but in a considerable number of school districts all school library media centers are automated.

For many school library media centers, efficiency of library procedures has been central to their library automation projects. It is obviously more effective and easier for library media center clients if the catalog is available on several networked computers in the library media center (and perhaps throughout the school) than to have groups of people attempting to search a card catalog at the one time. Automated circulation procedures reduce the turnaround time of items in the library collection and, therefore, result in increased availability of resources for use by other borrowers. Reporting functions provided in automated circulation system software allow the school library media center collections to be developed to more closely reflect school needs. Strengths and weaknesses in the collection are easier to detect through collection usage statistics generated by the system. Further, usage statistics available through the system can be used for forward planning and as the basis for some performance indicators for the library media center.

While conversion of manual library systems is an intensive process that may require increased staffing support in the short term, once the conversion has been completed there will be some efficiency outcomes, particularly in the saving of clerical staff time on the processing of books and other resources, typing catalog cards, filing catalog cards, catalog maintenance, routine circulation procedures such as loans and returns, preparing overdue reports and notices, and carrying out inventories of the collection. There may be some savings in professional staff time in, for example, preparing bibliographies, locating suitable resources for classroom units of study, and in preparing management reports. However, although automation can result in more efficient procedures and savings in time, most school library media specialists find that demands on their time and use of the services actually increase after automation. When resources are easier to find, more people are prepared to try to find them. When the systems work better, more people are prepared to use the services. So while automation should make the school library media center more efficient and more effective, this is not likely to mean that less professional staff time will be needed to provide services.

However, in relation to the use of computers in school library media center administration, it is important that this should not be seen as being unrelated to the educational needs of the students in the school. The school environment provides a basis for the learning experiences of the students, and the school administration and structures are part of this environment. It needs to be remembered that while library automation projects make the library media center more efficient, they also provide students with an example of the use of information technology in an application that has immediate relevance for them. It is a responsibility of the school library media specialist to ensure that the application is appropriate and effective so that students are exposed to a positive experience of computers in the school library media center.

As well as being more efficient, and providing students with an example of technology in action, the automation of library media center procedures can increase access to information within the school for teachers, school administrators, and students. By providing more effective search systems with more access points to the information contained in databases such as the school library media center catalog, the automation of school library media center functions contributes to the information-rich educational environment that is recommended in the library media center guidelines from the American Association of School Librarians and the Association for Educational Communications and Technology, *Information Power: Building Partnerships for Learning* (1998). Further, through the use of a range of information technologies for different purposes, students learn and practice information search skills that are so important in today's world. For example, access to an automated library system not only increases access to resources, it also offers learning opportunities for students who, when searching a relevant database such as the library catalog, find information in a range of formats in all subject areas. But it is not just the automated library catalog that offers such learning opportunities. Students may help to operate an automated circulation system or to create local databases that can be made available through the automated system.

The use of computers in school library media center organization and management can range from the use of fully integrated automated library systems that provide facilities for most of the administration and management functions performed in the library to small, specific-purpose packages designed to automate a single function, such as compiling overdues lists. Increasingly, school library media centers are choosing multifunction integrated systems so that management functions are handled by a single suite of software from one vendor and running on a network of personal computers. This approach has many advantages for the library, including access to all library data from any part of the system and reduced training time for staff because they have only one set of programs to learn.

OPTIONS FOR LIBRARY MEDIA CENTER AUTOMATION

Whether schools are considering library media center automation for the first time or evaluating their current system and considering alternative ways of implementing library automation, a number of options will be available to them. Because of their particular situation, many schools will not be able to make choices about all matters related to library media center automation; some or even all the decisions will have been made by a school district administration or a state or provincial education authority or a library authority. When this is the case, it has to be viewed as part of the external environment within which the school operates, and account has to be taken of it in any environment audit as part of the strategic planning process. However, many other schools will be making all the decisions for themselves.

Where some or all of the decisions are to be made by the individual school, there are many options and combinations of options. The decisions that are made at this stage will have a profound effect on conditions for access to information in the school, library media center staffing, and ongoing budgeting, among other things. Decisions may need to be made about whether to join an automated library network (either an existing network or a new one) with other libraries or to go it alone with automation; what type of computer hardware to use as the basis of the system; whether to have a fully integrated library management system (covering the major library functions, such as cataloging, circulation, serials control, acquisitions/ordering, budgeting, statistics, inventory) or to automate only some functions; whether to use software developed specifically for library automation or to use a general-purpose system, such as a database or bibliographic system. Some decisions, once made, will influence others. For example, if the school library media center decides to join a network of local libraries, then they may be required to have particular hardware or to adopt specific procedures. The options are discussed here separately.

- **Join a library network, or automate the school library media center as an independent system?**

For many schools, there will be no decision to make about networking because there will be no network to join. However, for others it will be an issue, and some may have little choice but to join a network. For those who go it alone, all decisions will normally be made within the school, and the library automation system will be set up within the school library media center. The library functions to be automated will be decided within the school, and the resulting system may automate just a few library functions or it may be a full integrated library system, perhaps linked to the school management systems and perhaps to the Internet. Going it alone no longer means isolation.

Networks may be set up as networks of school library media centers in a district or local area, as networks of all the different kinds of libraries in a city or town, as statewide networks of school library media centers or libraries in general, or as national networks. If libraries other than school library media centers are involved in the network, then school needs may or may not have a great influence on decisions about the network. The libraries in a network normally share a computer system and software and have a binding agreement of some sort (usually a legal agreement) regarding such things as financial commitment to the network, cataloging standards, and services to be provided through the network. Sometimes a school district or education authority might make these commitments on behalf of the school library media centers in the network. Some networks are heavily centralized and run from a central office that is separate from the libraries involved; other networks are run as cooperatives. Sometimes only cataloging is shared through a network; sometimes most or all administrative functions are shared, including cataloging, circulation, purchasing, and inter-library loans. It is usual that each participating library has a catalog of its own collection, generated through the central system (whether that catalog is online, on CD-ROM, or in another form), but also has access to all the catalog records of all the libraries in the network.

It is the potential for resource sharing (through access to the catalogs of all participating libraries) that is one of the main advantages of library networks. In addition, it may be possible to introduce cost savings through the sharing of catalog data as well as resources. Another benefit is that each library has access to more sophisticated computer equipment and software than it might be able to afford alone, and each library receives the benefit of the network specialist staff who make decisions and provide advice. The main disadvantage of joining a network is that, to a certain extent, the individual library loses control over its own decision making and future direction. The extent to which this happens will vary from network to network and may depend on the stage at which the library actually joins the network. There is also a possibility that in a large network that includes many different kinds of libraries the needs of small school library media centers might be ignored or compromised in favor of the larger institutions. These particular needs of school library media centers might encompass such things as having curriculum-related information attached to catalog records, having a graphical user interface that can be changed depending on the grade level of the students using the school library media center, and possibly having the capability to handle bulk loans to a classroom for the duration of a curriculum unit. In making a decision to join a network, a library usually measures all these things against the perceived benefits of network membership. Further, with developments in client/server technology as a basis for library automation systems, it may be possible for the different libraries in the network to take data in generic form from the network computer (the server) and format it in their own way on their own (client) machines and even to offer additional services through their own machines. Thus the continually developing technology is opening up new possibilities and overcoming some of the long-standing disadvantages of wide area networks as a basis for library automation.

In 1998, the American state of Minnesota was in the process of selecting a vendor for a statewide library automation system (provisionally called MnLINK) that would serve university, public, school, and research libraries. The system was to comprise two main sections: an integrated library system covering most of the main library functions and a communications gateway to facilitate links between libraries in the system. The initial funding came through a $12 million appropriation from the state legislature. While many schools expressed interest in the network, their level of participation was clearly going to depend on such things as network fees and the software selected as the basis of the system (of one of the software packages under consideration, one school library media specialist noted that it didn't seem to be an elementary library system and another commented that it required a dedicated workstation in each school library media center, which reduced the possibilities for integrating the school library media center catalog with the school network). These considerations reflect the advantages and disadvantages discussed earlier.

In the Australian state of New South Wales, the Department of School Education has taken a very different approach to school library automation. The OASIS (now Alice/Annie) software was provided free to all public (state) schools, and assistance was provided with computer hardware. The aim was to have all the school libraries in the state automated by the end of 1996. The schools used the software and hardware to set up their own school library systems (linked to an OASIS school administration system). However, because the software incorporates a communications system, and all schools were using the same system, it was possible for school libraries to communicate with one another and to set up networks of local schools with a union catalog. The software provides for cataloging, circulation, acquisitions/ ordering, statistics, serials control, inventory, and record keeping; in addition, catalog data can be loaded into the system from a CD-ROM or from online sources such as SCIS (the Australian national schools catalog and curriculum information system).

- **The school library media center as part of a schoolwide administration system or a stand-alone library system?**

One approach to school library media center automation is to see the school library system as part of the total school administration system—a system that could incorporate information about staff, students, accounts, timetable, reports, curriculum, school buildings and facilities, textbooks, equipment—and library media center resources and usage. The advantages of such a system are that all school information is stored centrally; information is made available easily through the school network to all who are authorized to use it; and data are stored only once on the system, which makes for easy maintenance and updating of files. For instance, the library media center circulation system would make use of the student information stored in the school's student files, the library media center budgeting system would make use of overall school budget plans and information stored in the school budget files, and scheduling groups for library media center use or for special programs would be done with the aid of the school scheduling or timetabling system.

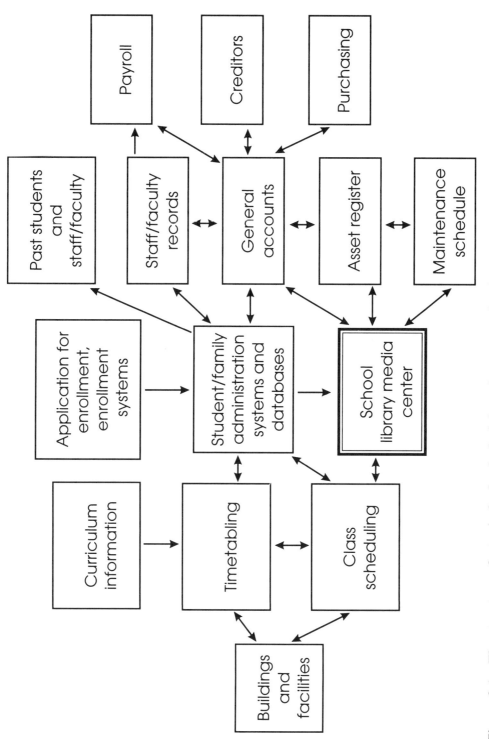

Figure 2.1 The structure of a typical school administration system that incorporates a library media center management system.

When a school system is well managed, there are distinct advantages for the school library media center in being part of it. There will also be advantages for the school (apart from advantages related to information access), in that the systems would be based on the same computer network and be maintained by the one technician. The technician's work is simplified because all modules operate in a similar way, and the users have only the one interface to learn to be able to use the various aspects of the schoolwide system. However, there may be disadvantages. Although a particular school administration system may well suit the school as a whole, the library media center module may not provide the kind of functionality that the library media specialist or the school would like. In addition, when decisions are being made related to the school as a whole, the needs of the library media center may not be given the same weight as they would be if it were just a library automation system that were being considered.

Several school administration systems incorporate a module or modules for the administration of the school library media center, among them MacSchool from Chancery Software, which incorporates MacSchool Library, and Administrator Plus (which has a library component).

- **An integrated, multi-function library system or automation of just one library function (or a couple of functions)?**

There are many possible variations on this set of options. Some school library media centers wish to automate as many functions as possible; others, for various reasons, may be looking at using computers for just one or two functions. Still others may want to automate just one or two functions now but also want the capability to extend their library automation project later, using the same suite of software and gradually building up to an integrated system.

An integrated, multi-function library automation system has many advantages, which will be discussed in more detail in the next section. This kind of system provides for all the major library functions, including cataloging, a public access catalog (OPAC) for library users, circulation, acquisitions/ordering, serials control, budgeting, and audiovisual media management. This means that the library media center databases (such as the catalog and the database of user information) are shared by all elements of the system, and data is entered only once into the system. The modules are designed as an integrated whole and work together in a seamless way. There is only one interface for the library media center staff to learn to use. Further, at the selection stage, there is a wide range of systems from which to choose, from relatively cheap systems for very small schools to sophisticated, minicomputer-based systems for larger schools. For school library media centers that are automating outside of a library network or a school administration system, this is currently the most popular path to library automation.

Some school library media centers choose an integrated, multi-function library system but begin implementation with one or two modules and then add modules to the system over time either as money is made available or as staff time is provided. This scenario operates best if the system was initially chosen with this in mind; it is easier to integrate modules that were designed to work together than to pull together disparate systems— although the latter has been done successfully, it usually requires a higher level of staff expertise. An advantage of this approach is that it enables the school library media center to spread the expenditure over a long period; a disadvantage is that it may cost more to purchase each module of the system separately. Depending on the way in which the integrated library system is designed, one module may have to be purchased first; with some earlier systems, this was the circulation module (which provided for a collection database and a user database), but it is much more common now for the catalog database to be the core database of the system and hence the first to be implemented. However, some vendors of integrated systems market the system as a single package, with no modules being sold separately, and so taking this approach may impose limits on the choice of an automated library system.

While an integrated, multi-function library system may be seen as the most desirable option for the school library media center that is going it alone with library automation, there are, nevertheless, good reasons why some school libraries media centers might be considering the automation of just one library function or a few library functions. A very small school of one or two teachers might want to have a catalog database to teach the students the basics of searching as well as to provide access to a collection but might not want to have a circulation system or a periodicals management system, for instance. Other schools may be looking at an interim system to store catalog data and produce a printed catalog while a decision is being made about an integrated system; provided that the interim system creates catalog records in a standard format (MARC), then it should be possible for these records to be loaded into the new system. It may even be that one of the criteria used to select the new system is its capability to accept records from the interim system or the capability of the vendor of the new system to convert the catalog records.

There are still other reasons for which some school library media centers might be looking to automate just one function or a few functions. The most common of these is the school library media center that is part of a multi-library network through which some but not all of the main library functions are automated. In this case, the school library media center may need to develop its own budgeting system—perhaps one that can incorporate data downloaded from the network system. Or there may be a need for locally produced bibliographies that relate to curriculum needs within the school and that incorporate material not in the network catalog or bibliographies that are in a format that cannot be produced through the network system. Again, it may be possible to download data from the network system to a local bibliographic system as the basis for this work.

- **Using specific-purpose library software or using general applications software?**

Most school library media centers automate using software designed specifically for library automation—either integrated, multi-function software, or smaller packages for specific library applications. Others decide for various reasons to use general purpose applications packages—such as database management or information retrieval systems, bibliographic packages, spreadsheets, and word processors—for various aspects of library automation. All these general-purpose packages have many potential uses in the library, and indeed it is quite possible to use an application development/database management package such as Oracle or a bibliographic package such as Pro-Cite to produce a library catalog. While there are some advantages for the school library media center in using software (such as a database package) that is already in use elsewhere in the school, there are also problems, not the least of which is that there will be a lot of work involved in adapting the package to meet library needs, particularly for such major library applications as creating a catalog.

However, sometimes a school library media center that has an integrated library automation system based on commercial library system software may use a general applications package to do just one or two tasks that can be better managed on a smaller system; desktop publishing for the production of bibliographies or brochures is a relatively common example. Other library tasks that have been handled by general applications software include producing current awareness bulletins, managing inter-library loans, developing a community information file, planning the budget, and scheduling library use by classes and groups.

- **Software Options: Purchasing software designed for the purpose or using "free" software or developing a system in-house.**

There are many decisions that have to be made by school library media specialists about the type of library automation software to be used. A major one is a selection decision from among the following options: to purchase commercially available software designed specifically for the purpose; to use "free" software that is available in the public domain or software provided as a donation; or to develop a system in-house, that is, to have the software written specially for the particular library. Today, most school library media centers consider only the first option, though school libraries in developing countries with free access to CDS/ISIS through UNESCO might find it a attractive means to automation.

Because there are a large number of commercial systems available to suit almost any need and budget, purchasing a commercial library software package for an integrated system or for some library functions has been the most popular option in most countries in recent years. It is also the one most often recommended by education authorities and consultants. The systems on the market vary in size from such very large, mainframe-based systems as VTLS and DRA to smaller systems for personal computers and local area networks—systems such as Alice/Annie/Embla, Athena, Winnebago, and Follett. In addition, there are hundreds of packages available that are able to perform just one or two library functions. These include cataloging systems, circulation packages, overdues systems, inter-library loan systems, as well as software for such purposes as bibliography management and newsletter production.

Among the advantages of purchasing commercial software is that the vendor will normally provide ongoing support for the system installation and further development of the system, there are other libraries that have had experience with the system, ongoing system development will usually have resulted in close tailoring of the system to meet library media center needs, manuals and other support materials will be available, and installation on a number of school sites will usually mean that "bugs" have been removed from the system. To maintain commercial viability in a competitive field, the vendor has to continue to develop the system, and so updates are available to library media centers that have purchased the system. This, in effect, allows ongoing development costs to be shared. A disadvantage if the system is a popular one is that a single library media center will not necessarily have its particular needs considered because many library media centers will be providing feedback to the developer. Some library media specialists also argue that, despite the number of systems on the market, they are unable to find a commercial system that exactly meets their needs.

Some other library media centers—usually though not invariably those with severe budget constraints—have chosen to use free library software to automate their libraries, rather than purchase a system. There are various sources of free software. Some—particularly microcomputer software for particular functions in small libraries—are in the public domain and available copyright free. This might be through downloading software from Internet sites, or it might be through an association or organization. UNESCO makes CDS/ISIS available free to libraries in developing countries, and it has been used by school libraries. One of its strengths is that it has been adapted to accommodate a number of non-English alphabets; another is that additional program extensions are available from a number of sources to adapt the basic system or to add functionality. An international listserv provides support and information for librarians who are using the system. However, it has to be emphasized that in this regard, CDS/ISIS and FILMS (from Functional Solutions) are exceptional.

While the idea of a free library system is an attractive one at first glance, the reality does not always bear this out. Apart from CDS/ISIS and FILMS, the documentation for free software is usually poor and sometimes nonexistent. There is seldom any customer support if the library media center has problems. Because the developer is not getting any money from it, there will seldom be ongoing development of the software. If "bugs" appear or if extra programming has to be done, the library media center will usually have to employ a programmer, who will, in turn, probably be working from poor documentation on the system and so will take longer to do the job. Horror stories abound about the way the program code for such systems has been written—some originated as student projects—and good programmers consequently will tend to steer clear of patch-up jobs on these systems. Some libraries have spent a great deal of money and staff time on a "free" system only to find that they still have an unsatisfactory system. There have even been articles written for professional journals about "the costs of a free automated library system" (see Parnell & Patterson, 1983). While CDS/ISIS has been very popular with users in many developing countries, it needs to be pointed out that, though the software comes free, the libraries still need to invest in staff training, database creation, and user education, among other things, so that the system as a whole is far from being free.

The third software option is for the library media center to write its own in-house library system or to have one written to its specifications. This may be done because the library media specialist cannot find a commercial package to meet the local needs—something that is increasingly unlikely as the commercial systems become more flexible and offer a range of options that allow each library media center to tailor the system to suit their own needs. Sometimes this option is considered because either the library or the system developer plans to market the completed system to other libraries as a commercial system—this was common in the early days of school library automation, and some of the current systems on the market began in this way. However, a considerable investment is required now to develop a system to the point where it is commercially viable. Sometimes this option is considered in a school when the price of an automated library system seems high to decision makers who are accustomed only to purchasing educational software or word processors: in this case, it is tempting to accept the offer of a parent or computer teacher to "write a system for the library media center." Library automation systems come at a high price because they are complex and time-consuming to write and to test fully—something that is not always apparent to an enthusiastic person who has programming skills but knows little about libraries. And then, where will the enthusiastic volunteer be when the system needs updating or there are bugs to be removed?

- **Hardware Options: Mainframe or minicomputer with terminals or a LAN or another option?**

To a great extent, the hardware decisions will be dictated by the decisions made in relation to other options for school library media center automation. If the school library media center is automating as part of a multi-library network, then the type of hardware that is used in the school may be dictated by the network contract—though there may well still be some decisions to be made, particularly regarding the number of access points to the system and the type of access that each one will provide. Some commercially available integrated library automation systems will run only on one type of hardware, while others are portable across a range of hardware platforms.

Some library media centers automate using hardware that is already available to them in the school, particularly where a school already has a substantial school network in place. For other libraries, the hardware to be used for library automation will be governed by the functions to be automated, the size of the library, the number of users, the size of its databases, the size of the system, the number of access points to the system, any requirements for access from outside the library media center, and so on. It may be that the school or school district already has a supply agreement with a particular hardware vendor, in which case the system would be selected with this in mind—in other words, this would be taken into account in the planning process as a factor in the external environment.

The basic hardware options for school library media center automation include a large computer (mainframe or minicomputer) with terminals (this computer may serve only one library, or, perhaps more likely, it may be shared with other functions in the school such as school administration, or it may be shared by all libraries in a multi-library network); a standalone personal computer (usually as the basis for an automated library system in a very small school library media center or to automate just one or two functions in a library, such as desktop publishing or budgeting and accounting); a number of personal computers linked in a local area network (LAN), with file server, printers, and perhaps CD-ROM drive, and other peripherals being shared by all the computers in the network; or a large microcomputer or supermicro supporting "slave" machines or "dumb terminals." In practice, with new developments in networking technology and the increasing power of personal computers, the distinctions between these options are blurring, and it is possible that library media center automation could be based on more than one of these options.

In most school library media centers where automation is being considered today, the school library media specialist is looking for a system to run on a local area network. This means that the main hardware decision to be made will be the kind of network. Some library system vendors sell their system only for installation on a particular kind of network; others make strong recommendations about the kind of network. It is a good idea to heed these recommendations: they are usually based on a combination of knowledge of the system software itself and the network environment for which it was optimized, and they take into account the experiences of the school library media centers that have bought and installed the system. A good vendor will want the system to look good in your library media center, not just out of vanity but because this will reduce the number of complaints about aspects of the system that are not working as well as they could. But be aware that the person whose responsibility it is to purchase the network hardware for your school or school system will be charged with trying to get the least expensive network that will actually run the automated library system that you want. If the minimum hardware configuration necessary to run the system is selected, it may run slowly, special features may not work well, and the school library media center may be locked out of any software updates that are written to take advantage of more powerful hardware.

INTEGRATED LIBRARY/ INFORMATION SYSTEMS

As indicated previously, the most common approach to school library media center automation today is the integrated, multi-function library system through which a range of the library media center procedures are performed. This kind of system can be used within the individual school or by the school library media center as part of a wider network of schools or libraries. It can also be used within the individual school library media center as part of a local area network through which members of the school community are provided with access to the school library media center catalog, other databases, CD-ROMs, and even online access to external databases and the Internet. In addition, library media center staff (but not others unless authorized) have access to library functions such as cataloging, ordering, budgeting, and circulation through the network. Used in this way, the integrated library system provides the school community with the basis of a powerful information and resource management system that is also efficient and effective in administrative terms.

The integrated approach to school library media center automation is based on the assumption that the media center can be viewed as a system in its own right in addition to being part of such wider systems as the school and the school district or education authority. The school library media center carries out a range of technical service activities as well as providing services and undertaking activities related to the educational program of the school. These activities include selecting library media center resources (or resources to which the media center will provide access); acquiring the resources; accessioning, cataloging, and preparing them for circulation (with barcode labels and possibly pockets for cards); storing and providing access to them; circulating them; including them in bibliographies; and, finally, withdrawing them from the collection. Figure 2.2, page 44, shows the classic "life cycle" of an item in a school library media center collection. Of all the procedures listed, only the selection of the item and the final removal of the item from the library media center collection would not normally be included in the automation process, though whether it would be appropriate to automate all the procedures in any particular library media center is a decision that would have to be made by the school library media specialist, taking into account local conditions and the needs of the school community. Even the procedures of selection and ultimate disposal could be assisted by the use of information technology: for instance, an online database of book reviews or the Amazon.com site on the Internet could be searched for an

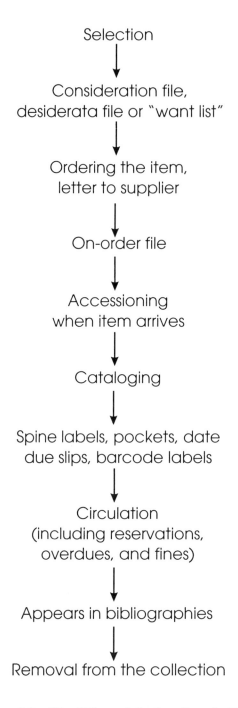

Figure 2.2   The "life cycle" of an item in the library media center collection—Procedures.

assessment of an item before purchase, and borrowing statistics compiled through the automated library system could help in a decision about whether to discard the item from the collection.

Integrated library systems generally provide modules for the major technical services and user services functions listed in Figure 2.2, plus a public access catalog (OPAC) to enable the users to search the catalog and any other databases incorporated into the system. The catalog database is usually the heart of such a system, forming the basis not just of the OPAC but also of the circulation system and the inventory module as well as providing data that can be used by the ordering module. Integrated systems usually incorporate at least the cataloging system and a circulation system; in addition, most have modules to handle a range of other library media center functions. Depending on the system, these might include modules for ordering materials for the library collection, the organization and circulation of periodicals/magazines, maintaining a booking system for films and other audiovisual materials, the management of inter-library loans, statistics generation and reports, and communications facilities for access to external databases or CD-ROMs. Not only do these integrated systems vary in the functions they perform; they also vary in the ways in which they perform them and in their effectiveness.

Some of these systems are sold as a hardware and software package in which both must be purchased together; for others, the hardware and software can be purchased separately. With some, all the software for the integrated system must be purchased at one time; others can be purchased module by module as the library media center raises the money or when each of the parts of the system is to be implemented.

Many integrated library automation and information systems are now available for school library media centers. A select list is provided as an appendix to this book, and a page on the "School Libraries Online" Web site provides not only a list but also interactive links to the Web sites of the vendors. Among the systems are Dynix (Ameritech), Alice for Windows (also known in various versions and in places as OASIS, Annie, and Embla), Alexandria, Book Mark, AIMS, Winnebago, Athena, The Eloquent Librarian, Library Pro 2.0, Mandarin (SIRS), CHILDS (Children's Interactive Library Display System from Sunrise Software), and Follett. Although they are all very different from one other, these systems all provide for the automation of most aspects of library administration, including cataloging, circulation, ordering, financial management, statistics and reporting, and other functions. However, the systems do vary in size, cost, capabilities, and ease of use so that there are systems that can meet the needs of very large

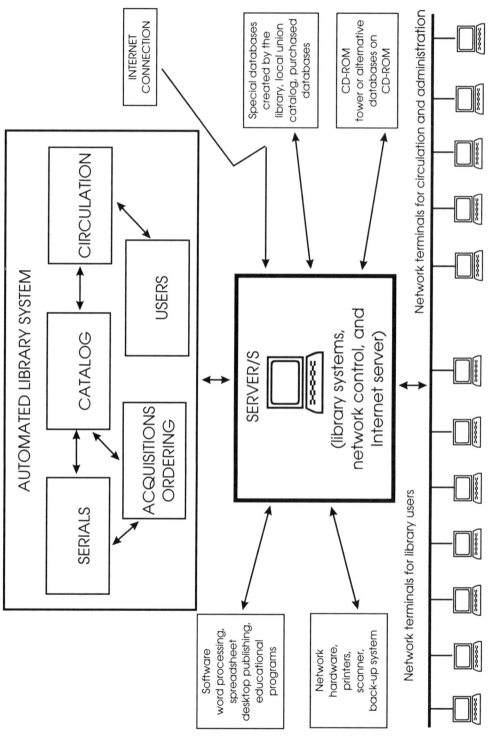

Figure 2.3   The components of a typical integrated library automation system for a school library media center.

libraries at one end of the scale and very small libraries at the other end—and everything in between. In each case, the basis is the one integrated software package that can be running on a standalone personal computer or on a local area network (LAN) in the library or on a minicomputer (usually through a network).

Not only do these systems handle most of the basic library functions but many are capable of being linked with the school's computer-based administration system as well (for budgeting, record keeping, and so on) and with library and information systems outside the school (for information retrieval). Thus, information about borrowers can be loaded into the library media center system from the school administration system; catalog records can be loaded in from an outside cataloging source. Word processors and desktop publishing facilities linked to the library system can enable the library media center to prepare bibliographies and other documents from its own catalog and other sources and present these in an attractive format to meet the needs of particular users. The statistics and information management features of automated library systems can enable the library media specialist to assess usage of the library media center and its services and to plan ahead on the basis of reliable information about current use.

THE LIBRARY MEDIA CENTER CATALOG

The library media center catalog may be computerized as part of an integrated library system; it might also be computerized separately or as the first step on the way to implementing an integrated system over a longer term. The catalog is an area of school library media center administration in which computers have had considerable impact over the years. Cataloging is a highly skilled, labor-intensive procedure that provides the main means of access to a library's resources. Without a catalog, the books and other materials held by a library media center would be almost useless; certainly, it would be extremely difficult for users to find what they needed. Yet traditional, manually created card catalogs have proved cumbersome, inefficient, and difficult to use (especially for young children). Some library media specialists have seen the trend toward computer-based cataloging as providing an opportunity to re-assess the aims and objectives of library cataloging and to develop catalogs that are more closely tuned to users' needs.

The earliest applications of computers in cataloging were creating a catalog database that could be used to produce a printed book catalog or a catalog on COM (computer output microform) microfiche. The catalog data would be entered into the computer and stored on tape or disk. Every three months (or six months or a year, depending on the library) the tapes would be sent to a bureau where updated microfiche catalogs, or printed book catalogs, would be produced from them. Only a few schools anywhere in the world seem to have created microfiche catalogs in this way, though some school systems or school districts have done so. The advantages of computer-produced microfiche catalogs were that it was a quicker process than typing and filing sets of catalog cards; the microfiche catalogs usually took up less space; and it was possible to have multiple copies of the catalog fiche so that copies could be placed in teachers' rooms or wherever there was a microfiche reader. The disadvantages were that access was required to expensive mainframe or minicomputer hardware or a bureau service, microfiche readers had to be provided for people to use the microfiche catalog, ongoing charges had to be paid to the bureau for updates, and between updates the catalog gradually became less accurate as books were added to or withdrawn from the library collection.

Rather more common in school library media centers were computer-produced printed book catalogs or indexes. These could be produced by a bureau from computer tapes or disks in a process similar to producing microfiche catalogs; however, from the late 1970s, there were also microcomputer-based packages available that could be used for this purpose. In the early 1980s, some school districts in the United States and Canada created catalogs for their schools using a central minicomputer-based system, while in Australia, some university/college computer services units provided a service to schools who wished to produce either printed book or microfiche KWOC (Key-Word-Out-of-Context) indexes to their collections (Jennings & Schmidmaier, 1983, 2). This was found to be a cost-effective alternative to the card catalog (Rogers, 1984, 6). The teacher librarians were pleased with the quick production methods and with having multiple copies of their catalog for use throughout the school; against this, some were concerned about their dependence on an outside agency to maintain their catalog should that agency wish to withdraw its services. Another problem arose when the library media center wished to automate its circulation system: the indexing/cataloging and circulation systems could not be linked directly.

Other schools tackled the problems associated with manually produced card catalogs by automating catalog card production. It was obvious that creating sets of catalog cards manually for each new item that was acquired by the library was both labor-intensive and inefficient. The same data had to be typed on the shelf list card, the author card, the title card, any subject cards, and on the loan card, then any necessary headings had to be typed on the cards. Then each card had to be proofread separately. This opened the way for errors in cataloging. It also meant that school library media specialists were often reluctant to use all the desirable subject headings for each item, because even more cards would have to be typed and checked. One early solution to this problem was a catalog card duplicator—the catalog data was typed onto a stencil and then copies were made onto catalog cards using a small, handheld duplicator; however, headings still had to be typed onto the cards, and the process was extremely messy. The memory typewriter provided the next solution, enabling the production of multiple cards with one set of data input, although, again, the headings had to be typed onto the cards individually. Catalog card production programs, developed for a range of microcomputers in the 1980s, provided the next solution to the problem of automated catalog card production. By 1986, the author identified some 60 of these programs when compiling her directory of *Computer Software for School Libraries.* Some sold for as little as U.S. $10. It was only with the increasing availability of automated library systems based on personal computers and local area networks that these catalog card production programs were gradually replaced, though some school library media centers are still using them. Where these card production systems allowed for the storage of the catalog data on disk, the database thus created could sometimes be used as the basis of a computer-based catalog when an automated library system was introduced, with attendant savings on the cost of data input for the new system, and time savings.

Computer-based catalogs, whether part of an integrated library system or implemented separately, allow library media center users to search for the materials they need through a personal computer or terminal. Most provide for searches by author, title, subject, and/or keyword, perhaps Dewey number; some add still more access points (illustrator, date, curriculum level, keyword in a note); most provide for more complex Boolean searches as well. Because the system is interactive, it is relatively easy for users to test ideas and to try multiple search strategies. Users may be able to format their search results into the school's required bibliographic format for research papers and projects and load them into a word processor. If a printer is attached, users will be able to print out their search results. Not only is this easier for the user but it is more accurate than copying from the screen and means less time is spent at the computer by each user. If the catalog is part of an integrated library system, then users will be able to see which of the items produced by their search are actually on the library media center shelves at the moment and which are out on loan (and perhaps even when those items are due back).

Some school library media centers have a catalog with most or all these features but based on a CD-ROM rather than with the catalog database on the hard drive of a personal computer or file server on the network. Some multi-library networks now provide each participating library with a catalog on CD-ROM or a copy of the union catalog on CD-ROM; this is normally updated regularly with a new CD-ROM. Some bureau services will take catalog records on disk and provide updated CD-ROMs regularly. An advantage of the CD-ROM system is that multiple copies of the catalog can be created easily and cheaply; these copies can be placed in classrooms, teachers' rooms, and other libraries—anywhere where there is a CD-ROM drive on which the disk can be used. Since more personal computers come with CD-ROM drives built in, this can be a very attractive idea. However, with recent improvements in network file servers and hard disk technology, the CD-ROMs can appear to be very slow by comparison—to the point where some school library media centers are loading the data from reference CD-ROMs onto their network to improve access speeds.

The last few years have seen many new developments in automated library systems (including systems for school library media centers). These developments are changing our ideas about what an automated library system should be and particularly about how a library catalog should operate. There is, for instance, a trend toward graphical user interfaces and the use of color and even sound in library catalog interfaces. The catalog database itself may incorporate reviews, pictures (such as cover illustrations), lists of contents, and other material, along with the catalog record itself and circulation information. In addition, the catalog may incorporate links to other related resources so that the user is led to material inside and outside the library media center that could be relevant to the search. It might also link the user to the catalog of another local library that has relevant resources—for instance, to the catalog of the local public library or a university or college library (via a direct link or via the Internet).

For example, the CHILDS system uses a combination of color graphics and simple commands to provide a search interface for children and a loans system that enables them to check out and return their own library books. The Dynix system can be installed with Dynix PAC for Windows, a multi-color graphical user interface that allows library users to search easily across the library catalog, CD-ROMs, and other databases. Alexandria can be installed with a colorful graphic catalog search interface called Kid's Catalog. An extension of the Annie system, the Book Wizard, CD-ROM provides a graphical environment through which users have access to reviews of books and cover illustrations as well as catalog information (this system also uses a quiz to lead children to fiction books that match their interests and reading abilities). The AIMS system enables librarians to scan reviews and summaries or contents pages into the library catalog. These developments mean that the library catalog is no longer just based on bibliographical information; it can also incorporate graphical search assistance tools, review information, summaries or abstracts, and images such as cover illustrations. It is not just the library catalog that is changing; as suggested in the description of CHILDS, there are also developments in circulation systems that are changing the ways in which libraries do things. The most obvious of these changes is *patron self-check*, the facility to allow library users to check out their own books automatically and to extend the loan period on books that they have borrowed.

Another clear trend, highlighted previously, is the development of a closer nexus between the school library media center catalog system and wider information systems, particularly the Internet. On the one hand, the school library media center catalog might be made available for searching via the Internet, which would mean that students and teachers could search the catalog from home (or from another library or community center) and perhaps even place holds on items that they need. The Eloquent Librarian has a tool called GENCAT through which a library database such as a catalog can be made available on the Internet's World Wide Web, while Follett has the Telnet QuickLink facility through which people outside the school can access the library media center catalog on the Internet via telnet, and Dynix has options for both telnet and Web access to the library catalog.

On the other hand, library catalogs can provide access to Internet resources for users in the library media center, in addition to the more usual function of providing access to information about resources within the library media center. The Dynix graphical OPAC allows the library media center to provide links to World Wide Web sites and community resources as well as to the catalog and an online library bulletin board. When a library media center user does a search for resources on a particular topic, he or she is provided with information about resources (books, audiovisual materials, and other resources) in the library media center and is given active links to Internet resources that match the search query. Library Pro 2.0 allows school library media specialists to catalog Web addresses so that patrons can locate materials and to make the school library media center catalog searchable through an Internet World Wide Web browser such as Netscape (which provides an easy-to-use graphical interface).

Today, most library catalog systems are based on MARC (MAchine Readable Cataloging) records. MARC, a standard bibliographic format for computer-based records, contains the descriptive cataloging data for a book or other item; the subject entries; the classification number (or call number); and other information, including price, vendor, date of purchase, funding and notes. The MARC record also includes information needed by the computer system to process the records; this information is in the form of tags. When the library media specialist catalogs an item for the library collection into the automated system, the screen display will guide the input, and the MARC tags will be created automatically by the system. When MARC records are added to a catalog from another source—for example, an online source or a CD-ROM of catalog data—then the MARC tags will come as part of the record. Most automated library systems can import (or add) catalog records in MARC format and export MARC records to disk or directly to another system; these are the two critical requirements in relation to MARC. Though such a format does not matter to the library media center users who would never see information in this form, it does matter if cataloging records from other sources are to be used in the system or if records created through the system are to be loaded into other systems (for example, when a new system is purchased a few years into the future).

Sources of catalog records in MARC format include:

- library networks (where member libraries can use catalog records created by other libraries in the network);

- commercial or cooperative online information services (utilities), such as OCLC, whose WorldCat database provides catalog records in MARC format, among others;

- the Library of Congress on the Internet and some other state library or school library systems on the Internet, such as Blue Skyways (Kansas), Sunlink (Florida), and Texas Library Connection;

- other Internet sources, such as Marcive's WebSelect;

- software systems such as Bookwhere 2000 and EZCat that can be used to search Internet MARC sources and download;

- commercial vendors of MARC catalog records on CD-ROM and online, such as Brodart's *Precision One* CD-ROM and Internet service and the *Alliance Plus* CD-ROM from Follett;

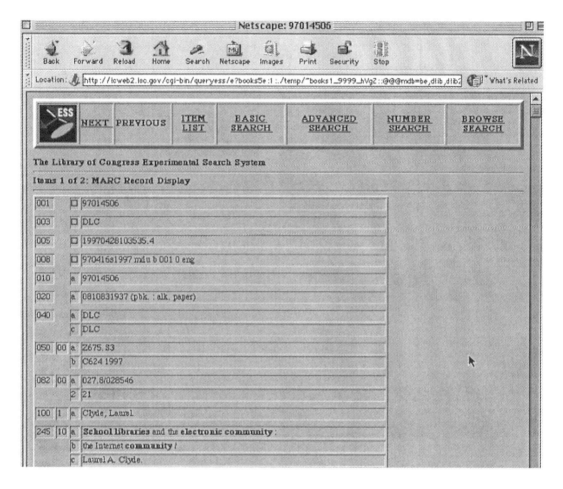

Figure 2.4   Part of a catalog record in MARC format from the Library of Congress.

- booksellers and library suppliers (such as Baker and Taylor in the United States) who provide books ready processed for libraries (complete with MARC records on disk);

- some automated library system vendors who provide databases of catalog records with their systems (for a fee); and

- bureau services that specialize in transferring card catalog data or non-MARC catalog records on disk to MARC format.

   In Australia, a national project originally called ASCIS (the Australian Schools Catalogue Information Service), now SCIS, has had an important influence on the development of school library catalogs. In the early 1980s, a research project established that there was considerable overlap among the collections of school libraries around the country that served similar age groups. It was also recognized that a great deal of professional time was being wasted because thousands of teacher-librarians were, of necessity, cataloging the same items (Macdonald, 1983, 42–44). This substantially reduced the amount of time that the teacher-librarians could spend working with library clients and developing library programs and services. In addition, it was felt that access to high-quality catalog data at a reasonable price would result in school library catalogs of a higher standard, which would not only be more effective for information retrieval but also as tools to teach search skills. Originally (in 1982) a dial-up online search service that provided catalog records in MARC form to schools in print form (as card sets) and on disk for loading into computer-based catalogs, SCIS now makes its database available via CD-ROM and through SCISWeb on the Internet, and MARC records can be downloaded directly. By 1998, schools were achieving a hit rate as high as 95 percent to 97 percent when searching for catalog records on the system (Roche, 1998; Hopkins, 1998), with a download time of under 30 seconds for multiple records. SCIS now includes curriculum information as well as catalog records in MARC format; it can therefore serve as a selection tool, helping teacher-librarians locate records on particular topics at particular grade levels. In addition, it is no longer strictly an Australian service, since it is used in New Zealand and a number of Pacific countries.

THE CIRCULATION SYSTEM

Just as there is an enormous range of automated catalog options available to school library media centers, so there are many different options for computer-based circulation systems. It has already been indicated that these options could include implementing an automated circulation system as part of an integrated school library system (Alice or Dynix, for instance) or as part of a computer-based multi-library network. A circulation system may be implemented in a school library media center as a separate system, and there are software packages available for this, though it is more common now to automate circulation as a module or part of an integrated library automation system.

The circulation system or module tracks the entire library collection, reducing book losses and improving the collection of fines (if these are charged). Lists of overdues or books out (by home room, for example) are easily printed as needed. Different fines, borrowing limits, loan durations, and grace periods can be set, depending on need. The system alerts people staffing the circulation desk to fines owed, overdue items, too many items checked out, or items on reserve for someone else. The following functions are normally covered by the circulation system or module:

- processing loans,
- processing returns,
- tracking overdues,
- recording and tracking reservations,
- information about any item in the collection,
- information about the current location of any item in the collection,
- information about any registered library user,
- information about what any registered user has on loan,
- providing different loan periods and different loan limits for different groups of borrowers,
- bulk loans to classrooms or teachers for curriculum units,
- statistics on collection usage and borrowing patterns, and
- information for collection maintenance.

In addition, in some integrated library systems the inventory function is part of the circulation module.

Computer-based circulation systems generally allow for the entering of loans data via a barcode reader (or light pen or barwand or barcode scanner). This is quicker than writing the details and more accurate. All items in the collection have a barcode label (usually inside the front or back cover or on the front or back cover beside the spine) that identifies the item, and borrowers have a card with a barcode label for their user number. To register a loan, the barcode reader is passed over the barcode label on the borrower's card then over the barcode label in the book. Details of borrower and book appear on the screen as confirmation that the loan is recorded. When an item is returned, the barcode reader is passed over the barcode label on the item to record the return, and then the item is re-shelved. In most systems, it is also possible to enter loans and returns data through the keyboard so that, if necessary, the library media center can operate without a barcode reader (though this is slower and less accurate, it can help in a difficult situation).

There are a number of different barcode systems in use today, and most circulation systems can operate only with one or two, so that in effect, when a circulation system is chosen, a barcode system is also chosen. The type of barcode system used becomes a particular issue if a library is switching from one automated library system to another, but it is also relevant when barcode readers are being purchased—a barcode reader has to be able to read the library media center's barcodes, just as the automated system has to be able to process them. Currently, the most popular barcode systems in libraries are Codabar and Code 39, but there are others. Some automated library systems will print barcode labels for items as they are added to the collection; otherwise, vendors supply barcode labels, or they are purchased through a secondary supplier.

Not all automated circulation systems use barcodes, however; some use OCR (optical character recognition) systems, which use standard letters and numbers that are read by an optical character reader rather like a barcode reader in operation. The problem at present is that currently the optical character readers are generally rather more expensive than barcode readers, so school library media centers have been advised to avoid systems that require them. Their advantage is that they display information about the item in a form that can be read and understood by humans; however, many barcode systems now add printed information in normal letters and numbers to the barcode label, and in a school library media center setting, this information may include the name of the school and the title and accession number or call number of the item.

One aspect of the circulation system is dealing with items in the library collection; the other is dealing with the borrowers. In the school library media center setting, teachers and school administrators will normally have library cards with a barcode label just as they have public library cards. In a secondary school, the students can be issued barcoded library cards too, though if the school has an ID card, then the library's barcode label might be placed on the back of the ID card. In situations where a card is lost, then most automated circulation systems allow library staff to record a loan by typing in the borrower number or the name of the student. In elementary schools, this becomes more difficult, particularly in the lower grades; not only are the children often deemed unable to take care of a library card, but as one library media specialist has reported, "the little ones don't even know their last names" (Hatton, 1998). Different schools have developed a number of strategies to handle this problem, including keeping alphabetical class lists in a folder at the circulation desk with the barcode label beside each name, asking children to memorize their class and a short number and having the circulation desk staff type the information in for each loan (if the school has a lunch program or other program that uses the same system, then this helps), creating borrowers' cards with barcode label but having the class teacher keep them, keeping the cards at the circulation desk and using a symbol on each one that represents the child (having each child draw the symbol?) so that they can find their cards in the class box even if they cannot read. It is worth noting, though, that school library media centers trust children to take books home and keep track of them, so should they also be taught to keep track of a card? Where cards are used, plastic cards can often be purchased from the automated library system vendor or from third-party suppliers. However, another option is to do the job in-house, using the personal computer and word processing program to create the cards, then pasting on a barcode label and laminating the card.

A feature that has been included in some circulation systems in recent years—or sold separately as an add-on to the circulation system—is *patron self-check*. In these systems, the library users run the books that they want to borrow through a special unit that records details of the items (from the item barcode) and then requests that they either swipe their library card or enter name or borrower number through a keypad. The swipe systems generally require the use of a special card with magnetic stripe, but where such cards are used in the school to record attendance (with students swiping their way into classrooms), then they might also be used as library cards for a self-check system. If students have to type their borrower number or name into the system, then the problems mentioned previously might arise in using the system in an elementary school. If a patron self-check system is to be effective, then it is necessary that the library media center also has a security system to prevent students taking items out of the library that have not been properly checked out. Security systems are discussed later in this chapter.

A range of statistical reports can generally be obtained through automated circulation systems, including printouts in the form of tables and graphs. In addition, the retrieval of information about loans or borrowers is not limited to one or two access points: Usually the computer-based circulation file can be searched by author, title, call number, accession number, keywords (for the item); by name, class, and borrower's number (for the borrower); and often by other access points as well. The statistics-gathering process is made much easier with automated circulation systems. Most library media centers need to keep circulation statistics. The reasons include:

- the need to be aware of those sections of the collection that receive heaviest use and those that are less well used so that new book purchases and promotions of certain types of materials can be planned,

- the need to be aware of which groups of users borrow most and which users borrow least so that user needs can be met and so that library promotion activities can be targeted to those who are not heavy borrowers,

- the need to document requests for funding,

- planning for staffing of the circulation desk so that the periods of heaviest borrowing are those for which the highest level of staffing is available,

- future planning needs of the library media center, and

- preparation of the annual report.

Other advantages of the computer-based circulation system include the ease and accuracy of recording loans via the barcode reader; the ability to retrieve information using a variety of online access points; the long-term saving of staff time; the absence of filing problems and the ease of retrieval; the speed of transactions; the ability to cater for multiple loan periods for different classes of borrowers with ease; the ability to generate statistics on item usage and borrower patterns. Disadvantages are less clear from this description, but relate to establishment costs for the computer hardware and software; changes to the library furniture to incorporate barcode readers and computer terminals, the cost of barcoding all items in the library collection, and the necessity to number or label the library users.

OTHER ADMINISTRATIVE FUNCTIONS

While cataloging and circulation are the major library functions that come to mind when library media center automation is being considered, there are a number of other library functions that can also be automated and that normally form part of an integrated automated library system. These functions include the purchasing (ordering/acquisition) of library materials and accessioning them, serials (magazine) control, management of audiovisual and multimedia materials, inventory/stocktaking, collection assessment and evaluation, budgeting and accounting, general statistics and record keeping, and library promotion and publicity. All these functions will be discussed.

Ordering and Acquisitions

It is through the acquisitions system that the library media center tracks the ordering of new items for the collection and the addition of new items to the collection and keeps a record of payments made and due. However, most acquisitions systems are rather more sophisticated than this, particularly in an integrated library automated system, where the catalog database and collection usage statistics are linked to the acquisitions module. The following are functions commonly performed by automated acquisitions systems:

- maintaining a file of purchase requests from students, teachers, and school administration (with information about bibliographic verification of those items by the library media specialist);

- maintaining a consideration file or desiderata file or want list of items that the library media center would like to order when funds become available;

- printing purchase orders (with covering letters) or submitting orders online;

- maintaining a file of items on order (which may be linked to the catalog database so that items are indicated as being on order when library users do a catalog search);

- tracking orders, reporting incomplete orders, and generating reminders and claims for items that have been on order for longer than a time specified by the school library media specialist;

- providing reports on funds spent, funds committed, and funds available;

- managing multiple sources of funds for purchasing, such as annual funds from the school, special grants, and allocation of funds to particular departments in the school for library media center resources;

- providing reports on suppliers, including time taken to fill orders, completeness of orders, pricing, and performance statistics;

- providing search access to information about particular items that are on order, through multiple access points, including author, title, ISBN/ISSN, keyword, and order number;

- printing vouchers to go to the school's accounting department for payment or online transfer of payment requests;

- transfer of order information to the catalog system when the item arrives in the library media center.

Serials Control

Serials (also called periodicals and magazines) have features that are significantly different from those of books (albeit both are printed materials), and so they require different treatment through an automated library system. The main difference is that while a book is purchased, arrives, is paid for, and is cataloged, a serial title is by subscription (usually on an annual basis) and keeps on arriving, with a consequent need for library holdings records to be updated with each issue. Serials may be published daily, weekly, fortnightly, monthly, quarterly, or annually (and there are a number of other possibilities). Thus funds have to be allocated for serials on an ongoing basis; the arrival of each new issue has to be recorded; and if the serial is circulated, then it has to be on the basis of the particular issue that is borrowed rather than the title. In addition, some library media centers route each new issue of a serial title to the people in the school (such as subject specialists) who most need to see it before placing it in the collection. However, as with books, MARC records are available for cataloging serial titles. The following functions are commonly performed by serials management modules of automated library systems:

- ordering a new serial title and paying the first subscription;

- alerting to the need for a subscription renewal and renewing the subscription when due;

- canceling the subscription;

- recording the arrival of each issue of the serial;

- alerting to nonarrival of issues and printing claims (or sending them electronically);

- creating a routing list for each new issue of the serial;

- managing funds and allocating the subscription against the appropriate budget line;

- tracking the performance of suppliers;

- recording information about binding (if the library media center has back issues of a serial bound);

- providing for searching on title, author, subject keywords, and perhaps other fields or elements, to display holdings data; and

- transfer of data from the serials system for display in the library catalog in response to user requests.

Management of Audiovisual and Multimedia Materials

Audiovisual and multimedia materials are managed in different ways in different library media centers; some simply treat them in the same way as books, catalog them in the same way, and lend them through the circulation system in the same way. For various reasons, including security and cost, other school library media centers want to manage them apart from the other resources of the library media center. They may want to keep them in a separate room and sometimes to restrict their circulation to authorized people, ensuring that copyrighted software and videos are not copied and that the user has the right equipment and knows how it works. The materials treated in this way might include laptop computers, overhead projection units, scanners, video recorders, videos, CD-ROMs. The following functions are commonly performed by the audiovisual and multimedia materials management modules of automated library systems:

- ordering and payment if purchased, otherwise ordering and payment for hire;

- maintaining equipment inventories;

- recording the availability of manuals and other operational tools;

- cataloging of equipment and software or disks;

- circulation of equipment and software;

- keeping track of software and other licenses;

- maintenance schedules for equipment;

- recording checks on videos, CDs, and other media for damage;

- compiling lists of resources as appropriate for inclusion in bibliographies and other listings;

- provision of information for the catalog system so that user searches locate not only the material on the open shelves of the library media center but also the materials covered by the audiovisual and multimedia module.

Inventory or Stocktaking

Inventory or stocktaking is the process by which the school library media specialist ensures that all items that should be in the library media center collection are in fact there and that the materials on the shelves are the materials that should be there. During inventory, the shelf list file is compared with the items on the shelves; for this reason, the shelf list is arranged in shelf order. With an automated system, there is no need to create a separate shelf list file; the inventory module provides for this to be done through the catalog database. Every item on the shelves is recorded using the barcode reader (a small portable barcode reader with a memory is particularly useful for this task because the contents of the memory can be dumped to the inventory system from time to time, and there is no need to tie up one of the library media center's computers with inventory tasks); those items legitimately out on loan are already indicated through the circulation system records. Once the process of going through the collection with the barcode reader is complete, the inventory module will produce a list of items that are not on the shelves and not on loan; this is the list of missing items. Statistical summaries are compiled and printed out in a variety of formats, including graphic formats. Most library media centers do an inventory on an annual basis, though the rate of loss from the collection might suggest that it be done more or less frequently. One of the most useful outcomes of an inventory is an indication of titles that need to be replaced, but it also gives an indication of patterns of loss that might be of assistance in establishing monitoring procedures.

Collection Assessment

The inventory provides some of the information that is necessary for collection assessment; in addition, information about usage or nonusage of items in the collection or areas of the collection is provided by the circulation system. The latter might include reports that show the circulation of items within a particular call number range or the kinds of books or authors that are borrowed most by children in particular grades. The catalog database might be used to produce reports showing the number of items in the collection (perhaps in particular areas of the collection) of a particular age (recorded as date of publication or date of acquisition). The database might, for example, be used to produce a table showing the average age of the library materials in each main area of the sciences. In the state of Missouri, the state media center standards are linked to the age of the collection: for certain sections of the Dewey classification (such as some of the science and technology areas) it is recommended that at least 70 percent of the resources have a copyright date within the last 12 years. There are similar requirements in other places, too. Once problem areas of the collection have been identified, though, then library media specialists and often teachers need to go over the reports and the items identified and make decisions about withdrawing items from the collection or purchasing new items. Even if there are no immediate problems, if teachers are involved in resource selection, then it would be useful for them to know what is being used, by whom, and how much. This could help them to identify areas in which resource promotion is needed.

Other sources of information about the collection and its use include user studies, analysis of the inter-library loan statistics and the items borrowed through inter-library loan, shelf availability studies and comparison of the shelf list/catalog records of library media center holdings with lists or directories of recommended resources for particular subject areas or age levels.

At the level of the individual item in the collection or of items being considered for inclusion in the collection, information technology can also be of assistance. Catalogs of other school library media centers on the Internet, or publishers' databases, or the Web sites of major online bookstores might be used to identify possible titles for purchase. Internet review sources might provide further information and evaluation of those titles.

Once the item is in hand, readability tests will help to determine the suitability of the item for a particular student group. Readability of text depends on a number of factors, which may include size of the font, space between the lines, difficulty of the vocabulary, number of syllables per word, predictability of the text from supporting pictures, any repetitive elements in the story, length of the sentences, sentence structure, page layout. There are many different measures of readability, and they do not all measure the same things. However, most tests give a reasonably useful guide, and the usefulness and reliability increase if more than one test is used. There are now computer-based tools available to calculate the readability of a piece of text quickly and easily; some of the tools calculate readability using several formulas. The *Microsoft Word* word processing system comes with the Flesch-Kincaid readability index (four measures of readability) as part of the Grammar Check (on the Tools menu); *Microsoft Word* in Office 97 also has a readability statistics feature. *WordPerfect's* Grammatik function provides several different measures of readability. There is also a readability calculator on Kathy Schrock's Web site for teachers—type in 100 words of text, and you will be provided with a readability estimate.

Budgeting and Accounting

Most integrated library automation systems include modules or functions to support budgeting and accounting; some of this functionality might be provided through modules already discussed, such as acquisitions/ordering and serials management. Information may be provided through the budgeting and accounting system in tabular or graphical form for inclusion in the library media center annual report and in other reports. It may also be possible to load statistics and budget reports into a spreadsheet package such as *Excel* to produce further analyses of expenditure or to develop future budget projections. It should also be possible to transfer budget and other financial information to and from the school administration system.

If more detailed analyses of statistics and budget are required, then statistical packages such as *SPSS* or *StatView II* can be used, while packages such as *DeltaGraph* and *Persuasion* can display statistical calculations, tables, and graphs in an attractive form for use in reports or for presentations.

Library Promotion and Publicity

In the area of library publicity and promotion, the use of computers has enabled school library media specialists to produce materials that are more attractive and have a more professional appearance without spending enormous sums of money. Desktop publishing packages such *PageMaker* or *Quark XPress* (or even simple ones designed for schoolchildren such as *Publish It!)* can be used to produce newsletters, bibliographies, bookmarks, library orientation booklets, study guides, leaflets to advertise library activities, certificates of various kinds, stationery, and forms. Much of this material is ephemeral; it needs to be updated regularly to reflect new activities, and yet having a uniform "house style" is desirable, so that materials are clearly identified as coming from the library media center. Desktop publishing allows for the quick and easy updating that is so often necessary in the school environment while making use of a few standard design features.

Graphics packages such as *Bannermania* and *McBillboard* can be used to produce posters and signs advertising library media center activities; in addition, some page layout and word processing systems can be used for this.

At another level, computer-based library media center orientation programs have been developed in some schools to introduce newcomers (teachers, students, parents) to the resources and services of the library media center. Some of these programs have been based on simple sequences of screens of information, with the user at the keyboard controlling the speed at which the screens are presented. *PowerPoint* can be a useful tool for this. Other programs have been designed to scroll through a sequence of screens automatically. Still others have been designed to be displayed through Internet browsers such as Netscape and are often more interactive. However they are set up, these library guides or library tours can be effective as a basic introduction to the library media center—especially if they can also be viewed on the network from outside the library media center. In addition, a Web site created by the library media center can be a useful way of promoting the programs of the center as well as providing access to resources.

Other Functions

Information technology can be used for a wide range of other functions in the school library media center. The following list, while being far from exhaustive, does give an idea of the possibilities:

- developing a union list or catalog of all the videos (or CD-ROMs or serials) held by the school library media centers in the district;

- inter-library loans management;

- scheduling the use of library facilities;

- providing for booking sessions in the school library media center for classes via an online booking form on the school network;

- bibliography production;

- providing a current awareness service for school staff;

- maintaining mailing lists and sending out circulars;

- project management (either to manage a major project, such as introducing a new automated library system, or to manage an on-going activity, such as a whole-school reading program); and

- developing local indexes to serve particular purposes, such as indexing poems in the anthologies available in the school or the hymns in the different hymn books or short stories in the short story collections.

It may be that the integrated library automation system will handle some of these functions, such as management of inter-library loans or the development of a union list or catalog for the district or bibliography production. However, these could also be done with specialist software developed for the task. Other functions can be handled by generic software packages. For example, maintaining mailing lists and sending out circulars could be done with any standard database management program that will work with a word processor, or it could be done with a program such as *Microsoft Office*. Scheduling the use of the facilities might be done with *Excel* or with a specialist scheduling package. For project management, a specialist package such as *Lotus Agenda* or *MacProject* could be used, as could personal information systems such as *Focal Point II*.

THE SECURITY SYSTEM

Security systems are completely separate systems from the integrated library automation system or the circulation system, though they support the circulation system by ensuring that the items that leave the library are items that have been properly checked out to legitimate borrowers. Some systems actually are connected to the library media center computer system. There is usually some kind of tag inside each item in the library media center collection, and a gateway or other barrier at the exit to the library sounds an alarm if a tagged item is taken through the system. The aim of installing such a system is usually to reduce theft from the collection and to reduce the amount of time spent by library media center staff in monitoring the library media center exits. The security system can be viewed negatively: a sign that library users are not trusted. It can also be presented positively: it will mean that all items in the collection are available to all library media center users, and the library media center's budget can be spent on new items instead of on replacing items that disappear. Another advantage of security systems is that library users can usually bring their bags and other books into the library—most systems are sensitive enough to detect a tagged book hidden in a briefcase or backpack.

Different security systems operate in different ways—a situation made even more complex by some of the vendors offering different kinds of systems. Some security systems are bypass systems; that is, the security target (usually a small metal "bug") is not desensitized before the item is borrowed. The user hands the item to the person on the circulation desk, the item is checked out, the user passes through the security gate, and the item is handed to the user on the other side of the gate. This type of system requires that the security gates be near the circulation desk and that there is a place for return of items before the user comes through the gates into the library. Staff time is saved because items do not have to be desensitized and sensitized again as part of the circulation process, but users cannot carry the items into the library while they are checked out (without setting off the alarm). A full circulation system is more expensive, because equipment or procedures (depending on the type of system) are needed to desensitize the items when they are borrowed and then to sensitize them again on return. This also takes time. On the other hand, use of this kind of system means that the security gates can be separated from the circulation desk, and users can carry items that they have borrowed into the library and out again without setting off the alarm. Checkpoints have both a full circulation system and a bypass systems; 3M produces a full circulation system; while Sermme Theft Control System is a bypass system.

Some of the security systems operate using radio waves to detect the security target in a book or other item; some use electromagnetic waves. While there is no proof that electromagnetic waves cause health problems, many people have reservations about exposure to electromagnetic waves on a long-term basis, and this has influenced the selection decisions of some library media specialists. Newer systems are now being produced using a micromagnetic system (Sensormatic), and other methods are being tested by some companies.

The type of security target used by the system can influence library resource processing procedures. The round metal targets used by some systems have to be hidden in some way, and many library media specialists have found that students can be quick to realize how the targets work—which will mean that they rip out the target to steal the book. The most common way of hiding these targets seems to be to put them under a book pocket on the inside cover of the book and to put a date due card into the pocket. Other systems use sensitized metal strips that can be hidden in the spine of the book or between pages close to the spine. It seems that these targets are more difficult for students to detect and remove.

While there are enormous variations, the equipment and supplies required as part of a security system include the security gates (with or without a locking bar that stops the user passing through the gate when the alarm begins to ring), desensitizing and sensitizing equipment (for full circulation systems), and a supply of security targets (needed on an ongoing basis) sufficient for the items in the collection plus new purchases. Some systems provide special tags for such items as reference books that are never loaned; these tags cannot be desensitized. Some systems require special tags for use with computer software, videos, and CD-ROMs. Depending on the system, it may be necessary to purchase a special small desensitizer/sensitizer to use with audio- and videocassettes. There will be costs associated with a maintenance contract or payment for occasional maintenance and repair. There is staff time involved in tagging the collection and operating the system.

Despite the costs, some school library media centers have found that the system pays for itself within a few years; a reduction of the annual loss rate to under one percent of the collection is not uncommon, with the figure of 0.5 percent being most often mentioned during a discussion of security systems on the Australian teacher-librarians' listserv OZTL_NET for more than a month in 1998. However, most people recognized that security systems were at best a deterrent: if a student is really determined to steal a book, then there is not much that can be done—a situation faced by other institutions, such as stores, that also use security systems. Thus security systems are not the complete answer to all security problems, though there is considerable evidence that they are effective.

SYSTEM MIGRATION

System migration is what happens when the library media center changes from one automated library system to another. The process is also known as installing a second generation library system. There are many reasons why the library media center might change systems. The current system might be too small for a library media center where the school population and the collection are growing. The system might be based on older hardware that needs to be replaced. The company may be phasing out the system in favor of a new system running on newer hardware or based on a new operating system. Many vendors are now phasing out DOS-based systems, for instance, and redeveloping their systems for the Windows environment. Local support may be no longer available for a system that was purchased some time ago. The library media center may decide to join a multi-library network where a different system is used, or the library media specialist may decide to make a change to bring the school library media center into conformity with other libraries in the area that are using a different system. And then, alas, some system developers and vendors do go out of business or sell their system to a competitor, and this situation may well mean that development work on the system ceases.

The process of system migration is not quite the same as it was for selecting the original system. For one thing, the external environment will have changed. There will have been changes in technology, in the types of automated library systems available, and in the general level of acceptance of technology in the community. The internal environment will also have changed. Both the library media center and the school will by now have accumulated a store of experience in dealing with library automation and the associated issues. The expectations of the users of the school library media center will have risen since the first system was installed. Changes in the school curriculum, with new emphasis on student learning, may mean that aspects of the system that were not rated particularly high when the first system was chosen may be considered more important now.

Ending the chapter on this note is designed to emphasize two points made in Chapter One: Information technology is constantly changing, and those changes bring changed expectations and new ways of doing things; and the process of managing information technology in the school library media center is indeed a cyclical one.

REFERENCES AND BIBLIOGRAPHY

American Association of School Librarians and The Association for Educational Communications and Technology. (1998). *Information power: Building partnerships for learning.* Chicago: American Library Association.

Breeding, Marshall (1997). Library software: A guide to the current commercial products: 1997 update. *Library Software Review.* 16(4): December, 261–76.

Brophy, Peter, *et al.* (1997). *Self-service systems in libraries: Final report.* Lancaster, Lancashire: Centre for Research in Library and Information Management, University of Central Lancashire.

Bruce, Harry (1994). Media center automation: A watershed for the school library media specialist. *School Library Media Quarterly.* 22(4): Summer, 206–12.

Butterworth, Margaret, ed. (1997). *Information technology in schools: Implications for teacher librarians.* 4th ed. Perth, Western Australia: Australian Library and Information Association, School Libraries Section.

Cibarelli, Pamela (1996). Library automation alternatives in 1996 and user satisfaction ratings by operating system. *Computers in Libraries.* 16(2): February, 26–35.

Clyde, Laurel A. (1986). *Computer software for school libraries: A directory.* Wagga Wagga, New South Wales: Alcuin Library Consultants.

———. (1995*). Information technology in Australian school libraries: A survey of readers of* Access. Reykjavík: Lindin.

———. (1996). *State of the art study of information technology in the libraries of the Nordic countries: Iceland.* Reykjavík: Félagsvísindastofun.

Costa, Betty (1981). Microcomputers in Colorado—It's elementary! *Wilson Library Bulletin.* 55(9): May, 676–78, 717.

———. (1982). An online catalog for an elementary school library media center. *School Library Media Quarterly.* 10(4): Summer, 337–46.

Day, Teresa Thurman, Bruce Flanders, and Gregory Zuck, eds. (1994*). Automation for school libraries: How to do it from those who have done it.* Chicago: American Library Association.

Dillon, Ken, ed. (1997*). School library automation in Australia: Issues and results of the national surveys.* 2nd ed. Wagga Wagga, New South Wales: Centre for Information Studies.

Furrie, Betty (1991). *Understanding MARC (MAchine Readable Cataloging).* 3rd ed. McHenry, IL: Follett Software Company.

Hatton, Sally (1998). Email message to the LM_NET listserv for Library Media Specialists, 19 October.

Hopkins, Darryll (1998). Email message to the OZTL_NET listserv for Australian Teacher Librarians, 23 March.

Indermaur, Jean (1996). Automated library software systems: The next generation. *Access.* 10(3): August, 24–26.

Indermaur, Jean, and Pru Mitchell (1997). Selecting a second generation library automation system: A checklist. In Dillon, Ken, ed. *School library automation in Australia: Issues and results of the national surveys.* Wagga Wagga, New South Wales: Centre for Information Studies, 127–43.

Jennings, Lois, and Dagmar Schmidmaier (1983). *KWOC indexing in secondary school libraries: An evaluation.* Sydney, New South Wales: Kuring-gai College of Advanced Education.

Johnson, Claire, Pru Mitchell, and Robin Wake (1997). School library automation: Migrating to second generation systems. In Butterworth, Margaret, ed. *Information technology in schools: Implications for teacher librarians.* 3rd ed. Perth, Western Australia: Australian Library and Information Association, School Libraries Section, 79–90.

Lighthall, Lynne (1996). The sixth Canadian school library automation survey. *Feliciter.* 42(5): May, 34–51.

Long, Marie, ed. (1969). Data processing for school libraries. *Drexel Library Quarterly.* 5 April, 63–123 (special issue).

Macdonald, Colin (1983). Towards a national cataloguing service. *Orana.* 19(1): February, 42–44.

McCusker, Mary L. (1967–68). Implications of automation for school libraries. *School Libraries.* 17: Fall, 23–27; 18: Fall, 15–22.

Muirhead, Graeme, ed. (1997). *Planning and implementing successful system migrations.* London: The Library Association.

Parnell, Stephen, and Rodney Patterson (1983). The costs of a free automated circulation system: Adapting CIRSYS to an academic library. *RivLibFile.* 4(2): Winter, 10–18.

Paxton, Ellen (1997). MARC for teacher librarians: An introduction. In Dillon, Ken, ed. *School library automation in Australia: Issues and results of the national surveys.* 2nd ed. Wagga Wagga, New South Wales: Centre for Information Studies, 91–114.

Peterson, Miriam E. (1957). Automation—implications for school libraries. *School Libraries.* 7: October, 10–13.

Reiss, Marguerite (1969). Ordering, processing and retrieval—done by computer. *School Libraries.* 18(2): Winter, 23–28.

Roche, Maggie (1998). Email message to the OZTL_NET listserv for Australian Teacher Librarians, 16 February.

Rogers, Kathryn (1984). Information retrieval at John Paul II, Marayong. *Library Newsletter (Catholic Education Office, Sydney).* 23(13): 5–6.

Solomon, Paul (1994). Children, technology, and instruction: A case study of elementary school children using an online public access catalog (OPAC). *School Library Media Quarterly.* 23(1): Fall, 43–51.

Valenza, Joyce Kasman (1998). *Power tools: 100+ essential forms and presentations for your school library information program*. Chicago: American Library Association.

INTERNET SOURCES

Blue Skyways (Kansas)
<http://skyways.lib.ks.us/kansas/>

Bookwhere 2000
<http://www.bookwhere.com/> and <http://www.risinc.com/>

Library of Congress
<http://lcweb.loc.gov/catalog/>

Marcive
<http://www.marcive.com/web1.htm>

MnLINK
<http://www.mnlink.org/>

OCLC
<http://www.oclc.org/>

School Libraries Online (International Association of School Librarianship)
<http://www.hi.is/~anne/iasl.html>
For the interactive list of automated library systems on School Libraries Online, see <http://www.hi.is/~anne/libaut.html>

Schrockguide for Educators—Kathy Schrock
<http://discoveryschool.com/schrockguide/index.html>

Sunlink (Florida)
<http://www.sunlink.ucf.edu/>

Texas Library Connection
<http://www.stcc.cc.tx.us/tlc/tlc.html>

Understanding MARC Records (booklet from the Library of Congress)
<http://lcweb.loc.gov/cds/marcdoc.html>

CHAPTER THREE

for
Information Access

INTRODUCTION

"Tapping into information sources worldwide." "A world of information at our fingertips." "The libraries of the world are just a few keystrokes away from everyone." These slogans encapsulate both the prospects that information technology offers to schools and the hype surrounding the electronic information industry. Online information services, the Internet, CD-ROMs, an automated library catalog, databases available on the school's local area network (LAN), the fax machine, and even the telephone do enable school library media centers to tap into a wide range of information sources inside and outside the school. However, since there are so many options for information access, an important part of the role of the school library media specialist becomes selecting from among the many information sources available to ensure that the information needs of members of the school community are met. The slogans also, by implication, highlight the increasing importance of information skills. Students need opportunities to develop information skills that will help them to become effective users of these information sources, and so they need to have experience working with these sources in the educational setting.

All members of the school community have information needs, many of which can (and should) be met through the school library media center that uses a wide range of print and computer-based information retrieval systems and resources. Students need information relating to their school subjects; their hobbies and special interests; the school clubs to which they belong; their sporting, cultural and recreational activities; vocational preparation; and personal development. Teachers need information relating to new developments in education and teaching generally and to their particular teaching areas and academic interests. School administrators need information on significant developments elsewhere; information for planning initiatives in courses, buildings, or other special programs; important documents and research reports that may assist with planning; information on new technologies and tools (for instance, new computer packages for school administration); and information on programs and projects that have been trialled in other schools. Parent groups and school councils or school board representatives need information that will help them to make appropriate decisions in relation to the school.

School library media specialists have an important role in relation to the use of information technology for information retrieval. Information storage and retrieval are basic to the functions of libraries, whether they are carried out manually or assisted by automated processes. Computer-based information management and information retrieval tools in the school library media center can help to teach students basic skills in these areas and provide constant reinforcement of those skills. Access to online information services and the Internet, computer-based listings of all or part of the school library media center collection (for instance, periodicals or videotapes or special collections such as careers pamphlets or local history materials), a public access catalog (OPAC), and computer-based bibliographies are examples of applications that might be appropriate. In addition, it is possible to purchase curriculum-related databases on floppy disk or CD-ROM, ready for loading onto the school's network or for use on a personal computer in the library media center.

In a school library media center, computer-based information retrieval has two main aspects: access to information that is held within the school library media center collection and access to information outside the school library media center (and the school). The latter (accessing external information sources and services) is becoming more important at a time when it has ceased to be possible for any school library media center to hold even the most important resources to support the school curriculum, much less all the resources that students and teachers are likely to need.

ACCESS TO INFORMATION WITHIN THE SCHOOL

Within the school library media center, computer-based information retrieval systems can take many forms. One that has already been discussed is the catalog of the school library media center's collection of resources. As we have seen, the computer-based catalog might be created as part of an integrated library automation system, or it might be created as a stand-alone system or as a part of the catalog of a multi-library network. Because the school library media center catalog is normally one of the largest databases, if not the largest, created by the school, it will be an important resource for information skills instruction as well as for providing students with an example of information technology in action. Computers might also be used within the library media center to provide access to other indexes or databases created by the library media center, such as an index to magazine articles or an index to the vertical file or to databases and reference works purchased from other sources, such as databases on floppy disk or encyclopedias on CD-ROM. Access might be provided to all or most of these via a school network so that they can be searched not just in the school library media center but also from other locations around the school. In this section, indexes and databases created within the school library media center will be discussed, along with databases purchased on disk and databases and reference works on CD-ROM.

Indexes

Indexing software or bibliographic software (such as *Pro-Cite* or *Inmagic/DB Textworks*) can be used to create indexes that can be searched using either a stand-alone computer or a computer attached to the local area network. Some automated library system catalog modules can also be used to create indexes and secondary databases; when this is the case, the advantage is that the index is searched in the same way as the school library media center catalog, and indeed it might even be possible to incorporate the index into the catalog. If this were the case, then a catalog search on any topic would produce not only a listing of relevant items in the school library media center collection but also relevant entries from the index.

Indexes that fill a need in one school may not be used at all in another—and it is important that the index be designed to fill a real need if it is to be used. Examples of computer-based indexes that have proved effective in different schools include the following:

- an index to the vertical file (or pamphlet file or clippings file);

- an index to poems or short stories in anthologies held by the school library media center so that poems or short stories by particular authors or dealing with particular topics can be found quickly;

- in a church-run school, an index to hymns in different hymn books used by the school;

- an index to recipes in recipe books and magazines;

- an index to a collection of careers pamphlets;

- an index for items in the school archives so that they can be accessed by people preparing displays for important school functions;

- an index to a magazine that is held by the school library media center and for which a commercial computer-based index is not available—this might be, for example, an index to a local magazine that contains information that is important for local history or geography, or it might be the school magazine; and

- an index to an important local information source, such as a newspaper.

The most important thing about these locally created indexes is that they meet an identified information need within the school.

At one Western Australia primary school, for instance, the school library was given a subscription to the *Australian Geographic Magazine*, a well-produced, attractive magazine with many curriculum applications, particularly in geography, social studies, science, and history. To provide better access to the information in this magazine, an index was created that complemented the computer-based school library catalog and was integrated with it. When the children and teachers searched the school library catalog to locate material for classroom work, they retrieved a list of books and audiovisual materials in the school library, together with references to any relevant articles in *Australian Geographic Magazine*. Library users could elect to restrict their search to the journal index ("I want to know what there is in *Australian Geographic Magazine* about penguins"), or they could undertake a search of the whole catalog, covering books, magazines, and other resources ("I want a list of everything available in the library that has information about penguins"). After this successful venture, the school library went on to create other indexes that could be searched via the catalog.

In-House Databases

Anneli Ahtola has said that "in-house database building can be an activity that helps libraries to survive in today's competitive information world" (1989, 36). It is claimed that in-house databases can help to develop and maintain links between the library media center and the community, and they generate opportunities for cooperation with local organizations and businesses. In addition, locally oriented and collection-specific databases can assist local networking as well as add significantly to the resources available to the library media center users. The possibilities for databases created within the school library media center are virtually unlimited but those possibilities that are taken up should be ones that have been evaluated carefully with the school needs and available resources in mind. A database can be created for almost any subject field and for material in almost any format; it can cover the subject in depth or provide an overview; and it can provide coverage at the school, local, state, national, or international level. A database created in-house can provide access to a topic for which no commercial information retrieval tool currently exists or where the commercial tools are at a level or provide a depth of coverage that is inappropriate for the users in the school. A database created in the school library media center might be designed to provide access to information on a topic that is of local concern or to provide a local viewpoint on a topic of wider concern.

Databases created within the school library media center can be used to teach or reinforce information search skills. If the databases are linked to the school library media center catalog, then information from a variety of sources will be retrieved with each catalog search. If the databases are searched separately, however, then they will be smaller and easier to comprehend than a large catalog database, and so they may be easier for young people to search. Nevertheless, their main advantage is that they can be used to provide access to local information or special collections in the school that have immediate relevance for the students and that are not available via the computer in any other way. Bibliographic software or database management software, such as *Access, Foxbase, Pro-Cite*, or *Inmagic/DB Textworks,* can be used to create local databases, which can then be searched using a stand-alone computer, or the database might be made available via the library media center network. Alternatively, it may be possible to use the library catalog module of an integrated automated library system to create additional databases.

As with indexes, databases that fill a need in one school may not be used at all in another, and so local needs should be analyzed before a decision is made to create a local database. The external and internal environments should also be taken into account; for example, it needs to be confirmed that no similar source already exists, that there will be support locally for that database, that the teachers will be able to use it in the teaching/ learning setting, and that the resources needed for the project (including time, personnel, skills, software, hardware, funding) are available. Examples of databases that have proved to be useful and effective in particular schools include the following:

- a database of local authors and their works (this is particularly effective if the database entries can be linked to the holdings of the school library media center through the catalog);

- a database of information about pioneers of the district, graves in an older graveyard, or names of people listed on a local war memorial;

- a database of local history materials either held in the school or accessible to the school community;

- a database of the paintings or prints or other artworks on the walls of the school, with information about each one, about the artist, and a link to any relevant information held in the school library media center collection;

- a database of birds or animals or plants seen in the vicinity of the school; and

- a database or directory of resource people in the local community who are prepared to speak to classes on specialized topics.

In some schools, children have been involved in creating special databases—for example, of well-known people who have lived in the district or of the gravestones in a local graveyard or of local birds and plants. Being involved at this level gives children an understanding of database concepts that will help them when they come to search other databases. It also provides an understanding of the particular subject area and of ways in which information can be organized and presented to others. The databases are then available for use by other classes. The newer versions of database software and of computer-based library catalogs will allow students to incorporate photographs and drawings into the database. Today, the Internet, through the World Wide Web, also provides a tool for making these databases more readily available and in a format that is both attractive and relatively easy to use.

Prepared Commercial Databases

Many commercially produced databases on a wide range of topics can be purchased on floppy disk or on CD-ROM for use in the school library media center or via the library media center or school network. Some provide very simple keyword search facilities for young children, while others aimed at more experienced users in secondary schools incorporate facilities for more complex searches and data manipulation. Some allow the users to specify the format in which the results of the search will be printed. Some of these prepared commercial databases, such as *Men of Science, Countries of the World, The Olympic Database*, and *Birds of Antarctica*, are designed for use within the context of particular subjects or units in the school curriculum. In addition, other resources are now being made available on disk. Examples include bibliographies on disk, collections of newspaper and periodical articles on disk, and disks containing illustrations and graphics for use in publicity materials created by the library.

Many of the prepared commercial databases that were available in previous years on floppy disk, such as *The Presidents*, are now available on CD-ROM; in fact, this illustrates a trend toward CD-ROM as the medium for supplying this kind of information. There are three main reasons for this: first, CD-ROM has a much larger storage capacity, and so larger databases can be supported; second, the use of CD-ROM makes it possible to include more complex images, sound, and video or animation; and third, the price of CD-ROM has actually come down over the last six or seven years and is more affordable for schools. As an extension of this trend or migration, some of the databases are now moving to the Internet as well.

Databases and Reference Works on CD-ROM

Many databases and standard reference works are available on CD-ROM for use on stand-alone machines (with CD-ROM drive) in the school library media center or to be loaded onto a CD-ROM tower (a CD-ROM server that provides access to a number of disks at the same time) and be accessible through a network in the school or the school library media center. CD-ROM technology is improving all the time: One has only to look at the early text-only CD-ROMs and then the newest multimedia CD-ROM encyclopedias with their color video sequences, interactive information skills tutorials, and other features to see this. Many reference works that were originally sold as printed works, as well as in the form of databases on disk, are now available on CD-ROM—a format often much cheaper than the printed versions and easier to search. As with databases in other formats, these reference tools and databases on CD-ROM can extend the scope of the school library media center collection considerably while also providing facilities for information skills work.

Reference sources available on CD-ROM today include standard reference works such as encyclopedia, dictionaries, and atlases; indexes to magazines and newspapers; databases for students as well as professional databases; full-text collections of indexed articles for students on particular curriculum topics; collections of artworks and historical photographs; collections of computer programs; and a range of other types of information. Most reference CD-ROMs are updated regularly on payment of a subscription. Some occupy just one CD-ROM disk, while others are much larger. For example, National Geographic has released a CD-ROM product called *The Complete National Geographic*, with 108 years of the magazine on 30 CD-ROM disks, incorporating photographs, maps, charts, and stories—all fully searchable. This enormous electronic archive will be of use to history students as well as for work in geography and general science. Articles can be bookmarked electronically (so that the user can find them again quickly) and printed in color or black and white.

Of all the information sources on CD-ROM, electronic encyclopedias have been the most popular with school library media centers in the United States and probably elsewhere too. This is clear from analyses carried out by the author of information provided to the *CMC (Computers in the Media Center) Newsletter* over a period of five years. Each year, the editor of the newsletter, Jim Deacon, surveys his readers to collect information about the information technologies they are using in their school library media centers. Analyses of the data for 1993, 1995, and 1997 illustrate trends in use of computer-based resources and services (see Clyde, 1998, for details). The ten most often owned CD-ROM titles in 1997 (among the school library media specialists who read *CMC News*) are shown in Table 3.1. The CD-ROM title reported most often was the Grolier electronic encyclopedia (listed by 105 of the 160 respondents, or 68.18% of the 154 CD-ROM users). This CD-ROM had also topped the list in the 1993 and 1995 surveys, as the table shows. In fact, in both the 1993 survey and the 1995 survey, three of the top ten titles had been encyclopedias, the other two being *Compton's Multimedia Encyclopedia* and *Information Finder/World*

Book Encyclopedia. In 1997, these three were still in the top ten, though *Compton's* had dropped to tie for tenth place. They were joined for the first time by a fourth electronic encyclopedia, *Encarta,* in fourth place. There are other indications of the popularity of CD-ROM encyclopedias in the responses. Two other general encyclopedias, *Encyclopedia Americana* and *Encyclopaedia Britannica*, were among the top 20 in 1997. Many schools reported having two or three CD-ROM encyclopedias, and some schools had four.

Table 3.1
Survey of Readers of *CMC News*, 1993, 1995, 1997:
CD-ROM Titles in Use (the top ten).

RANK	1993 SURVEY	1995 SURVEY	1997 SURVEY
1	Grolier's Encyclopedia	Grolier's Encyclopedia	Grolier's Encyclopedia
2	Compton's Encyclopedia	SIRS	SIRS
3	TOM	Newsbank	Information Finder/World Book
4	Newsbank	Information Finder/World Book Encyclopedia	Encarta Encyclopedia
5	Information Finder/World Book Encyclopedia	MAS (EBSCO)	Newsbank
6	MAS (EBSCO)	Compton's Encyclopedia	MAS (EBSCO)
7	SIRS	TOM	DISCovering Authors
8	Mammals (both titles)	Mammals (both titles)	TOM
9	Microsoft Bookshelf	DISCovering Authors	Time Almanac
10	World Atlas	ProQuest/Resource One	UMI ProQuest and Compton's Encyclopedia

Reprinted with permission from *Teacher Librarian: The Journal for School Library Professionals.*

The second major category of CD-ROMs used in school library media centers in the United States in the years covered by the analyses was current information sources (articles in full text and indexes to current material). These sources provide students with access to articles and papers covering curriculum-related topics and current issues. In 1993, four of the top ten CD-ROMs fell into this group—*TOM* (Information Access Corporation) in its different versions, *Newsbank, MAS* (Magazine Article Summaries—EBSCO), and *SIRS* (Social Issues Resources). (See Table 3.1.) In 1995 and 1997, these four were joined by *ProQuest* in tenth place. Apart from *ProQuest*, the relative positions of these information sources changed through the period, though not greatly. The exception is the *SIRS* standard system, which moved to second place in 1995 (after being seventh in 1993) and not only retained that position in the 1997 survey but was used by more respondents in 1997. If use of other *SIRS* products, such as *SIRS Government Reporter* and *SIRS Renaissance,* is taken into consideration, then the position of this company as an information provider to school libraries appeared even stronger. As was the case with general encyclopedias on CD-ROM, some schools reported having more than one of these current sources/indexes on CD-ROM.

In 1997, the general encyclopedias on CD-ROM and the current information sources and indexes almost completely dominated the top ten positions. If the *Time Almanac* is counted as a current news and information source, then the only other disk is the literature reference source, *DISCovering Authors*, at seventh place; this first appeared in the top ten in 1995, though it was in the top 20 in 1993. The *Mammals* multimedia encyclopedias on CD-ROM, which had appeared in the 1993 and 1995 top ten lists, dropped to 13th place in 1997.

Other CD-ROM titles listed by five or more respondents included *Microsoft Bookshelf* (a disk that includes dictionaries, a dictionary of quotations, and other reference sources), *Facts on File* (current information), *Monarch Notes* (a literature guide), *US History, US Presidents, WilsonDISC, The New York Times, Magill's Survey of Science, Countries of the World,* and *Granger's Index to Poetry.* Twelve people mentioned having a World Atlas CD-ROM and others an atlas or PC atlas; these disks extend the concept of the print atlas through the use of still and moving images, sound, and interactive features as well as maps. Professional databases on CD-ROM (that is, databases indexing and abstracting the professional literature for teachers and school administrators and other education databases) were represented only by ERIC (the education database of the Education Resources Information Center of the United States Department of Education), which was cited by four respondents (one had the *SilverPlatter* version, one had the *Dialog OnDisc* version, and two did not indicate the version). Thus in 1997, as in the earlier years, the CD-ROM titles mentioned most frequently were reference works of one kind or another, from the standard encyclopedias and atlases to indexes/abstracting services, current information sources, and other research tools.

The disks related to specific curriculum areas were a much more varied group, but apart from curriculum-related reference works such as *Mammals*, cited earlier, they each tended to be cited only by two or three people at most in 1997. Among these titles were *Rosetta Stone, Rainforest, World Religions, Dinosaurs, Desert Storm, Audubon's Birds, Macbeth, Window on Korea, Mayo Clinic Family Health*. In all, more than 220 different titles (not all of them information sources, though information sources predominated) were mentioned by the 154 respondents who had CD-ROMs in 1997.

Messages on Internet listservs for school library media specialists confirm the general impression given by the preceding analyses. The types of CD-ROMs mentioned most include electronic encyclopedias and other standard reference works such as dictionaries and atlases and current information sources and indexes. However, while newspapers on CD-ROM did not figure largely in the responses of the readers of *CMC News*, databases providing the full text of a newspaper have been discussed from time to time on the listservs (with the *Sydney Morning Herald* and *The Australian* being mentioned in Australian discussions, the Canadian newspaper databases being cited by Canadian teacher librarians, and *The San Francisco Examiner* and other newspapers by school library media specialists in the United States).

While the analyses indicate that the school library CD-ROM market, though growing, has been remarkably stable, there are hints in them of changes under way. The move to the use of local area networks in schools is suggested in the 1997 responses. It was clear that more school library media centers were making their CD-ROMs available via networks, whether within the library media center or throughout the school. New networked versions of the electronic reference works and current information sources/indexes reflect this.

However, the survey results contained suggestions of further changes. Even as early as 1997, a few schools were moving away from networked CD-ROMs to the provision of online access to some of these sources, usually in conjunction with the continued use of sources on CD-ROM. In December 1997, Jim Deacon reported in a *CMC News* editorial that he had noticed that not only was there "a lot of emphasis on the Internet" at computer conferences, but "many of the library products that we use standalone or networked with CD-ROM towers are moving to online versions." Among these were *Britannica* (which had developed a sophisticated Web site as a basis for its online products), SIRS (another company with a comprehensive Web presence), *Grolier's*, UMI, and EBSCO's *MAS FullText Ultra*. The latter, designed for elementary and high school students and available online through EBSCOhost, provided full-text access to more than 400 publications plus indexes to others. EBSCO claimed that this service provided more than double the coverage of their school CD-ROM services such as *MAS FullTEXT*.

There are several factors behind this trend to online access. The first is increased access to the Internet in schools and thus to online sources available via the Internet. Secondly, with more powerful computers and faster modems or net connections and lines, accessing the Internet is no longer necessarily a case of "World Wide wait." Thirdly, the online versions of these reference sources are updated constantly, whereas CD-ROM updates usually range from quarterly (for news sources) to annually (for standard reference works). Fourthly, we have seen the emergence of hybrid forms of these reference works that take advantage of the strengths of both media (CD-ROM and the Internet). This is manifested in CD-ROMs that can be updated by downloading from a Web site; CD-ROM systems that search both the CD-ROM (for static information) and the Internet site (for current information) when a search is done; and CD-ROMs with "hot links" to a carefully selected range of Internet sites, as well as more static information on the disk itself. The use of these features requires not only a computer with a CD-ROM drive but also access to the Internet, either directly or through the school or school library media center network. Some of the services, such as UMI *ProQuest*, have a site license arrangement that allows the school library media center to provide access to students and teachers from home as well as from inside the school. These systems represent a compromise between access to information within the school library media center (on CD-ROM) and access to external information sources and services. However, even among this group, the trend seems to be more toward full online access to the databases and services, with *The Electric Library* (a service from Infonautics Inc.), for instance, taking this path.

ACCESS TO EXTERNAL INFORMATION SOURCES AND SERVICES

In terms of the computer-based information resources outside the school library media center that could make a contribution to meeting the information needs of members of the school community, the most important are the Internet; the commercial online information services such as DIALOG (available internationally from Dialog Corporation) and SCIS (from the Curriculum Corporation in Australia); the catalogs of other libraries, such as national libraries and local public libraries; and the hybrid CD-ROM and on-line services mentioned in the previous section. Over the last few years, more of the commercial online information services, library catalogs, electronic bulletin boards, community freenets, and other computer-based services have been moving to the Internet, so anyone with access to the Internet now has access to all these online resources. Some (such as the Library of Congress catalog) are free; some (such as Dialog's databases) require a paid password. Because it is now such an important part of the on-line world, the Internet will be discussed first in this section, followed by commercial online information services.

The Internet

The Internet has its origins in networking experiments to link the computers of research institutions and universities in the United States more than a quarter of a century ago. The result of this was a national network called ARPANET, through which communications protocols (standard ways of sending and receiving messages and files and of communicating between computers) were developed. Among these protocols was what is known as TCP/IP (transmission control protocol/Internet protocol), still the basis of the Internet to such an extent that the Internet is sometimes defined as "a network that is based on TCP/IP." ARPANET has since been decommissioned, but the success of this early networking ensured that the network links remained and increased, first through a "backbone network" based on five supercomputers in the United States under the auspices of the National Science Foundation (1985) and then through the development of other powerful high-speed networks at the local, regional, and national levels. As time went on, more computers joined this network, via dedicated data lines and the telephone networks, and since many of these computers were also linked to other computers, the complexity of the networks increased. Thus the Internet is a massive network of networks that now links machines in almost 200 countries.

While the networks that form part of the Internet usually have some form of network governance of their own, the Internet as a whole is a concept rather than an institution as such. There is no real organization at the international level, though there are many institutions that have an interest in issues related to the Internet, and there are committees and groups that work on developing standards for various aspects of the Internet. The owner of each computer that is linked to the Internet makes decisions about that computer and the information that is stored on it within the context of the laws of that particular country. The Internet transcends national boundaries and any set of rules and regulations, though some degree of regulation is possible within some sectors of the Internet. It has grown primarily because of the possibilities it offers for cheap electronic communications and access to information worldwide. However, this free-form structure makes it impossible for one person or organization to control the net, something that many people who are new to the Internet have trouble coming to terms with. It is both positive and negative in its effects: positive in that access to information is increased and any person with access to the Internet can use it for communication and information provision; negative in that precisely this characteristic means that a very great deal of unorganized information of doubtful quality is made available.

Although the Internet has been in existence for more than 25 years, it was only in the 1990s that it began to be widely used outside the universities and research centers within which it originated. The main reason for this has been the development since 1991 of user-friendly Internet access software and Internet services that can be used by people with only a minimal knowledge of computer systems. The first of these user-friendly services was a menu-based system called Gopher; this was closely followed by the World Wide Web. With the addition of graphical interfaces that can support multimedia, the World Wide Web has become the best-known part of the Internet. This has happened to such an extent that many people quite wrongly assume that the Internet is just the World Wide Web and associate the use of the Internet only with the use of Web browser software such as *Netscape* or *Microsoft Internet Explorer*.

Although the basis of the Internet is physical (or satellite) connections, the Internet is rather more than the machines and telecommunications links or the software through which it is accessed. It is also databases—information in many different forms and people communicating with one another in a variety of ways. In addition, the Internet is an enabling technology—it links other technologies and makes them available to a wider audience in another example of the trend toward the convergence of technologies that was described in Chapter One. These other technologies linked through the Internet might include computer-based library catalogs that can be searched via the Internet; commercial online information services, some of which can be accessed directly via a modem and telephone line as well as via the Internet; electronic mail (which is part of the Internet but is also available outside of it); video and audio services; Internet telephone and fax; and the CD-ROMs that form the basis of some Internet services. In recent years, still another type of convergence—this time related to software—has increased the capability of the Internet as an enabling technology. Originally, each separate part of the Internet, and each of the different Internet facilities (such as telnet, Gopher, file transfer protocol or FTP, electronic mail, Internet Relay Chat or IRC, the World Wide Web) required different software for access. Now, however, the Web browsers are being developed into tools with which users can explore most aspects of the Internet, not just the World Wide Web. Figure 3.1, page 88, illustrates the convergence of technologies and services via the Internet and Web browser software. In this chapter the Internet will be discussed as a means of access to information; in the next chapter it will be discussed as a communications medium.

A key to finding and describing resources on the Internet is the URL (*uniform resource locator* or *unique resource locator* or *universal resource locator*). This system provides a unique Internet address for every resource on the Internet, whether it is a database, Web page, image, sound file, document, software program, or piece of hardware such as a Web camera. The URL is based on the computer on which the resource is located, the specific location on the computer (the directory or folder and the path to that directory or folder), and the filename or other identifier of the resource. In addition, the URL indicates the type of resource. A URL for a Web page begins with *http://* (which indicates that this is a hypertext-based resource, that is, a resource with links to other resources), followed by the computer domain name and the path on the computer. For example, the URL for "School Libraries Online," the Web site of the International Association of School Librarianship, is <http://www.hi.is/~anne/iasl.html> for the home page. It is on a mainframe computer at the University of Iceland at *www.hi.is*—in Anne Clyde's public space at */~anne/*—and with the filename of *iasl.html*. The filename extension (*.html*) indicates that this is a *hypertext document*, that is, a Web page written in HTML (hypertext markup language, a way of marking up or tagging the text in a document so that it can be interpreted by a computer system). Some URLs are much shorter and simpler; however, some are very long and complex indeed. Once known, though, the URL can be used to find any resource on the Internet, and it is thus an essential tool for work with the Internet.

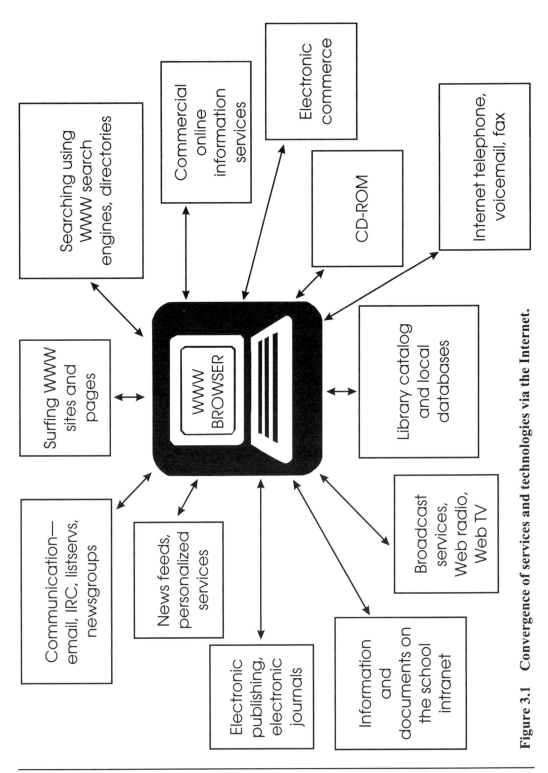

Figure 3.1   Convergence of services and technologies via the Internet.

Both the number and range of information resources now available through the Internet are enormous. In terms of helping to meet the information needs of the various user groups in the school, the Internet has many possibilities, with coverage of almost every topic at a variety of levels. The examples given here are selected simply to give an idea of some starting points for each group (URLs are provided at the end of this chapter).

For teachers and school administrators, there are Web sites provided by education authorities and school districts, educational research organizations, commercial organizations, and individual teachers, among others. The Web site of the United States Department of Education's ERIC service provides free search access to the full ERIC database of more than a million bibliographic records—bibliographic information and abstracts or summaries for books, articles in professional journals, research reports, conference papers, dissertations, tests, audiovisual materials—plus a document ordering service. In addition, full-text information is now being added to the service. Additional resources and links on the Web site make this a rather more appealing way to access ERIC than the CD-ROMs described in the previous chapter. Australia's EdNA, Canada's SchoolNet, Iceland's ISMENNT (the Icelandic Education Network), and the National Grid for Learning in the United Kingdom are all examples of national Web sites designed for educators. Other particularly useful sites for educators include the Blue Web'n database of "blue ribbon" Web sites from Pacific Bell, Pro-Teacher, Scholastic Internet Center, and Kathy Schrock's Guide for Educators. Resources available include electronic journals and newsletters, book reviews, lesson plans and curriculum units, policy statements, computer software, the archives of electronic discussion groups (listservs and newsgroups), and electronic conferences.

For school library media specialists, there are Web sites from the professional associations, including the previously mentioned "School Libraries Online" from the International Association of School Librarianship, the American Association of School Librarians (AASL), various state associations, the national associations of other countries such as Canada, and the International Federation of Library Associations and Institutions (IFLA) with its Section of School Libraries and Resource Centers. The Internet Public Library has a useful collection of reference resources and other materials in its divisions for children and young people. The LION (Librarians Information Online Network) Web site of the School District of Philadelphia (United States) Library Services has links to Internet resources covering every aspect of school librarianship, including school library media center automation, children's literature, and management. Professional journals that are available online include *School Library Media Research* from AASL, and *D-lib Magazine* from UKOLN (a magazine that deals with digital libraries).

Among the Web sites for students are directories that are specifically designed to lead them to sites that are educational, fun, and safe, as well as Web pages on a wide range of topics to meet the needs and interests of young people. Homework Central provides thousands of links to resources on subjects covered in the school curriculum and to recreational and personal development sites covering everything from careers selection to pet care to reading to fashion to pop music. This is not a resource just for home use; it could be useful in the school library media center setting too. Other interesting Web sites include Teenhoopla (from the American Library Association) and Nickelodeon (all kinds of activities for children).

As the World Wide Web and the Internet have grown, search engines have been developed to help users find the pages and information that they need. The first was Yahoo! but there are now many others, including HotBot, AltaVista, Lycos, InfoSeek, and Excite. All are different, both in the ways in which they are used and in the Internet resources that are searched. Each search engine consists of two main parts: the search engine itself (the software that actually does the searching) and the database of resources that is searched by the search engine. Some search engines search just World Wide Web resources; others search the Web plus Usenet newsgroups and directories and other services. Most of the search engines rely on software "robots" to build and index their databases (which can explain some of the strange responses to searches), though Yahoo! is indexed by human indexers. The databases are of varying size, and it is important to note that no one search engine covers all of the Web, much less "all of the Internet." The last three years have seen a further development: the creation of "meta-search engines" that take a search query, send it on to a selection of search engines, and then format the results for the searcher. Among these are Inference Find, Dogpile, AskJeeves, and SavySearch. In addition to the general-purpose search engines, there are search engines for specific purposes or for specific user groups. For example, there are now some search engines designed for children, providing a simple and attractive search interface and based on databases that have been reviewed to ensure that the resources included are suitable for children; two useful ones are Yahooligans from Yahoo! and KidsClick!

In some school library media centers, the Internet is being used only as a source of information. The school library media specialist carries out searches to meet the specific needs of teachers or students and provides the information to them, just as information from print and audiovisual sources is provided in response to reference questions (Clyde, 1997b). In other school library media centers, however, teachers and students can use the Internet and carry out searches for themselves, either from a single stand-alone computer that is linked to the Internet or through the school's local area network. When students are able to use the Internet themselves through the school library resource center, there will be a need for appropriate guidance and instruction; this may be provided as part of an information skills program, often in cooperation with classroom teachers.

Commercial Online Information Services

The commercial online information services, based on large central mainframe computers, have been with us for almost 30 years, initially serving a client group consisting mainly of academics and librarians, who used them via dedicated terminals and lines. However, with the advances in microcomputer technology since the late 1970s, online information services have reached a wider audience who rely on them as a means of locating information that would be either impossible or too time-consuming to find manually. As demand for these services has increased, so the number and variety of commercial online information services has grown. The development of the Internet—specifically the World Wide Web—has provided further impetus for growth: not only is it usually cheaper to use these services via the Internet than through the telephone line but the Web now provides an interface that is much more user-friendly.

The online information industry is based on online information service providers or utilities or hosts, who make available a number of databases—sometimes their own databases, sometimes databases created by others, sometimes a mixture of the two—and carry out the necessary management functions. These functions will include advertising the service and its databases, preparing guides for accessing the system and searching the databases, providing facilities for access to the system (either via a dial-up connection or via the Internet), running a billing system to collect money from users and to pay royalties to the database owners, and providing a telephone "help desk" or online help for users who have problems. Some of the online information service providers have hundreds of databases on their system; others have just one or two. While many are international in their appeal and customer base, others have been developed to serve customers in a particular country or region or even town.

The earliest online information services were generally bibliographic; they either provided cataloging information for libraries, or they consisted of references to books and journal articles and other documents, usually with abstracts. ERIC, mentioned above, was one of the first of these. Once people had the bibliographic citation and the abstract, they could make a decision about their need for the item, and if necessary it could be ordered in print form via an inter-library loan. In recent times, however, the trend has been towards full-text databases that provide not only the bibliographic citation and abstract but also, if desired, the full text of the item itself. Full-text databases contain the complete text of books, newspapers, dictionaries, encyclopedias, parliamentary papers, laws, legal judgments, patents, research reports, company reports, directories, magazines, and other material. Some databases, such as the United States census database and financial databases, are based on numeric or statistical information. With the trend toward full text, some databases contain the full text of the most recent items but bibliographic information and abstracts for older material. Document delivery services are an extension of online searching of bibliographic databases or databases of reviews: if a searcher locates a reference to an article or document and perhaps an abstract, but does not have access to a copy of the item in a nearby library, and cannot wait for the normal inter-library loan processes, then a document delivery service will provide a copy of the full text of the item in print form (usually faxed) or in electronic form via electronic mail or FTP. Sometimes document delivery services are provided by the database provider; sometimes by a third party. A popular document delivery service is UnCover on CARL. Users can search the UnCover database for free, and if they locate a reference to an article that they would like to have, then they can pay (online) for document delivery by fax or airmail.

The organizations and companies involved in the online information industry are varied. There are several large international online information services, such as Dialog, DataStar, Questel/Orbit, and OCLC (Online Computer Library Center), that make available a wide range of databases on a multitude of topics aimed at different groups of users. The ERIC database is available on Dialog, OCLC, and Questel/Orbit, for instance; in addition, Dialog has the LISA (Library and Information Science Abstracts) and Library Literature databases, which provide access to the professional literature of librarianship (including school librarianship). Library Literature is also available through OCLC. Other bibliographic databases on Dialog that could be useful for schools include Enviroline, Energyline, Magazine Database, and Newspaper Abstracts Daily. On OCLC, the Readers Guide Abstracts database indexes current general periodical publications, many of which carry articles that would be at an appropriate level for secondary school students. Useful full-text databases on Dialog include newspapers such as the *Washington Post* and the *New York Times*. Dialog has had a long-standing Classroom Instruction Program, while OCLC has a strong record of working with school library media centers and school authorities to develop programs that will support learning in schools. In addition to the large online information services, there are many small online information service providers who have just a few databases (or even one database), often catering to a niche market consisting of people living in a particular geographical area or people interested in a particular topic or members of a particular profession or trade.

While many of these commercial online information services provide a free online trial of their service, or a "database tour," for real applications a subscription has to be paid. This may be in the form of a flat monthly or an annual fee, or an annual subscription plus payment for each search or simply payment for use. Some services provide some information free but charge for other information. Instructions for use of the service plus the necessary user identification and passwords are provided when the subscription

Table 3.2
Types of online databases/services.

TYPES OF DATABASES/ SERVICES	EXAMPLES
Cataloging information services	OCLC (WorldCat), SCIS, British Library, Library of Congress
Bibliographic information services	Dialog (ERIC, Energyline, Books in Print), Questel/Orbit (ERIC, Energyline), OCLC (ERIC, Library Literature), DataStar (Psychological Abstracts), Dansk Bibliotekscentralen (Artikelbasen)
Full-text or statistical information services	Dialog (The New York Times, The Times of London, Facts on File), Dow Jones, NEXIS/LEXIS, EBSCOHost (MAS)
Local or special-interest services	Orðabók Háskólans (Iceland) NAMLIT (Namibia), SABINET (South Africa), WALIS
Document delivery services	CARL (UnCover), Dialog, British Library

is paid. The searching of an online information service usually requires a systematic approach and the development of some necessary skills—often through practice. A searcher may need to use a set of commands that have been specified for that service and to follow procedures. Where a service has a Web interface, searching will normally be easier and more intuitive, though some Web interfaces also assume considerable skills on the part of the user (particularly where the information in the database is complex).

A survey of Australian school users of online information services, carried out by the author with Joyce Kirk and reported more than ten years ago (Clyde & Kirk, 1989), showed that schools saw the major advantages of using online information services as being related to better and faster access to information or access to current information than is possible with manual services. Other benefits were seen to be contact with other schools and other students via the electronic mail systems of some of the online services, access to school library media center cataloging information, removal of pressure on existing resources in the school library media center, and access to a resource to teach students about technology. Some schools highlighted the value of online information services in information skills development. While problems were identified, particularly in relation to cost (in what was then a dial-up environment), the schools using online information services were using them for a range of applications and across many subject areas and seemed convinced of their value. The major changes in the years since then have been in improved access to the services (particularly through the Internet) and in the increased number of schools using the online information services.

INFORMATION SEARCH SKILLS

Through online information services, the Internet, and media such as CD-ROMs, it is now, theoretically at least, possible for children and teachers in schools to have access to massive amounts of information. This has implications for curriculum development, teaching and learning styles/strategies, information skills instruction, and for the school library media center as the school's major information access point. However, while it is theoretically possible for children in schools to explore information from a wide range of computer-based sources, in reality this access is governed by technological and intellectual factors. The technological access is related to access to the equipment and the online password or connection; intellectual access relates to the skills necessary to actually use the system to locate information. In this section, resources for the development of skills for intellectual access will be discussed; in the next section, "Hardware and Software," discussion will focus on the technical requirements for access within the school.

Online information services and the Internet, as well as other electronic information sources, have much to offer schools in terms of the currency of information available through them and the opportunities for networking and sharing information. As a management tool, using these information search systems offers considerable savings in time and often in costs over the use of information from other sources. Most importantly, the computer-based information sources can play a part in helping students develop information skills. Current curriculum theory draws heavily on ideas about resource-based learning, individualization of instruction, and the need for all people to develop lifelong learning strategies to cope with a rapidly changing world. Online information services, the Internet, and other electronic information sources such as databases on CD-ROM are valuable resources. Not only do they provide access to information that is current and in many instances available in no other form, but they also provide students with opportunities to develop their skills in information use (Clyde & Kirk, 1989). In short, the application of these electronic information sources to school curriculum enhances students' physical and intellectual access to information and provides a valuable resource for information skills development.

For school library media specialists, an Australian CD-ROM (available internationally) called *Teaching Information Skills—Best Practice* is an important resource. Produced in Queensland for the Australian School Library Association, this interactive CD-ROM provides examples of "best practice" related to planning, teaching, and evaluating information skills programs across the curriculum. The practices demonstrated through the disk are based on the theoretical frameworks developed by Michael Eisenberg and Bob Berkowitz (United States), Ann Irving (United Kingdom), Judy Pitts and Barbara Stripling (United States), and on the Australian document *Learning for the Future: Developing Information Services in Schools*. Case studies come from elementary, middle, and secondary schools and from urban and rural schools. The CD-ROM was joint winner of the 1997 IASL/SIRS International Commendation Award for a significant project in the field of school librarianship.

There are also many resources on the Internet to support information skills work, particularly in the context of electronic information sources. "School Libraries Online" has a page of links called "Internet Resources Related to Information Skills." The resources listed include policy statements, curriculum units, lesson plans, articles, and evaluation tools. In addition, there are Internet listservs devoted wholly or in part to this topic; these include a "Big6" listserv established for discussion of teaching strategies, experiences, and resources related to the "Big Six" sequence of information skills developed by Michael Eisenberg and Bob Berkowitz in the United States and used internationally (Eisenberg & Berkowitz, 1990).

HARDWARE AND SOFTWARE

Using CD-ROMs requires appropriate computer hardware; for a stand-alone system in the school library media center this would consist of a personal computer, a CD-ROM drive (which might be built in as part of the computer), and usually a printer. The brand of computer doesn't matter, but to use the latest disks, it should have as much memory as possible and be as fast as possible. The printer will be needed so that users can print out the results of their searches and (with some disks) any notes that they themselves have made via the keyboard while using the disk. If users are to be charged for the printouts, then there needs to be some method of recording usage. If the CD-ROMs are titles such as encyclopedias and atlases that rely on color graphics in their presentation of information, then a color printer would be useful. Alternatively, if the CD-ROMs are being made available via a local area network in the library media center or the school, then the CD-ROM drive can be installed on a computer connected to the network. If access is to be provided to several CD-ROMs, then a CD-ROM tower or "jukebox" or multi-disk drive is needed on the network. Many CD-ROMs have their search software as part of the information on the CD-ROM itself; for others, the software comes separately on floppy disk. In the latter case, the software will need to be installed on either the stand-alone computer or the network server.

It should be noted that some CD-ROMs will operate only on a stand-alone computer; that is, they are single-user disks. Others can be mounted on a stand-alone computer or on a network, and still others are for network use only. Where a CD-ROM can be used in both environments, the school library media center may have to pay extra for a network license, depending on the disk and the vendor. The license may be based on the number of machines that can access the disk, or it may be based on the number of potential users in the school. Some producers of educational CD-ROMs are even willing to negotiate a license covering a whole school district.

Most people who use commercial online information services today will be using them via the Internet. This is especially the case since most of the older online information services have introduced Web interfaces, and many of the newer ones have been designed specifically to be used via the Web. Consequently, the equipment and facilities for access to commercial online information services will be the same as for the Internet.

Using the Internet requires appropriate hardware, software, and either a link to an Internet access provider or a school network that is linked to the Internet via a provider. However, within the context of these basic requirements, there are many options, though in fact, for each individual school the number of options will be limited by geography, funds, facilities, and the equipment already available in the school—in other words, by conditions in the internal and external environment of the school library media center.

For a single connection (one personal computer in a school or school library media center), what is needed is a personal computer, a modem, a telephone line, and software. The brand of computer doesn't matter, but, as with the computer for CD-ROM access, it should have as much memory as possible and be as fast as possible (unless it is to be used only for electronic mail, in which case, an older and slower machine can be used). The modem connects the computer to the telephone line and thus to the Internet access provider through whom the school has its connection; the higher the baud rate of the modem, the faster the information will come through (unless the speed of the modem exceeds the carrying capacity of the line, in which case, the line speed will be the determining factor in speed of access). Ideally, the telephone line should be a direct outside line, though it is possible (if less convenient) to use other types of lines. The other major requirement is for communications or Internet access software; this will often be provided (or at least recommended) by the Internet access provider and may be available on the Internet itself for downloading.

There are good arguments for using the same stand-alone computer for both CD-ROM access and Internet access. The same kind of basic computer hardware is needed for both, there is a need for the equipment for both to be placed in a location where it can be supervised easily, and both applications would benefit from access to a color printer. In addition, some CD-ROM encyclopedias and news/current information services on CD-ROM depend on Internet access for updates or so that users can take advantage of the Internet hot links that form part of the articles on some of these disks. However, accessing both CD-ROMs and the Internet from just the one computer places severe limitations on the number of users who can take advantage of these information sources.

For schools or school library media centers with a local area network, a direct connection to the Internet is possible from the network to the

Internet through the ordinary telephone line or a data line or ISDN line and a multiplexer or bulk modem or a system such as a LINUX box that links the school network to the Internet service provider. This kind of connection means that the Internet can be used at any time from any of the computers connected to the network—though it is possible to restrict access to particular machines or times. It is also possible to connect a small network (five to ten computers) to the Internet using an ordinary telephone line, a modem and router or hub plus WinGate software so that the machines on the network can access the Internet at the same time through the one line. WinGate software is available for downloading on the Internet, and payment can be made online. These network options really assume that there will be a person in the school or the school library media center with local area network management skills. Such skills will be at a premium as more schools establish high-bandwidth connections to the Internet, and some school library media specialists have already moved to acquire these skills through continuing education courses and professional development updates.

If the Internet connection is to be used for a variety of purposes, then it is probable that several applications packages will be needed in addition to the basic communications software that is recommended by the Internet access provider. The most popular World Wide Web browsers are *Netscape* (for PC and Macintosh) and *Microsoft Internet Explorer*, though there are others. At the end of 1998, some 74 percent of people accessing the "School Libraries Online" Web site were doing so using one of the versions of *Netscape* as their browser, suggesting that in the education sector at least, *Netscape* is the face of the Web. Electronic mail packages include *Eudora, Pegasus Mail,* and Microsoft's email system. There is also a range of different software packages for using other Internet tools and services, including, *WSGopher* and *TurboGopher* for Gopher, *Ewan* and *NTSC Telnet* for telnet, *mIRC* for IRC (Internet relay chat), and *FTP Voyager* or *Fetch* for FTP (file transfer protocol). It is increasingly the case, though, that Web browser software packages are incorporating facilities for using a range of other Internet services such as electronic mail and Usenet newsgroups.

While the hardware and software are essential for Internet access, it is, as previously discussed, through an Internet access or service provider that the connections are actually made. There are several ways in which schools can get access to the Internet. It may be that a national or statewide education authority or a school district establishes a wide area network with Internet connections for all the schools for which it is responsible; or else negotiates with a commercial provider on behalf of all the schools. A common method of access for schools in some countries is through a local college or university. Another common means of access is through a local commercial Internet access provider: a company or organization that provides Internet access and sometimes storage space for Web pages as part of a service package, for a fee. It is important that the Internet access provider be as close to the school as possible so that the costs of telephone access are reduced; some Internet access providers have established access points ("points of presence") within several local call zones in their region so that almost all (if not all) users have local call access.

The next chapter will discuss the use of information technology for communication rather than for information access. However, since the communications applications mostly depend on the Internet, the software and hardware used will generally be the same as described here for Internet access as will the conditions of access.

REFERENCES AND BIBLIOGRAPHY

Ahtola, A. Anneli (1989). In-house databases: An opportunity for progressive libraries. *RQ*. 29(1): Fall, 36–47.

American Library Association (1996). Access to electronic information services and networks: An interpretation of the Library Bills of Rights.

Anderson, Judith (1996). Internet use—a primary perspective. *Scan*. 15(4): November, 27–29.

Barker, Roz (1996). The Internet and information skills—a primary school perspective. *Scan*. 15(1): February, 14–15.

Berry, David (1996). What lurks in cyberspace? *Orana*. 32(1): February, 4–17.

Chambers, Liam, and Eamon Hayes (1998). Managing electronic resources. *Managing Information*. 5(10): December, 33–34.

Clyde, Laurel A. (1993). CD-ROM usage. *CMC News*. Spring, 5–7.

——— (1996). What CD-ROMs are other schools using? *Emergency Librarian*. 23(4): March-April, 51–53.

——— (1997b). *School libraries and the electronic community: The Internet connection*. Lanham, MD: Scarecrow Press.

——— (1997a). The Internet. In Butterworth, Margaret, ed. *Information technology in schools: Implications for teacher librarians*. 3rd ed. Perth, Western Australia: Australian Library and Information Association, School Libraries Section, 7–25.

——— (1998). The top 10 CD-ROMs. *Teacher Librarian.* 26(1): September-October, 54–56.

Clyde, Laurel A., and Joyce Kirk (1989). The use of electronic information systems in Australian schools: A preliminary survey. *School Library Media Quarterly.* 17(4): Summer, 193–99.

Deacon, Jim (1997). Editorial. *CMC News.* 18(3): Winter, 1.

Dillon, Ken (1996). Management of student access to the Internet: Issues and responsibilities. *Scan.* 15(4): November, 32–35.

Eisenberg, Michael, and Robert Berkowitz (1990). *Information problem-solving: The Big Six skills approach to library and information skills instruction.* Norwood, NJ: Ablex.

Hay, Lyn, and James Henri, ed. (1996*). A meeting of the minds—ITEC virtual conference '96 proceedings.* Belconnen, Australian Capital Territory: Australian School Library Association.

Herring, James (1996). *Teaching information skills in schools.* London: Library Association Publishing.

Oliver, Ron (1996). Information access and retrieval from electronic information systems: What do our students need to learn? *Access.* 10(1): March, 20–22.

Valauskas, Edward J., and Monica Ertel (1996). *The Internet for teachers and school library media specialists: Today's applications tomorrow's prospects.* New York: Neal-Schuman.

Wilson, Elizabeth A. (1996). *The Internet road map for educators.* Arlington, VA: Educational Research Service.

INTERNET SOURCES

AltaVista
    <http://www.altavista.digital.com/>

American Association of School Librarians (AASL)
    <http://www.ala.org/aasl/>

AskJeeves
    <http://www.askjeeves.com/>

Association for Teacher Librarianship in Canada (ATLC)
    <http://www.sbe.saskatoon.sk.ca/atlc/index.html>

Bell and Howell Information and Learning (formerly UMI)
    <http://www.umi.com/>

Blue Web'n
    <http://www.kn.pacbell.com/wired/bluewebn/>

Canada's SchoolNet
    <http://www.schoolnet.ca/>

CARL
    <http://www.carl.org/>

Compton's Encyclopedia Online
    <http://www.comptons.com/>

Dialog Corporation
    <http://www.dialog.com/>

D-lib Magazine
    <http://mirrored.ukoln.ac.uk/lis-journals/dlib/>

Dogpile
    <http://www.dogpile.com/>

EdNA
    <http://www.edna.edu.au/>

The Electric Library
    <http://www.education.elibrary.com/>

Encyclopaedia Britannica
    <http://www.eb.com/>

ERIC
    <http://ericir.syr.edu/>

Eudora
    <http://www.eudora.com/>

Excite
    <http://www.excite.com/>

Grolier Online
    <http://go.grolier.com/>

Homework Central
    <http://www.homeworkcentral.com/>

Homework Helpers
    <http://www.radix.net/~mschelling/homework.html>

HotBot
<http://www.hotbot.com/>

InfoSeek
<http://www.infoseek.com/>

Inference Find (Wisdom Dog)
<http://www.iwisdomdog.com/>

International Federation of Library Associations and Institutions (IFLA)
<http://www.ifla.org/>

Internet Public Library
<http://www.ipl.org/>

Internet Public Library—Reference Room (a variety of online reference works)
<http://www.ipl.org/ref/>

The Icelandic Education Network—ISMENNT
<http://www.ismennt.is/>

KidsClick!
<http://sunsite.berkeley.edu/KidsClick!/>

LION—Librarians Information Online Network (Library Services,
School District of Philadelphia, USA)
<http://www.libertynet.org/~lion/lion.html>

Lycos
<http://www.lycos.com/>

Microsoft Internet Explorer
<http://www.microsoft.com/windows/ie/default.htm>

National Grid for Learning (United Kingdom)
<http://vtc.ngfl.gov.uk/>

Netscape
<http://www.netscape.com/>

Newsbank
<http://www.newsbank.com/>

Nickelodeon
<http://www.nick.com/>

Purple Moon
<http://www.purple-moon.com/>

SavvySearch
   <http://www.savvysearch.com/>

School Libraries Online (International Association of School Librarianship)
   <http://www.hi.is/~anne/iasl.html>

School Library Media Research (AASL) (formerly School Library Media Quarterly)
   <http://www.ala.org/aasl/SLMR/>

Schrockguide for Educators—Kathy Schrock
   <http://discoveryschool.com/schrockguide/>

SIRS
   <http://www.sirs.com/>

TOM (Information Access Company)
   <http://library.iacnet.com/noframes/supertom.html>

Virtual Reference Desk (links to online dictionaries, encyclopedias,
   reference materials)
   <http://www.refdesk.com/>

Webster's Dictionary Online
   <http://www.m-w.com/>

WinGate
   <http://www.wingate.com/>

Yahoo!
   <http://www.yahoo.com/>

Yahooligans
   <http://www.yahooligans.com/>

CHAPTER FOUR

for
Communication

INTRODUCTION

"A historic moment! FrEdMail to shut down June 30, 1999" (Rogers, 1999). This message was distributed through a number of Internet services in January 1999. For quite a few readers, it evoked feelings of nostalgia coupled with sadness, for it was through the FrEdMail (Free Educational) Bulletin Board System that many teachers and students around the world had their first experience of the wonders of electronic communication and the benefits of collaborative learning via email. Originally developed in 1985 "to connect students and teachers around the world," FrEdMail fulfilled this function for 14 years, using the venerable and hardy Apple IIe and IIGS computers. It served developing countries as well as schools in more affluent nations such as the United States where it was based. However, with the original FrEdMail computer in Bonita, California, which had run the system continuously for the 14 years, becoming outdated, and the uneasiness felt about the "Year 2000 Problem," the Global SchoolNet Foundation made the decision to cease supporting the FrEdMail Network in mid-1999. The decision reflects a trend already noted in Chapter Three, for the Foundation will concentrate its work in the future on "building the global learning community on the Internet" (Rogers, 1999). They already have a World Wide Web site with communications facilities available through it. This trend means that when we talk about electronic communications today, to a very large extent we are talking about applications of the Internet—though many private networks are still operating and will probably continue to do so.

Because of the dominance of the World Wide Web in recent years, the Internet is often thought of as primarily an information search medium; however, electronic communications (including electronic mail and online talk or chat services) have always been an important part of the Internet. Even today, there is some evidence that more people use electronic mail than use the World Wide Web. The communications facilities provided by the Internet make it possible for school library media specialists to take part in professional development activities (such as courses or virtual conferences) via the computer and for students to become involved in online activities such as international book discussions, to cite just two applications of Internet communications. In addition, it is increasingly possible to use these Internet-based communications facilities through the Web, using the Web browser as the basic software.

While email is the best-known form of communication on the Internet, there are others, including listservs and Usenet newsgroups (both based on email), IRC (Internet Relay Chat), MUD and MOO (multi-user environments), and computer conferencing. The Internet is being used as a carrier for Internet telephone and fax traffic. With Internet radio and Web TV (both still in their infancy), it became a true broadcast communications medium. In addition, through the Internet almost anyone with access can become a publisher by creating a Web page to communicate ideas or distribute software or provide a service. Further, we are now seeing the development of Web sites whose aim it is to form the basis of Internet communities. All these forms of Internet communication have present or potential educational applications, and some have the capacity to support school library media center administration as well.

ELECTRONIC MAIL

It has already been pointed out that electronic mail, or email, is one of the foundations of Internet communications, and any computer that provides access to the Internet will support at least this feature; some people only have email access to the Internet. Email can be one-to-one or one-to-many, and it can form the basis of electronic conferences and discussion groups. It has already developed its own user culture and conventions, so email messages do not look the same as paper mail. In addition, email communication is often less formal than paper mail.

Use of Internet email requires an Internet connection and an email address. The email address will be allocated by the Internet service provider or the system operator of a network that is connected to the Internet. The email address will usually incorporate the user ID or logon name of the user and the domain name (Internet address) of the host computer on which the user has an account (whether the computer of the Internet service provider or the network server of the school). The author's email address illustrates this format:

anne@rhi.hi.is

where *anne* is her logon name, and *rhi.hi.is* indicates a mailserver computer at the University Computer Services (Reiknistofnun Háskólans in Icelandic, thus *rhi*) at the University of Iceland (Háskóli Íslands in Icelandic, thus *.hi*) in Iceland (Ísland in Icelandic, thus the standard country domain *.is*). The symbol between the logon name of the user and the domain name of the computer system is the "at" symbol, @. Some email addresses are longer, but the principle is the same. An Internet email address, like a World Wide Web URL, provides a unique identifier, so that Internet email can be delivered worldwide.

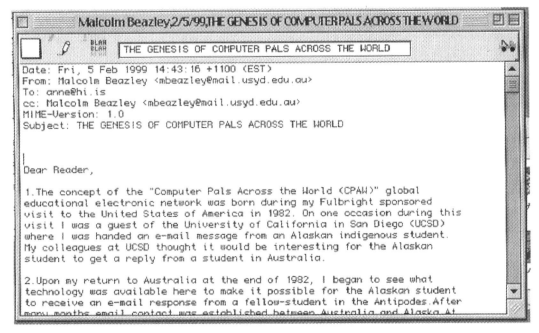

Figure 4.1   A typical email message as viewed through the Eudora email software. The message was sent by Dr. Malcolm Beazley AM, founder CPAW Global Educational Network <http://reach.ucf.edu/~cpaw>.

Email has advantages in comparison with alternative media for messaging and advantages that are related to intrinsic features of the email system itself. The advantage of email over telephone calls for messaging is that the communication is not dependent upon both or all parties being near the telephone at once. Thus, communication with other countries is not hindered by time differences or holidays. In addition, the receiver of a message can collect all relevant information before replying at a time that is convenient rather than interrupting other tasks to deal with a telephone call when it comes. Fax technology shares some of these advantages of email but is more expensive, though the introduction of fax via the Internet reduces the latter problem. The advantages of email over paper mail relate mainly to speed and cost; however, it can also be very convenient to have information in an email message rather than a letter, because it can be transferred easily to a document in a word processor or reformatted for other uses. It is also easier to forward an email message to another person, or to distribute it to many people at one time. Where the email system allows attachments (for example, if the *Eudora* email software is being used), then almost any computer-based file can be sent as an attachment to an email message: this file might be a photograph in digital form; a document such as a report or an article or even a whole book; a sound file (a school class singing the national anthem for a school on the other side of the world or a digital audio recording of a conference presentation); a computer program (an update to the inter-library loans system software or a new educational program); a copy of a World Wide Web page or link; or an animated greeting card.

Internet email has both school library media center management applications and curriculum applications along with applications that either fall outside the boundaries of these two categories or across them. For example, email can be used for administrative communication and as a means of information delivery. It provides an avenue for contact with the supplier/vendor of the automated library system; system updates might be delivered in this way as email attachments. The acquisitions/ordering module of the automated library system used by the school library media center might be using email to place orders with booksellers and other suppliers; the inter-library loans system might also be operating via email. Some providers of catalog records for automated library systems deliver those catalog records by email, at which point they are ready for loading into the school library media center catalog.

Email also provides a means of professional contact and communication among teachers and school library media specialists; listservs and newsgroups (discussed in more detail in the next section) are an example of this kind of application. In addition, there are many free (as well as paid) electronic journals and newsletters that are delivered by email that are very useful for school library media specialists. They include the following:

- **EDUPAGE**, distributed three times each week, is aimed at people working in all levels of education; it provides coverage of new developments in information technology, usually in the form of short summaries of reports in major newspapers and magazines. To subscribe to EDUPAGE, send an email message to <listproc@educom.edu> with <subscribe edupage> in the body of the message (but leave out the arrow brackets on either side of the email address and the message). The newsletter is produced in a number of languages other than English, and back issues are available via the Web.

- **Current Cites**, a monthly overview of published articles and books in the field of information technology, is aimed at librarians and school library media specialists. To subscribe, send an email message to <listproc@library.berkeley.edu> with the words <sub cites your name> in the body of the message (but replace the words "your name" with your own name and omit the arrow brackets). There is a Web site, and it is possible to subscribe to the email newsletter using a Web form.

- **The Scout Report** is a weekly electronic publication by Gleason Sackman that lists new resources and services on the Internet, including Web sites, listservs, and other resources. It is also available on the Web. To subscribe to the email version, go to the Web site and fill in the subscription form (see "Internet Sources" for the URL). Back issues are available on the Web site.

Electronic mail has been used in curriculum applications in a wide variety of ways: for information-gathering projects; for "keypal" projects; for tracking expeditions such as those of polar explorers; for process writing exercises; for communication with groups of school students in other countries and other regions; for extension work in foreign languages; and to support classroom work in media studies, science, social studies, geography, mathematics, home economics, language, and reading. It has found an important application in special education, since it is possible for physically or otherwise challenged students to communicate via email, without the recipient being aware of the disabilities of the sender; to the recipient, the sender appears to be just the same as any other email sender. Another important application has been in distance education at all school levels. Sometimes these curriculum applications of Internet email have also involved the use of other Internet resources, such as listservs and World Wide Web pages. Some examples follow:

- **Computer Pals Across the World** has had participating schools in many different countries, including the United States, Australia, New Zealand, Canada, the United Kingdom, Peru, France, Germany, Japan, Sweden, and China. The project matches schools in different countries and sets guidelines for their exchanges so that the use of electronic communications is firmly based in the educational programs of the schools. The language arts curriculum forms a focus for many Computer Pals projects, and students are able to share experiences, opinions, discussion of current events, social and cultural information, creative writing, and newsletters. Environmental monitoring projects, projects that record bird migrations, and projects that record oral histories or memories of events in previous decades are examples of other recent Computer Pals projects. Computer Pals Across the World was established by Dr. Malcolm Beazley in 1983 as the Australaskan Writing Project linking schools in Sydney, Australia, and Fairbanks, Alaska (United States). When other countries joined, the name was changed to reflect the increasingly international orientation. Computer Pals Across the World also links students studying by distance education, children in hospitals, and teacher education students.

- **Ask an Expert**. There are a number of "Ask the Expert" sites and email addresses through which children can email questions related to particular subjects. Many of these sites have university professors and graduate students answering the questions; others are operated by groups of teachers. The "Experts" locations include "Ask Dr Math," "Ask an Astronaut," "Ask Dr Science," and on a lighter note, "Ask a Magician." Some have guidelines for the email submission of questions; others take the work of children just as it comes. Many of these sites are listed on the "Ask an Expert" Web page (see the "Internet Sources" section at the end of this chapter). In addition, the Internet Public Library Web site has links in the children's and youth sections, through which young people can send email to authors.

- **The Global Schoolhouse**. "Linking kids, teachers and parents around the world" through a series of interactive projects, the site includes "community share" projects and expeditions that students can follow by email (and sometimes via the Web). The Global Schoolhouse Web site provides details of each project and the procedures for participation. The Web site itself is well worth a visit for an overview of the use of Internet communications in education.

While it has many advantages in the school setting, email is not without its attendant problems. It can be used very effectively, but it can also be abused. The abuse can be in both directions: students sending inappropriate messages and people outside the school preying on the students. School responses to this difficult situation can be divided into three basic categories: those who allow no email access for students, those who restrict student use of email to a supervised classroom setting (through a variety of strategies including teacher-controlled passwords), and those who allow unrestricted email access for students.

Some of the schools in the first group (those who allow no email access) originally had a free access policy. It was usually assumed that because the messages could be traced to the author through the system, bad behavior would be constrained. However, this proved not to be the case, and student misuse of the system resulted in a policy change. The misuse ranged from inappropriate messages to harrassment to obscene communications. Some library media specialists have argued that reading personal email on the library media center computers can tie up even a large network of machines and interfere with the work of other students, who are trying to get access for school projects and curriculum-related work on the Web. The reality may be that free access to email on the school or school library media center network works best in a situation where students' access to email is tied to their access to the network as a whole; if students abuse their email privileges and lose them, then they also lose access to CD-ROMs and other information sources on the network.

In those schools where access is restricted, it may be restricted to the classroom for keypal programs and other special projects, though it is usual to require special permission from teacher and parent for this use. Other applications for which email access might be permitted in these settings where access is restricted include access for foreign students who are sending email messages home; access for students in gifted and talented programs who need email to communicate with teachers who are not on the school site; and access for students who are taking part in foreign-language pen-pal programs.

In schools where unrestricted email access is allowed, there is sometimes a policy that requires a student reading personal email in the school library media center to give up the machine if a user with a classroom-related information need wants it. In others, there are no such restrictions. For some, free access to email from the school library media center or the school network recognizes that even if students are denied an email account on the school server, they can still set up a free account on Yahoo! or HotMail or Excite to read their email at school. In some schools, students are even encouraged to arrange for free email addresses so that they can use Internet email in the library media center. The rationale is that if they find an interactive Web site, but have no personal email address, they can still send questions and take advantage of the activities on the site through the school library media center computers using a free account. Further, encouraging students to use one of the free services means that the school does not have to maintain email accounts for perhaps hundreds of students (a saving in time and cost); from the student's point of view, this may be an attractive option, too, because they can take their email address with them as they move from school to college or work.

Given this variety of valid responses to student access to email in the school and school library media center, there is a clear need for each school or school district to consider the issues and establish a policy to guide school participation. The policy might address the restrictions (if any) on student use of email, the machines on which email can be used, the purposes for which it can be used, and the type of messages that can be sent. In developing the policy, the problems associated with enforcing it will have to be considered; for example, if students are not to have access to email on school machines, how will this be monitored? Through constant supervision of all machines? Through saving and checking all student email messages, with its attendant legal problems (some jurisdictions such as Connecticut require that notice be given of any monitoring of email and that it only be done where reasonable grounds exist to suspect that a person is violating the law) and ethical problems (library users have a right to privacy)? Against this, it should be kept in mind that on almost all systems, copies of email messages will be archived somewhere anyway, so email is never totally private, and users should be aware of this. Some schools require that parents sign a consent form for use of email at school and sometimes that the student (and sometimes the parent too) signs an ethical use agreement. If this is the case, it should be stated in the policy. In this situation, there also needs to be consideration of the information needs of the students whose parents do not sign a permission statement or agreement; what rights do they have to alternative sources of information to complete their curriculum-related work or for personal development? In response to issues such as these, some schools have moved from requiring parents and students to sign an ethical use agreement to printing the ethical use policy in the school handbook, along with other school policies (such as the discipline policy). School library media specialists will need to ensure that teachers, school administration, and parents have the information they need to make decisions in this complex and changing environment. In particular, since it is the negative aspects that have been presented so frequently in the media, they will need to be ready with examples of positive curriculum applications of this exciting communications technology.

Students need to be taught the basics of *netiquette* (good net behavior), so that their email messages do not offend other people and so that they don't abuse the system. The school or school library media center system needs to be secure enough, however, to withstand routine attempts by students to test the system; it should, for instance, prevent students from sending email under anything other than their own email address.

While the students need to be encouraged to take responsibility for their own use of email, through ethical use agreements and other strategies, they also need to be warned about, and as much as possible protected from, the undesirable behavior of others. They need to be taught safe computing, just as they are taught to look after themselves on the streets of their town: don't pass out your full name or address to a stranger online; don't respond to email advertisements that seem too good to be true (no matter what they are advertising); don't be drawn into private email exchanges with adults you don't know; if you feel uncomfortable about an email message you have received, show it to a supervising adult; and so on.

The school library media specialist will also need to be aware of those other hazards of email life—spam and email hoaxes—and to develop strategies for teaching people about them. Spam (or junk email) is sending unsolicited email messages (usually advertising of one form or another) to thousands, even millions, of recipients at one time. Because it costs virtually the same amount to send one or one million copies of a message, junk emailers buy mailing lists and send their message to everyone on the list, even when it might be very obvious to the most casual observer that the mailing is inappropriate for many of the people on the list. A lot of these spam messages come from an email address that is faked, and usually the only contact given in the message is a telephone number or a Web page URL. Honest retailers want people to know where they are; they don't need to hide. While some spam messages are offensive, and most are at least a bit on the shady side, the real problem comes when people find their email boxes cluttered with junk email or have to spend time dealing with several such messages each day.

Virus hoaxes are a variant of the chain letter, and they usually pretend to be helpful. The recipient is warned about a virus that can be transmitted by email and told not to open email messages with a particular subject line. The consequences of the virus are normally spelled out in fairly graphic detail. The recipient is also told to forward the message to as many friends as possible so that they will escape possible damage to their hard disk or their computer files or whatever. Herein is the real purpose of the exercise: The perpetrator has some fun watching the gullible recipients panic and spread messages all over the email system.

Unfortunately, each new generation of Internet users (several a year at the present time) has to be educated about both spam and virus hoaxes because these aspects of net life are not going to go away. This means that when the school library media specialist is planning email training for either students or teachers, there is more to be considered than just the technical aspects of getting online and the ways of composing an email message. There are resources on the Web that can help with this, including pages about netiquette, spam, and hoax virus warnings. Two of the latter have been created by organizations that monitor Internet hoaxes. See the "Internet Sources" section for further information.

Generally speaking, the hardware and software needed to use information technology as a means of communication by email are the same as for using it for access to information on the Internet, with the possible addition of specific-purpose email software. *Eudora* and *Pegasus Mail* are among the email packages currently available for both the Windows environment and the Apple Macintosh. However, some of the World Wide Web browsers are now incorporating email facilities. *Microsoft Internet Explorer* is one of these. In addition, free Internet email services (such as HotMail and MailStart) can be used to send and receive email messages via a Web page and using a standard Web browser.

INTERNET LISTSERVS AND NEWSGROUPS

Listservs and newsgroups both operate by electronic mail, and both are used to distribute information (such as announcements, advertisements, newsletters) as well as for communication. There are many thousands of listservs and newsgroups covering almost every subject and from different perspectives or for different groups of people, and sometimes messages are "cross-posted" between listservs and newsgroups that deal with the same topic.

However, the two systems are very different, both in the way in which they operate and the way in which they are used. Listservs operate through the normal Internet email system; newsgroups are provided through a network called Usenet (a relatively old international network that is based on mainframe and minicomputers using the UNIX operating system). Usenet is a network that is linked to but not, strictly speaking, part of the Internet. Listserv messages arrive in the subscriber's email box within a few minutes of being sent; the newsgroups are updated daily (or sometimes more often) through bulk feeds from computers on the Usenet network. While the listserv messages arc delivered to the electronic mailboxes of all the people who subscribe to a listserv, a user of a Usenet newsgroup has to go to the newsgroup to read the messages that are stored on the system and to reply to or post new messages. To see listserv messages, a user must subscribe to the listserv, but anyone with access to Usenet can read the messages of all but the closed newsgroups. While some people will have a preference for one of these forms of communication over the other, in practice it may be the content and quality of the newsgroups or the listservs in a subject area that govern the user's choice, and many people are subscribers to listservs and readers of newsgroups.

Listservs

Listservs are email discussion groups to which Internet users can subscribe—usually for free—by sending an email message to the listserv computer. Those who are members of a listserv send email messages to the listserv address. This mail is then distributed automatically to the email addresses of all the participants in the listserv. Each listserv has two addresses: the administrative address to which requests to subscribe are sent; and the address of the listserv itself, to which messages are sent for distribution through the listserv. When a listserv address is given in this chapter, it will be the administrative address. When someone subscribes to a listserv, they will get a response from the listserv computer that indicates, among other things, the address for participation and any procedures that apply to the particular listserv.

There are many thousands of listservs, covering almost every imaginable topic, and each listserv might have hundreds or even thousands of participants. Some listservs are closed; that is, only people who belong to a particular organization or group can subscribe. Others are open to anyone who is interested. Some are moderated—there is someone whose task it is to facilitate discussion and to screen out any inappropriate messages. Other

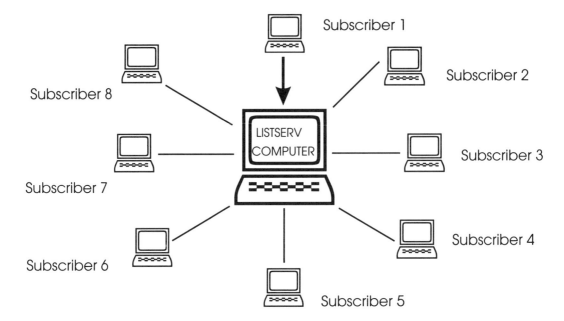

1.   Subscriber 1 sends an email message to the listserv address.

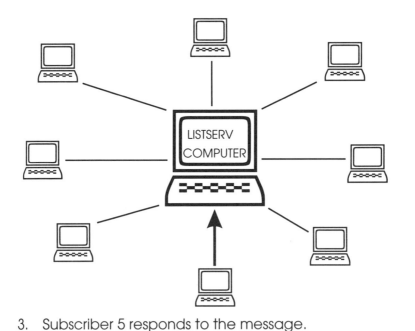

3.   Subscriber 5 responds to the message.

Figure 4.2   A listserv in operation.

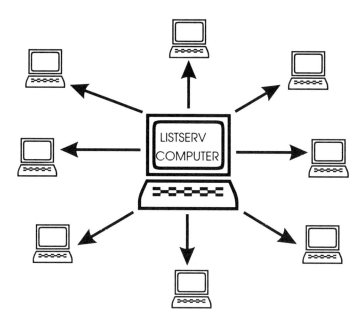

2.   Copies of the message are distributed to all subscribers.

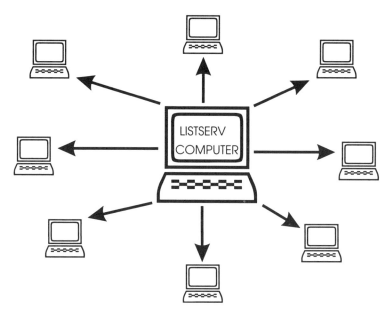

4.   Copies of the responses are distributed to all subscribers.

listservs are unmoderated, and people are free to participate as they wish. Some listservs are quite formal in their operations and may have documents that tell people how to participate, what topics can be discussed, and how to format their messages; others are very informal. Some professional listservs even have a system of subject headings for messages so that if people wish to screen out messages related to topics in which they are not interested, they can do so. This technique may be used where a listserv generates a lot of traffic (that is, a lot of messages come through the listserv each day). On some listservs, subscribers have the option of requesting the day's messages in digest form so that they receive fewer messages; on the other hand, the digests are often long and may include messages on many different topics related to the general topic of the listserv.

For people in the field of librarianship, listservs have become an essential form of professional communication. They have been adopted enthusiastically by the leading practitioners, and as a result, information about a new development may come through a listserv long before it appears in a printed journal or newsletter. In addition, the discussions on the listservs often focus on issues of the moment, before there is any coverage in print form. The listservs are also used for requesting (and providing) advice and mutual support and posting information about new publications or resources, among other things. Table 4.1 shows the purposes for which LM_NET (the largest listserv for school library media specialists) is used (information from Clyde, 1997). A discussion of LM_NET follows.

Table 4.1
General Classification by Topic or Purpose of LM_NET Messages over One Month.

TYPE OF MESSAGE	% OF MESSAGES
Discussion of professional issues	24.92
Locating information about resources	24.09
School library media center administration (including automation)	21.12
General professional contact and communication	9.08
Reference and information services	8.25
Curriculum applications and student projects based on the Internet	3.96
Miscellaneous	5.77
LM_NET administration	2.81

From *Managing InfoTech in School Library Media Centers.* © 1999 Libraries Unlimited. (800) 237-6124.

There are a number of professional listservs for school library media specialists; in addition, international virtual conferences in the field of school librarianship, such as the 1996 and 1997 ITEC information technology in education conferences (based in Australia), have been using listservs as the basis of discussion sessions (Hay & Henri, 1996; 1998). Listservs for schoolchildren are often associated with particular curriculum projects. Examples of useful listservs include the following:

- **LM_NET**, an "electronic community for school library media people on the Internet," is based on a computer at Syracuse University in New York State (United States), and managed by Professor Michael Eiscnberg (originally at Syracuse University) and Peter Milbury (Chico High School in California). Established in 1992, it had more than 5,000 members by the end of 1998, including many people in other countries. To subscribe, send an email message to <LISTSERV@listserv.syr.edu> with nothing in the subject line and with <subscribe lm_net your name> in the body of the message (but replace the words "your name" with your own name, and leave out the arrow brackets). The listserv also has a Web site where messages are archived and can be searched by topic and date.

- **OZTL_NET** (Australian Teacher-Librarians' NETwork) is an Australian listserv for teacher-librarians that also has members in other countries. It is "intended to be an effective management tool" for teacher-librarians, with a focus on topics of interest, including "the latest issues and developments that relate to and impact on school library services, operations, and activities" (from the Web page). OZTL_NET is managed by Lyn Hay and Ken Dillon at Charles Sturt University in Wagga Wagga, New South Wales. To subscribe, send an email message to <OZTL_NET-request@listserv.csu.edu.au> with the word <subscribe> in the subject line (leave out the arrow brackets) and nothing in the body of the message. As with LM_NET, OZTL_NET has a Web site with a message archive.

- **IASL-LINK** is a closed listserv for members of the International Association of School Librarianship (IASL). Based on a computer at the University of Iceland and managed by Professor Anne Clyde, it provides a means for communication among members of the Association and a distribution system for notices and other information. IASL members can subscribe by sending an email message to <majordomo@rhi.hi.is> with nothing in the subject line and with the words <subscribe iasl-link> in the body of the message (leave out the arrow brackets). The IASL-LINK listserv has a Web page on "School Libraries Online," but messages are not archived.

Listservs for students are mostly related to curriculum applications, particularly Internet-based projects. The following is an example:

- **KIDSPHERE** is a listserv for elementary and secondary school students and their teachers. It has been used as the basis for several international projects. To subscribe, send an email message to <joinkids@vms.cis.pitt.edu> with nothing in the subject line and the words <subscribe KIDSPHERE your name> in the body of the message (but replace the words "your name" with your own name, and leave out the brackets).

There are a number of online directories of listservs available to help school library media specialists to identify listservs either related to particular subject fields or for particular groups such as elementary school students. Of these, one of the largest is Liszt, which listed and indexed more than 90,000 listservs in October 1998. Others include the List of Lists and the Official Catalog of Listserv Lists.

Usenet Newsgroups

Although Usenet is not, strictly speaking, part of the Internet, the distinction is probably irrelevant in practical terms because most people who have access to the Internet also have transparent access to Usenet (access that makes it look like part of the same system). Many Web-based search engines now also search Usenet, and some Usenet newsgroups have Web pages and make available searchable archives of their messages on the Web. This provides yet another example of the impossibility of drawing meaningful boundaries on the Internet.

With more than 70,000 Usenet newsgroups, most Internet service providers who provide access to newsgroups as part of their service only get a news feed of a small proportion of the total number of newsgroups available. Some Internet service providers who provide connections for schools deliberately restrict access to Usenet to avoid problems with the adult material that is carried on some sections of the system. This means that even where Usenet is available, it may be that not all newsgroups are received.

Usenet consists of groups or collections of messages, called "newsgroups," each one dealing with a different topic or a different aspect of a topic. Usenet newsgroups are not really "news" except that items of news are discussed in some newsgroups. As was the case with listservs, there are newsgroups representing almost any subject and a wide range of views and tastes. There are Usenet newsgroups for teachers and for school library media specialists. There are also newsgroups covering issues of current concern to schools.

The names of newsgroups are written as a series of *domains* (groups of letters) separated by dots, with the domains being hierarchical in their structure, that is, going from the general (k.12) to the more specific (library), as in the newsgroup called k12.library (for school library media specialists). The name of the newsgroup is important, because this is what is used to find it on the Usenet system. When newsgroups are being read via the World Wide Web, their names can be presented as URLs. Some useful newsgroups include the following (the newsgroup name is given first, followed by the URL form):

- k12.chat.teacher <news:k12.chat.teacher>

- alt.books.reviews <news:alt.books.reviews>

- rec.arts.books <news:rec.arts.books>

- alt.censorship <news:alt.censorship>

Within each newsgroup, messages are organized in threads or topics. Someone introduces a discussion (or thread) topic, such as on the k12.library newsgroup, problems associated with selecting a second-generation library automation system. All subsequent replies and other discussion related to that thread appear after the first message and are linked to it. Sometimes, as discussion goes on, a thread spawns other threads (for example, complaints about the follow-up service provided by automation system vendors, discussion of the details of a particular system, horror stories about the automation process), and each of these threads will have replies and discussion listed under the first message. This means that readers of a newsgroup don't have to look at all messages; rather, they can follow threads according to their interests.

As with listservs, newsgroups may be moderated or unmoderated, they may be private or open to anyone who wants to participate, and there may be conditions for participation. As with listservs, postings to the news-group may be archived on a Web site (or in an FTP archive), where they can be searched and read, sometimes for years after the original discussion.

The Frequently Asked Questions (FAQ) file that is provided by many newsgroups is often very useful as an overview of a topic. These FAQ files are created by members of newsgroups (and sometimes listservs too) and posted to the newsgroup on a regular basis. They are an attempt to avoid the situation where every new reader of a group asks the same questions, to the irritation of the regulars. Some of these files represent the best collection of fact and opinion related to their topic, especially since many experts contribute to newsgroups and listservs; some have actually been published as printed books.

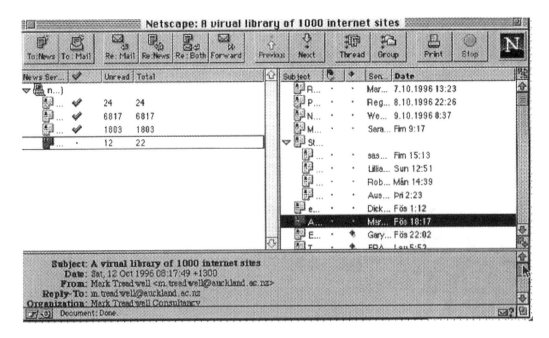

Figure 4.3   A message on the Usenet newsgroup k12.library.

In the school setting it is important to be aware of the nature of some of the newsgroups. Those whose name begins with the *comp* domain are related to computer science and are on a fairly technical level. Other major groups are *news* (usually announcements rather than news as such), *sci* for scientific discussion of a topic, *rec* for recreational discussion (that is, for people for whom this topic relates to a hobby rather than a profession), *biz* for business, and *soc* for social. The *k12* groups are for elementary- and secondary-school teachers. The *alt* (alternative) groups can be unconventional and very open in their discussion of all kinds of issues. It is to these groups that people are usually referring when they complain about inappropriate content and "adult language" in the newsgroups. This categorization of newsgroups by domain can give a useful indication of focus: for example, the newsgroup called rec.arts.books is for people who enjoy reading and want to discuss books with others rather than for librarians in their professional capacity.

To use Usenet, newsreader software is needed. An example is *Free Agent* for the Windows environment. As in other areas, though, it is increasingly the case that the World Wide Web browsers such as Netscape can be used for access to newsgroups if they are available on the system. Furthermore, some of the Internet search engines search Usenet newsgroup messages as one of the search options (in which case, they also provide a link to any relevant messages found), and the Excite search engine also provides newsreader facilities so that users can browse the newsgroup messages through the Excite pages. In addition, information from selected newsgroups is carried on some Web sites and electronic bulletin boards where it is thought to be of interest to the people who use the board or Web site. Further, messages are sometimes *cross-posted* from a newsgroup to a listserv dealing with the same topic. Depending on how the systems are set up, this may be done automatically or else a person who is both a subscriber to the listserv and a reader of the newsgroup may do the posting. In other words, there are many ways in which people can read newsgroup postings even if the school library media center (or the Internet service provider) blocks newsgroups.

There are a number of online directories of newsgroups that will help school library media specialists identify newsgroups related to particular subjects or for particular groups of people (such as science teachers or guidance counselors). At Reference.com on the Web, there is a guide to Usenet, a searchable directory of newsgroups, plus an option for searching the messages within newsgroups and then browsing related messages. There is a simple search option and an advanced search. Further, it is possible to create active queries that are run automatically for the user over a number of days so that a discussion can be followed over time. Other directories of newsgroups include Tile.Net and the "Search for Usenet Newsgroups" site. In addition, there are some newsgroups (such as news.announce.newusers and news.newusers.questions) whose function it is to provide information about newsgroups, including new newsgroups.

ONLINE CHAT

In the form of a text-based mainframe system called "talk," chatting online has long been a part of Internet life. Today, there are two main forms of chat, IRC (Internet relay chat) and the newer Web-based chat rooms. Both provide online forums for people to meet together online and hold discussions. However, they operate rather differently and look very different to the users. Both will be discussed here. While people can take part in other Internet discussion groups such as listservs and newsgroups by reading and replying to messages in their own time, chat (in both forms) requires that participants all be online at one time.

IRC (and its many variants) operates directly on servers rather than through a Web connection, and IRC software (such as *mIRC for Windows*) is needed to connect to a local server and to take part. IRC is text based; users have only their typed words and generally accepted abbreviations (such as *BTW* for *by the way*) with which to communicate ideas and thoughts. The system operates in "real time;" that is, all text from all people in a channel appears on the screen as soon as it is entered. As users type their own words, they can see new comments from other users appearing in another area of the screen.

Users entering the IRC system first select a channel from among those on offer. Each channel can accommodate hundreds of people, and there are many different channels operating at any one time. Generally, the channels will be dealing with different topics—though some are just places to meet up online and talk about anything at all. Users can start their own channels, and it is also possible to participate in several channels at one time (though this tends to be a strictly recreational application, since serious discussion is just about impossible if someone is monitoring chat across more than one channel).

Not all people who have access to the Internet have access to IRC. Some Internet service providers block IRC for a variety of reasons; sometimes it is blocked at the school level. The reasons will probably be different at these different levels. The Internet service provider is likely to be concerned about system traffic; the school is more likely to be concerned about potential access to inappropriate IRC channels or students wasting time (and occupying machines) for inconsequential chat on open channels.

Web-based chat rooms are not "real-time" applications in the same sense as IRC and its variants: messages are only sent or appear on the screen when the get/send button is clicked. They provide a graphical environment in place of the text-only environment of IRC: people can use small images to identify themselves rather than just a name or "handle," and they can post images that can be viewed by other participants. In addition, in most Web-based chat environments, a Web URL or email address can be posted as a "clickable" (interactive) link so that participants can move from the chat environment to view a Web page just by clicking on the URL, or they can invoke email by clicking on an interactive email address.

Several of the search engines provide access to Web-based chat rooms. For example, Webcrawler has several in operation, with various discussion topics, as does Excite. Some of the Web sites of professional associations have chat rooms. LM_NET, the listserv for school library media specialists (see the previous discussion under "Listservs"), also provides this facility, and chat times or topics are advertised through the listserv. A problem for international participants is created by the need for all participants to be online at one time, something that can mean a very early morning or late evening session for LM_NET participants who do not live in North America.

There are educational applications of both IRC and Web chat rooms—groups of students in different places might, for example, practice a foreign language or discuss a topical issue or wish to communicate with key-pals in real time. Another application is a professional one: the different chat systems can be used to hold online meetings when travel for face-to-face meetings is impossible. An IRC channel can be started by the person responsible for the meeting or activity, and the channel operator can, to a certain extent, control who uses the channel—both conditions that facilitate on-line meetings. Where chat in either form is used, organizers usually find it necessary to arrange contact details in advance and to ensure all participants share common objectives for the online session, so that educational or administrative goals are achieved.

Chat is popular because its real-time nature gives it an immediacy that is not always present in the other forms of Internet communication discussed so far in this chapter. Participants have a real sense of involvement in the ever-changing situation on their screens. The limitation in IRC is that participants must be able to type quickly while reading the comments of the other participants. Web chat rooms are slower.

However, as with the other Internet communications systems, there are potential problems that need to be addressed if IRC is to be used in the school library media center and if students are to be allowed to use the Web-based chat rooms through the library media center computers. One problem is the amount of time that participants will spend occupying the computers for chat when it is not part of an organized session. If the chat is recreational, should priority be given to library media center users who need to use the Internet for information searching for curriculum-related work? Another problem for schools is that IRC is by and large an adult world, and not all chat is suitable for young people. Although there are Web-based chat rooms specifically for children or teenagers, it is relatively easy for students to move from these to other chat locations. To what extent is supervision needed or possible? As with the use of email in the school or school library media center (discussed earlier in this chapter), policies and procedures will need to be established if access is to be provided to IRC or students are allowed to use chat rooms. In addition, students need to be aware of both their obligation to behave appropriately online toward others and of the need to exercise some sensible caution in their online activities.

The hardware required to use IRC and Web-based chat rooms is the same as that required for using the Web or email; there are no special software requirements for using the Web-based chat rooms, but special software is required to use IRC. The most popular IRC package, *mIRC*, can be downloaded from the Internet. It comes with excellent documentation, and there is online help on the mIRC Web site.

COMPUTER CONFERENCING

Computer conferencing is based on a link between Internet users that includes an audio and video connection. The link can be between two locations (for example, an instructor in one location and a class in another), or several locations can be linked. In each case, all participants can see the others through "windows" on their computer screens, and all can hear the others. In addition, slides can be shown and viewed by all participants, and the system can be linked to special equipment such as a microscope or a telescope so that everyone can see whatever feature is being discussed. Web pages can be used to provide support materials.

A major application has been in distance education at all levels and in the provision of professional development activities for people working in remote locations. Computer conferencing can be used to bring an expert into the classroom in a way that allows the students to ask questions and to engage in real dialogue with a person they can see and to watch demonstrations or slides or video clips presented by that expert. Another possible application of this kind would be for virtual author visits. In addition, it would be possible to connect classrooms so that students taking part in international or other projects via the Internet could see and talk to one another.

The use of computer conferencing requires that all locations in the linkup have a hardware and software configuration for conferencing. This includes the usual computer with a modem or network connection to the Internet, a sound card and speakers (for audio), a high-resolution color screen, a microphone, a video camera mounted on the computer, and conferencing software such as *CU-SeeMe* (from White Pine; it can also be purchased as part of a Cam Kit with the video equipment) or Microsoft's *NetMeeting*. If a large group is to watch a presentation or take part in the conference from any location, then a projection unit linked to the computer will be needed plus a screen. A fast Internet connection is important; on a slow connection, the picture will fall away each time someone moves. Some video chat rooms are now appearing on the Internet to link users of this equipment for professional or recreational discussions.

It will be clear from this description that computer conferencing is not cheap, and this is its major disadvantage for schools. However, as has been the case with other types of computer equipment over the years, costs are coming down all the time; an indication of this is that CU-SeeMe are now marketing their systems for home users so that users can "meet new friends," expand their "professional and social networks," and "watch entertaining cybercast events." (See the CU-SeeMe Web site for details.) Another problem is the one usually associated with real-time communication—all participants need to be online at the one time, and so time differences become an obstacle when working across time zones. In addition, a successful computer conference requires a great deal of preparation and organization.

OTHER FORMS OF INTERNET COMMUNICATION

This section will discuss briefly several Internet-related technologies that have in common only that they are used in one way or another for communication. They include multi-user spaces such as MUD and MOO and technologies such as Internet telephony, Internet radio, and NetTV.

MUDs are *multi-user dungeons* on the Internet, places where people can meet online in real time to take part in role-playing games or other activities. MOOs are MUDs that are "object oriented;" that is, they make available a range of online tools to assist users in creating virtual places such as towns or schools. Traditionally text based, MUDs and MOOs (particularly the latter) are now being enhanced through graphics and sound. Newer MOO software, such as *Palace*, enables participants to talk via typed text in a graphical environment, with the participants being represented on the screen by icons called avatars. This has made MOOs more attractive as venues for professional meetings and other serious applications, but they have long had a place in education as creative environments where students can work on collaborative projects. They also have applications in distance education (see Gibbons *et al.*, 1998).

Internet telephony is a relatively new communications application on the Internet, as is Internet fax. A standard Internet connection plus speakers and a microphone are all that is needed to make and receive telephone calls via the Internet, though more elaborate setups are possible too, and the software that is available tends to assume a fast machine with lots of memory. Telephone companies in many places are beginning to offer connections via the Internet, but rates vary, as do the kinds of connections supported. This is very much a developing field.

Internet fax, however, is an older and much more established Internet application, and many of the modems currently on the market support fax transmission. There are Internet services through which a message can be sent from the Web to a fax machine; there are other services that convert incoming faxes to email so that people who do not have access to a fax machine can still read faxes. Some services are free, but there are also commercial services that may offer more for the user. Further current information is available through a comprehensive FAQ document on the Web: "FAQ: How Can I Send a Fax From the Internet?"

The recent extension of the Internet into the field of broadcast media is reflected in such developments as Internet radio. Audio streaming software and systems allow radio stations to broadcast programs via the Internet as well as on air. These radio stations can highlight their Internet feed through their Web page; listeners need to have speakers on their machine (and sometimes headphones) and software such as *RealAudio* or Microsoft's Windows Media player (*NetShow*). As yet, it seems that while several radio stations are broadcasting some programming in this way (particularly in the United States of America), the numbers of stations and listeners are still fairly small. However, it is clear that there are many strategies being trialled for broadcasting via the Internet, and the future is likely to bring many more possibilities for broadcasting in different forms via this medium.

THE INTERNET FOR PUBLISHING: THE SCHOOL LIBRARY MEDIA CENTER WEB SITE

It has been suggested that a disadvantage of the Internet is that anyone can become a publisher. This point is usually made in the context of comments about the quality of the information available through the Internet. However, this supposed disadvantage is also one of the great strengths of the Internet. Almost anyone with a full Internet connection can become a publisher, presenting their ideas to a worldwide audience without spending much money (certainly a lot less than they would have to spend to create and distribute printed materials). Of course, there are some qualifications on this: they have to have a net connection through an Internet service provider who provides them with space for their Web pages (or they have to set up a Web server themselves, a more expensive proposition); they have to have the skills to create Web pages (not difficult to learn); and with many millions of competing Web pages, audiences are not all that easy to attract. Publishing and communicating in this way can be personally satisfying for the people involved because they have a medium through which they can express their creativity as well as provide information or services that might be useful to others.

School library media centers can become information providers on the Internet by developing either a home page on the World Wide Web or a full Web site comprising many pages of information. A school library media center presence on the Web can serve many purposes, including the following:

- to promote the school library media center as the school's information service;

- to facilitate communication by providing contact information related to school staff (including interactive email addresses);

- to provide information to the school community, whether or not the library media center is open and wherever the users happen to be;

- to provide search access to the school library media center catalog and other databases from remote locations (and from the library media center);

- to help users to explore quality sites on the Internet and to locate resources on the Internet for schoolwork or recreation;

- to help students develop information skills through information searching and participation in resource creation and evaluation (in developing a Web page);

- to provide links to Internet resources that will support particular curriculum units or activities in the school (with the lists of links being developed either by the school library media specialist, or by the teacher, or by both through cooperative work);

- to give students an opportunity to express their creativity through writing, art, design, music, or programming;

- to showcase the work of students by publishing that work of students in electronic form; and

- to provide a basis for school participation in collaborative projects via the Web with schools in other locations.

The school library media center is the major information center of the school, and so it is logical that the school library media center would be involved in any Internet-based information and publishing activities in the school, both in terms of information skills work and in terms of the skills of information access and organization that school library media specialists themselves can contribute to such activities.

What is actually happening in school library media centers in this regard? In August 1996, the author carried out a small-scale analysis of school library media center Web pages, using the international directories maintained by Linda Bertland ("School Library Pages") and Peter Milbury ("School Library and School Librarian Web Pages") as the basis (Clyde, 1996a; 1996b). While a little over half the pages in the sample of 50 were from school library media centers in the United States, the rest came from eight other countries.

The content and format of these pages were very different, suggesting that school library media specialists may have had very different aims in developing their pages, though some seemed to have no clear aim and no particular audience in mind. Only a few pages actually identified the intended audience in some way, either by a statement of purpose or by clear implication. Seven had been developed for students of the school to help them find Internet resources or to help them search for materials, while one was aimed at teachers in the school. One was developed for students, teachers, and visitors—a diverse group with very different needs; another was for students, teachers and parents. Six were clearly intended for online visitors from outside the school, because they were little more than sections from a school prospectus made available via the Internet. The intended audience for the other school library pages was impossible to discern from the pages themselves, and it may be that they had been created with no particular audience in mind. It is difficult to select and present information to meet the needs of users if neither the users nor their needs have been identified, and so these pages tended to include a miscellany of material and links at a variety of levels, usually without any indication of purpose and without any linking theme. It is interesting that eight of the home pages provided links to Internet resources for school librarians, suggesting that the school library staff themselves were among the main users of the pages in some cases.

Just as the intended audience for these school library media center Web pages varied, so did the contents. Table 4.2, page 132, summarizes the results of a basic content analysis of the school library media center Web sites/pages in the sample. Some 29 of the 50 pages provided information about the school library media center and ranged in length from a few sentences to quite long and detailed descriptions of buildings, collections, and services. Six had the mission statement and goals of the school library media center. Eight provided information about the staff (beyond just their names and positions), and some of these had links to the home pages of the staff members. Although 28 school library media center pages provided an interactive email address for contact with the staff, only 14 provided the street address (even the town, state or province, and country) of the school or the library media center. Six had a photograph of the school library media center, and four had photographs of the school library media center staff. Four carried a newsletter, or a news or update section, with information about current library media center activities. Two provided the library media center rules online, three had information for parents about Internet access and use (and access policies) in the school library media center, and three carried discussions of the changing role of the school library media center in an electronic age (apparently aimed at parents or online visitors). None provided search access to the school library media center's online catalog, though one Australian school library home page showed this as a future development.

Table 4.2
Features of School Library Media Center Web Pages, October 1996.

FEATURE	NUMBER OF HOME PAGES
Links to selected resources on the Internet	31
Information about the school library	29
Interactive email contact address	28
Link to a school home page	24
Date of the last update of the page	19
Links to Internet search engines	15
Address of the school/library	14
Counter	11
Information about Internet projects undertaken in and through the library	9
Research skills information, e.g., the "Big Six," "Be Definite," research guides	8
Links to Internet resources for teachers	8
Links to Internet resources for teacher-librarians	8
List of CD-ROMs in the school library	8
Book reviews, lists of books recommended by students, school book club choices, etc.	7
Photograph of the school library	6
Information (or links to information) about citing Internet resources in bibliographies	6
Links to HTML guides or information about creating a home page	5
Links to resources about the local area	5
News about the library or library activities	4
Information about the Internet for library users	4
Internet tutorial	4
Online reference desk for email inquiries	3
Information about Internet access and policies in the school and library	3
The library rules	2
Electronic magazines	1

From *Managing InfoTech in School Library Media Centers*. © 1999 Libraries Unlimited. (800) 237-6124.

The most common feature of the school library media center home pages was links to resources on the Internet (31 of the 50 pages provided at least some links). In its simplest form, this was done as a plain list, perhaps with a short description or annotation for each link. However, in some school library media centers, considerable thought had been given to how these links would be presented. Sometimes they were listed by broad topic or by school subject; sometimes they were presented under the name of the course for which they could be used; sometimes under the name of the teacher in whose courses they would be used; sometimes by curriculum unit or even under the actual assignment or project for which they would be used. Occasionally another classification scheme was employed—for example, a geographical arrangement (such as "resources in the school," "resources in our local community," "resources in our state," "resources in other places") or even an arrangement based on the main Dewey classes. Fifteen of the pages had links to Internet search engines such as Lycos, Yahoo!, and Alta-Vista, sometimes with an explanation of how this tool might be used to locate resources on the Internet. Eight of the pages had links to Internet resources for teachers, including links to online journals and to education and curriculum databases and services.

Several of the school library media center Web pages/sites were clearly designed (at least in part) to help school students (and sometimes their teachers) to use the Internet and to incorporate information and resources from the Internet into their work. Eight pages had information skills resources (or links to them) that were usually presented for students; the most popular was the "Big Six" information skills sequence developed by Michael Eisenberg and Bob Berkowitz, but two Australian pages presented information skills guides developed in Australia. Presented through the home page, these are always available when needed by students who are doing online work. To assist students to use Internet resources appropriately, six of the school library media centers had provided information (or links to information) about citing Internet resources and general information about preparing bibliographies. Four Web pages/sites had Internet tutorials designed to help students understand the Internet and to use it more effectively; one of these was presented as training for an Internet Driver's License.

When a school takes the step of moving from being not just a user of information on the Internet, but to becoming an information provider as well, then there are a number of issues to be considered and policy decisions to be made. The main thing that has to be recognized is that a complete change of orientation has occurred; the school is now an active participant in a global information system. Visitors to the pages could be located anywhere in the world, and they could be using the pages for a variety of purposes, including reasons quite unrelated to those that governed the development of the pages. The school is not protected in the way that it is in real life, and it will be judged in the same way that other information providers are judged. Regardless of the specific aims in creating the pages, the pages themselves become an ongoing public relations statement and help to define the image of the school and the perceptions that people have of the school.

If it is decided that the school library media center should have a home page or Web site, then many questions arise. What should be its purpose or aim? What needs should it serve? Who would be the users? How should it be designed, who should create it, who should maintain it, and what should be on it? It is impossible to deal with all these questions in this section. Nevertheless, they are important if a home page or Web site is to serve to promote the mission of the school library media center and the school, to further the educational aims of the school, and to promote the school library media center as the information center of the school.

It should be recognized from the beginning that the creation of a home page or Web site is not a once-only activity. It is rather the beginning of an ongoing process that lasts as long as the Web page/site is available for public viewing. The Web page or site will need to be maintained and updated regularly, again perhaps as a cooperative venture involving students and teachers and within the context of information skills work. Links to other pages will have to be checked regularly to make sure that they are still active and the information about the library kept up-to-date. New links and new content will be needed to keep the page interesting and relevant to the needs of users. Thus, when resources (personnel, time, money, equipment) are allocated to this task, it should be on an ongoing basis. Through the home page, the school library moves from being a user of online information to being an online information provider, a significant change that is appropriate in today's context but one that needs to be planned and managed so that educational goals are achieved through it.

In terms of creating and developing the school library media center Web site/page, the most common options are to have the work done by a specialist or the computer staff, to have the work done by the school library media center staff, or for the school library media specialist to coordinate a home-page project with students and perhaps teachers involved in the work. This is, after all, an opportunity to help members of the school community to develop information selection and presentation skills. The specialist may have skills in page design and page development that the school library media specialist initially lacks, but sooner or later the library media center staff will want to be involved, especially because it will then be easier for them to ensure that the Web page or site meets the needs of intended users and that information is updated as necessary. Even if outside expertise is used, the library media specialist will need to decide what information should go on the library media center's Web page/site—perhaps in consultation with others. It is the library media specialist, after all, who is the information expert and the person who knows the information needs of people in the school.

Because a Web page or site is so public and because it has so many implications for ongoing commitment of personnel and resources, it is important that the school (or the school district or education authority) has a policy related to school Web pages or Web sites. This might cover such things as a statement of the aims of the school or the school library media center in creating the Web site (as a guide to development of the site); who will act as Webmaster; who is ultimately responsible for the style and content of the pages; the responsibilities of other members of the school community in relation to the Web site; standards or guides for the evaluation of pages before they are mounted on the server; use of features such as the school badge; defining a "house style" for the Web site; the updating of the pages; any use of advertising or mention of product names. While the Web is an effective medium for the publication of student work, there are also questions about privacy and use of names and photographs on the site that have to be addressed at the local level and procedures that must be established. Recent cases of unwanted contact as a result of a photograph or an email address on a Web site have made it imperative that the school community take such things into account in their Web publishing activities.

The technical aspects of Web page creation are not particularly difficult to master, though creating pages that are effective for their purpose is another matter. Pages are prepared using HTML (HyperText Markup Language), a way of preparing text and other information so that it can be read by computer systems and Web browsers. There is plenty of online help available for those who want to begin this process; among the sources is "Resources for Creating Web Pages" (see the "Internet Sources" section for the URL). HTML is becoming more flexible with each new version of the HTML standard that is released so that Web page developers can add new features on an ongoing basis. At the same time, new programming languages such as Java, designed for the Web environment, offer even more possibilities for Web page design and what can be accomplished through a Web page. Software packages are now available to assist in the process of creating (or authoring) Web pages. These range from simple HTML editors that check the HTML tags in the document as it is being created to pagemaking packages that allow the Web page designer to work in a graphical environment and to create pages without writing the underlying HTML to full Web site management packages that not only include facilities for Web page creation, but also facilities for site management (linking the pages, maintaining a logical structure on the site, creating indexes, providing for global changes across all pages on the site). Among the best known of the Web page development packages are *Netscape Composer*, *PageMill* (Adobe), *HomePage* (Claris), and *HotDog 5* (Sausage). All have Web sites and the software can be purchased online. To take advantage of these packages, the school library media center will need additional software such as a picture editor and additional hardware such as a scanner.

To make the school library Web pages available on the Internet, access is needed to a Web server. Most Internet service providers allocate space on their Web server for their clients who want to create Web pages. If the school or school library media center has access to the Internet through a local Internet service provider, then it is quite possible that space for a small number of Web pages will be included automatically in the monthly access fee. Some local providers also have good rates for people who want to store more than the number of pages that they can have free. If so, then it makes good sense to take advantage of this, especially in the beginning. Each of the Internet service providers will have their own procedures for loading their clients' Web pages to their server, and the school library media center will need to follow these procedures.

While using space on the Web server of an Internet access provider can be very convenient, there may also be limitations on what can be done in this way and on the size and number of the pages stored. If the school or the school library media center decides to establish a large Web site with many pages—especially pages that are dynamic or need frequent updating—then it may be worth considering setting up a Web server in the school. This will mean a powerful computer that is permanently linked to the Internet plus a line and perhaps other hardware and cabling (depending on what is already in place as part of a school local area network). Both a fast machine and a high-bandwidth Internet connection are needed so that the Web pages are distributed at a reasonable speed to people outside the school. In addition, Web server software will be required to store the pages and deliver them in response to requests via the Web. However, many schools, including elementary schools, have successfully set up their own servers, some even offering host facilities for the storage of Web pages of parents, school board members, and others outside the school.

HARDWARE AND SOFTWARE

Much of the hardware and software required when information technology is being used for communication will be the same as when it is being used for information access. Thus the hardware and software requirements for using Internet email or participating in listservs or Usenet newsgroups are the same as those for using commercial online information services and the Internet, as outlined at the end of the previous chapter.

However, some of the applications outlined in this chapter on "InfoTech for Communication" do involve special requirements. Because their requirements are somewhat different in each case, they are discussed within the context of each application. Thus the use of computer conferencing requires additions to the basic Internet-linked computer, including video camera and conferencing software. Using the World Wide Web for publishing involves the same kind of hardware and software that was outlined for searching the Web in Chapter Three, but with additional requirements specific to Web page creation, such as a scanner and Web page development software. Establishing a Web server in the school introduces further hardware and software requirements.

REFERENCES AND BIBLIOGRAPHY

Baird, Val (1997). Publishing on the Web. In Butterworth, Margaret, ed. *Information technology in schools: Implications for teacher librarians.* 3rd ed. Perth, Western Australia: Australian Library and Information Association, School Libraries Section, 91–95.

Beazley, Malcolm (1987). The Australaskan writing project. *English in Australia.* 79: 51–57.

——— (1989). Teleliteracy for global understanding: Computer Pals Across the World. *Unicorn.* 15(4): 204–8.

——— (1989). Reading for a real reason: The Computer Pals Across the World project. *Journal of Reading.* 32(7): 598–605.

Clyde, Laurel A. (1993). Happy anniversary, Computer Pals. *Emergency Librarian.* 21(1): September-October, 57–58.

——— (1996a). School libraries: At home on the World Wide Web? *Scan.* 15(4): November, 23–26.

——— (1996b). The library as information provider: The home page. *The Electronic Library.* 14(6): December, 549–58.

————— (1997). *School libraries and the electronic community: The Internet connection.* Lanham, MD: Scarecrow Press.

Eisenberg, Michael B., and Peter Milbury (1996). LM_NET: Helping school library media specialists to shape the networking revolution in the schools. In Kuhlthau, Carol Collier, ed. *The Virtual school library: Gateway to the information superhighway.* Englewood, CO: Libraries Unlimited, 29–49.

Gateways: Information technology and the learning process—a collection of teacher practice from Australian schools. (1996). Tuggeranong, Australian Capital Territory: Commonwealth of Australia.

Gibbons, William J., Michael B. Eisenberg, Robert L. Heckman, and Adam Rubin (1998). Internet based distance education: From dungeons and dragons to degrees. In Hay, Lyn, and James Henri, eds. *A meeting of the minds 2: ITEC virtual conference, 97 proceedings.* Belconnen, Australian Capital Territory: Australian School Library Association, 179–85.

Hay, Lyn, and James Henri, eds. (1996). *A meeting of the minds: ITEC virtual conference, 96 proceedings.* Belconnen, Australian Capital Territory: Australian School Library Association.

————— (1998). *A meeting of the minds 2: ITEC virtual conference, 97 proceedings.* Belconnen, Australian Capital Territory: Australian School Library Association.

Rogers, Al (1999). A historic moment! FrEdMail to shut down June 30, 1999. Electronic mail communication, NET-HAPPENINGS listserv, 7 January.

Smith, Sally (1997). Telematics. In Margaret Butterworth, ed. *Information technology in schools: Implications for teacher librarians.* 3rd ed. Perth, Western Australia: Australian Library and Information Association, School Libraries Section, 75–77.

Stover, Mark (1997). Library Web sites: Mission and function in the networked organization. *Computers in Libraries.* 17(10): November-December, 55–57.

INTERNET SOURCES

"Ask an Expert" Web Site
    <http://www.askanexpert.com/askanexpert/>

Chat Etiquette: The Do's and Don'ts of On-Line Conversation
    <http://www.geocities.com/SouthBeach/Breakers/5257/Chatet.htm>

Computer Pals Across the World
    <http://reach.ucf.edu/~cpaw/>

Current Cites
    <http://sunsite.berkeley.edu/CurrentCites/cc.current.html>

CU-SeeMe
    <http://www.wpine.com/>

Edupage
    <http://www.educause.edu/pub/edupage/edupage.html>

Excite
    <http://www.excite.com/>

FAQ: How Can I Send a Fax from the Internet?
    <http://www.savetz.com/fax-faq.html>

Global SchoolNet Foundation's Global Schoolhouse
    <http://www.globalschoolhouse.org/>

HomePage (Claris)
    <http://www.claris.com/products/homepage3.html>

HotDog 5
    <http://www.sausage.com/>

HotMail
    <http://www.hotmail.com/>

Internet Public Library
    <http://www.ipl.org/>

List of Lists
    <http://tile.net/lists/>

Liszt
    <http://www.liszt.com/>

LM_NET Web Site
    <http://ericir.syr.edu/lm_net/>

MailStart
    <http://mailstart.com/>

mIRC
    <http://www.mirc.co.uk/>

Netscape Composer
    <http://www.netscape.com/>

The Official Catalog of Listserv Lists
    <http://www.lsoft.com/catalist.html>

OZTL_NET Web Site
  <http://www.csu.edu.au/research/cstl/oztl_net/>

PageMill
  <http://www.adobe.com/prodindex/pagemill/main.html>

Palace
  <http://www.thepalace.com/>

ProTeacher
  <http://www.proteacher.com/>

Reference.com
  <http://www.reference.com/>

Resources for Creating Web Pages
  <http://www.hi.is/~anne/internet3.html>

Scholastic Internet Center
  <http://scholastic.com/>

School Libraries Online—International Association of School Librarianship
  <http://www.hi.is/~anne/iasl.html>

School Library and School Librarian Web Pages—Peter Milbury
  <http://wombat.cusd.chico.k12.ca.us/~pmilbury/lib.html>

Schrockguide for Educators—Kathy Schrock
  <http://discoveryschool.com/schrockguide/>

The Scout Report
  <http://scout.cs.wisc.edu/scout/lists/>

Search for Usenet Newsgroups
  <http://alabanza.com/kabacoff/Inter-Links/cgi/news.cgi>

Tile.Net—Search for Newsgroups
  <http://tile.net/lists/>

CHAPTER FIVE

As an Educational and Recreational Medium

INTRODUCTION

Young people today are growing up in a world of computer-designed products, computer-generated images, computer-produced rock videos, computer-enhanced or even computer-created music, and computer-based communications. They belong to a world where information technology is the critical technology, where the use of computers has become so pervasive that it is no longer noticeable, where global networks carry information from continent to continent in fractions of a second, and where such concepts as *computainment* and *infotainment*, for all their linguistic clumsiness, encapsulate the idea that both entertainment and education are changing.

When most people think of computers in library media centers or information technology in school library media centers, they tend to think in terms of library automation or information retrieval (the latter particularly from remote online information services and the Internet). However, just as most school library media centers have developed holdings of audiovisual materials as well as print materials to support the educational programs of their school, many are now incorporating computer software into their collections or services, and for the same reason: to offer a range of learning experiences for the students. A wide range of computer-based educational materials is now available, and there are reviewing sources that can help teachers and school library media specialists select from those on the market or free on the Internet so that the resources made available through the school library media center meet the needs of the users. Computer-based resources may form part of the library media center collection of materials as well as be made available through its local area network (LAN). CD-ROMs and material downloaded from online information services and the Internet can also form part of the collection either for use in the library media center or loaned to students and teachers for use outside the library media center.

In this overview of current developments, the term *computer-based resources* will be used to cover information, education, and recreation resources for young people that are based on a range of technologies—all of them dependent on the computer. These resources include computer programs on floppy disk, resources on CD-ROM, online sources and services, resources downloaded from the Internet, electronic bulletin boards, and electronic mail (for information services or gaming). In terms of subjects or areas of interest, the range of computer-based resources is also wide. *Star Wars* and movie stars, aircraft and battleships, space stations and archaeological excavations, football games and chess tournaments, environmental simulations and ecological disasters, Beethoven and rap, Peter Rabbit's problems in the vegetable garden or King Richard II's problems on the battlefield, cooking or creating Web pages, learning to manage money or finding hidden treasure—all these and much more have been featured in computer-based recreational and educational packages in various formats. Information and education packages on floppy disk or on CD-ROM cover almost any topic or subject: mathematics, science, language study, literature, music, art, history, geography, home economics, and business studies, among others. Meanwhile, a young person with a personal computer, a modem, and a telephone line has access to a global information environment, an environment in which the boundaries of information and entertainment may become blurred, an environment in which projects can be carried out in cooperation with others, friends can be made, and hobbies can be pursued— or in which a young person can hide behind an alias and lead a fantasy existence as, say, the Captain Crazy or the Cyberwitch of the Internet.

Computer-based resources (on floppy disk or CD-ROM or downloaded from the Internet) may include applications packages (such as database packages, word processors, graphics packages, and Web page development software), educational software related to the school curriculum, computer-assisted learning programs, computer games, and computer-based literature (including "the disk of the book" and "the CD-ROM of the book"). These resources might also include educational robotics packages and other devices that use computers to control other equipment. Within the school library media center, computer-based resources of various kinds—from database packages to online services and self-instructional software packages—may be used in information skills instruction.

It is worth remembering that school library media centers are not just sources of material related to the curriculum; recreational, cultural, and general-interest materials also have a place in the collection. In addition, literature promotion or reading promotion programs have long been recognized as an important part of the work of the school library media specialist, whether related to classroom work or to the leisure reading interests of young people. It follows, then, that computer-based recreational materials should also have a place in the school library media center's collection. These materials could include interactive fiction packages on floppy disk or CD-ROM that allow the students to become participants in a story, taking on the role of a particular character and having an influence on the development of the plot. Interactive stories are now available on the Internet, too, with some even being developed interactively by the readers/participants. Other computer-based recreational materials include simulations, games, packages related to hobbies, and applications packages such as graphics packages and desktop publishing software (which allow students to explore their own creativity and enhance their leisure time). In addition, it should be acknowledged that exploring the Internet is itself a hobby for many young people, while others pursue such hobbies as stamp collecting or writing or chess via the Internet.

It is now fairly common for public libraries as well as school library media centers in some countries to provide resources on floppy disk for use in the library or for lending. As an extension of this, the Datalibrary (Data-biblioteket) in Copenhagen has been set up to provide computer programs and computer books for lending to users throughout Denmark. In the United States, the United Kingdom, Canada, Australia, New Zealand and elsewhere, some school and public libraries are providing access to CD-ROM resources within the library and sometimes outside the library via a local area network and/or via the Internet. The City of York public library system in Canada pioneered the lending of CD-ROMs as part of the normal lending services of the library (Shirinian & Nicholls, 1997). As more libraries and school library resource centers make their services available via the Internet, it is becoming increasingly difficult to distinguish between resources in the local collection and resources to which users have access through the library or library resource center.

It is worth noting that, as with books and audiovisual materials, the quality of these computer-based resources varies considerably, and selection will be an important issue for school library media centers. Not only are some of the materials of poor quality (in terms of the content and in terms of the programming or technology), but school library media specialists will also need to check for bias, appropriateness for age and interest levels of the users, ease of use, and price value. There is nothing new in this, of course—school library media specialists are accustomed to applying these criteria to a range of materials. However, applying them to, say, a multimedia CD-ROM or to an electronic bulletin board that makes available thousands of computer programs can present a special challenge.

In addition, there are a number of other administrative tasks associated with the incorporation of these resources or services into the school library media center collection and program. They include establishing procedures to check for damage when the items are loaned, any special technical requirements for the loan (such as special targets for use with the security system), shelving and safe storage, dealing with any copyright conditions or fees for use, supervision of use (in an online or Internet environment), the provision of appropriate equipment if necessary, maintaining schedules for use within the library media center, providing the necessary support equipment (such as printers), and providing user assistance (including troubleshooting).

School library media specialists have a key role in promoting the educational use of information technology and in coordinating the acquisition, cataloging or listing, and storage of hardware and software so that they are made available to all who need to use them, as well as in providing facilities for access to online resources. The school library media specialist's role should not just be that of a custodian of computer resources—that would achieve little benefit for the school. Rather, the role should be that of a facilitator who, through catalogs, bibliographies, and other aids, promotes awareness of resources and makes them available for use when needed. This does not necessarily mean that all resources should be housed centrally in the school library media center—only that they be coordinated centrally.

There are other advantages associated with having the school's educational computer resources managed through the school library media center. Because subject departments within the school, individual teachers, and the school library media center are all likely to purchase software and CD-ROMs, there will be financial and educational benefits if the school library media center is established as the clearinghouse for all such purchases; as, indeed, it should be for all educational media. This means that a record of all computer-based resources held in the school will be maintained and made available to staff and students through the school library catalog. It could also lead to the rationalization of purchases on a schoolwide basis, with cost savings as a result. Furthermore, there is a need for the provision of a range of services associated with computers, just as there is for those services related to other educational and recreational resources maintained through the school library media center. These services may include the maintenance of a schedule for group and individual use of equipment (perhaps with interactive booking forms available via the school or school library media center local area network) or the organization of a preventive maintenance program for equipment. They may also include a range of educational services such as user education or orientation programs to help both teachers and students use the technology effectively and programs that would familiarize parents with the technology.

CURRICULUM-RELATED APPLICATIONS

Information technology of almost all kinds can be used to offer a variety of learning experiences for students in schools, and the range of educational applications is increasing as time goes on. Some of these applications are appropriate for use with whole classes; others for individual or group use. While educational applications of computers once meant mostly resources on floppy disk, today it also means CD-ROMs, with the possibility that both the resources on floppy disk and the resources on CD-ROM might either be loaned from the school library media center collection or be made available via a local area network. Other computer-based educational resources might be used online (interactively) via the World Wide Web or downloaded to a computer in the school library media center or the local area network (LAN) from electronic bulletin boards or downloaded from the Internet using FTP (file transfer protocol). Some may even arrive as email attachments, ready for loading onto the network or onto a stand-alone machine. While all these formats have many things in common, each also brings with it particular conditions of use and particular administrative requirements.

A number of writers in the field of educational computing have attempted to categorize educational software and CD-ROMs in different ways. R. Jones (1981) lists ten possible educational applications of personal computers in elementary schools, simulations and models, demonstrations, computer-aided instruction ("course material imparted through the medium of the computer"), testing, drill and practice exercises ("consolidation"), a reference source (a database accessed in various ways), problem solving, educational games, acting as a control device (to take readings or control the operation of an experiment), and programming tools. Alfred Bork's list is rather different, incorporating, as it does, drill and practice, drill and practice with remediation, tutorial programs, testing, testing with learning, and "controllable worlds" as the main categories (Bork, 1981). The categorization that will be used in this chapter is an amalgam of categories drawn from educational reports and documents; it was originally developed by the author (Clyde, 1985) for a conference on the use of computers in school libraries, held in Perth, Western Australia, in 1985, and subsequently was amended several times to take account of new developments in information technology.

Information Technology As an Educational Medium

Computer-Assisted Learning
Computer-Managed Learning
Drill and Practice
Games
Simulations
Cooperative Projects
Information Technology as a "Learning Environment"
Reference Works and Databases
Applications Packages
Using Computers to Drive Other Equipment
Teacher Utilities

It is important, however, that these categories should not be seen as fixed; in fact, there are no generally accepted terms for the different types of educational programs, and different writers on the subject tend to use terms in different ways. Definitions, therefore, are not going to provide clarification, and attempts to categorize educational software may even hinder understanding of the range of materials currently available. It is probably better to use these categories as a general guide and to look at some of the range of educational applications and some of the programs being marketed or distributed, that could be included in the collection of a school library or to which access could be provided in some way.

Computer-Assisted Learning

Computer-assisted learning or computer-assisted instruction involves the use of the computer and its peripherals and software as the basic resource. The student works through a sequence of activities at the computer that are in a predetermined order that usually depend on the results achieved at each stage. Some of these materials have been transferred to the Web environment, often using interactive forms for the submission of responses. Much of the theory behind educational applications of this type relates to work done in the era of mainframe and minicomputers, before microcomputers and personal computers emerged in the late 1970s.

Computer-Managed Learning

Computer-managed learning or computer-managed instruction involves using the record-keeping facilities of the computer to keep track of the work done on the computer by students. Sometimes the computer is used to provide diagnostics as well. While it also makes use of computer-assisted learning features in most cases, it is the record-keeping facilities offered by the computer that are most critical in this application. It enables teachers to see how far each student has progressed on a range of tasks carried out on the computer, and may even give an indication of the time taken by the students and the particular areas of the computer-managed learning work with which they had problems.

Drill-and-Practice Programs

Drill-and-practice programs or tutorial and test, or read and respond— there are a number of names for this phenomenon. Information is presented to the student through the computer or other materials, and then recall or comprehension (and sometimes both) are tested, usually through multiple-choice exercises. Drill-and-practice packages are often promoted as a means of enticing students to do the repetitive work necessary for mastery of basic procedures in subjects such as mathematics and spelling. Examples of this kind of software include *Letterhunt* (Cambridge Micro Software) for spelling and *Math Blaster* (Blaster Learning Systems). *Let's Go Read: An Island*

Adventure (Dataflow) incorporates voice recognition technology in a phonics package for four- to six-year-olds. Much of the traditional library-skills software that was used, for instance, to teach the outline of the Dewey Decimal Classification fell into this category. Packages such as *Dewey Decimal System* (Right On Programs) and *Dictionary Guide Words* (MicroEd) are examples.

Educational Games

Educational games considerably extend the idea of the drill-and-practice programs, some of which were actually presented in the form of games (for example, using a computer-based version of *Hangman* for spelling drills). The better educational games have been almost indistinguishable from entertainment—the classic geography and problem-solving skills game *Where in the World Is Carmen Sandiego?*, which has been popular inside and outside the classroom for quite a few years, is a case in point. Originally marketed on floppy disk, it is now selling well as a CD-ROM in computer stores to people who plan to use it at home as a game for the family.

Simulations

Simulations, an extension of the game genre, provide students with an insight into particular situations, such as the causes of a war or of an economic recession. Alternatively, simulations give students a vicarious experience of something that would be impossible in the normal classroom setting—such as following an expedition or managing a town or conducting experiments that would either take too long or be too dangerous or too expensive to undertake in the classroom. Well-known examples of educational simulations include *Volcanoes* (an earth science simulation produced by Earthware Computer Services) and *Odell Lake* (for ecology). Simulations that, like Carmen Sandiego, have moved outside the educational environment and joined the classics include *SimCity* and similar packages, through which participants create new worlds as a cooperative venture. Some MOOs on the Internet (see Chapter Four) also provide this kind of cooperative and problem-solving challenge.

Learning Environments

At their highest level, simulations merge into learning environments. Through this application of information technology, participants can explore, set their own goals, and create new knowledge and new situations.

Through these learning environments, or "microworlds," students can explore relationships within a topic and learn through discovery or their own creativity. This kind of software is difficult to describe, because in essence it becomes what students and their teachers make of it. An early example was *Worlds Without Words* (4Mation Educational Resources). This educational adventure was based on nonverbal communication—no words appeared on the screen. Designed for large-group activity, it allowed students to explore the environment of an alien visitor through puzzles, games, and problem-solving techniques. It could be used with children from the kindergarten level onward, and with English-as-a-second-language groups. *Legoland* (Lego Media International) is a virtual reality environment for children as young as six, and involves a number of supporting packages and materials. Using *Legoland,* children can explore a world or build a world—in fact, they can create a world and explore it. As with simulations, some of the best virtual learning environments are now on the Internet, particularly in the world of MUD and MOO, where new graphical interfaces have enhanced the potential of this medium.

Reference Works and Databases

Reference works and databases (see Chapter Three) may be purchased on floppy disk or CD-ROM and used on stand-alone machines or on a local area network. In addition, many are now being made available online via the Internet or through mixed mode (on CD-ROM with updates via the Internet or on CD-ROM with hot links to relevant Internet sites). These reference works and databases allow students to search for information related to a topic and to explore the topic in a way that would not be possible with printed sources. Even the interactive encyclopedias, whether on CD-ROM or online, provide an environment for exploration that transcends what is possible in the print versions, with linkages and interactivity and with tools that allow students to build presentations with the material they have found.

Applications Packages and Other Tools

Applications packages—including word processors, database packages, spreadsheets, graphics software, desktop publishing systems, and Web page development software—allow students to perform a variety of tasks on the computer and have applicability across almost all areas of the curriculum. They also provide tools for teachers to develop learning experiences for their students and for the school library media specialist to develop a range of administrative and information services. Further, computers can be used to drive other equipment, including experimental equipment and data-gathering devices. The equipment can include remote sensing devices, Web cameras, and Lego-type equipment as well as robotics devices.

Information Skills

An important aspect of the curriculum-related use of information technology is for information skills work. This applies as much in the Internet environment now as it has in the past in the more traditional information technology media of floppy disk and CD-ROM. Today, it is generally accepted that the development of information skills should not be confined to library-skills instruction in library lessons; rather, it should be a broadly based, continuous process that cuts across the curriculum and throughout the school and that involves the school library media specialist and classroom teachers in cooperative planning and teaching as partners. Recent reports have emphasized the importance of information handling and information retrieval skills for children of all ages so that they will be able to cope with planning and decision making in an increasingly complex and technology-based world. The school library media specialist's role in this area encompasses not just the cooperative teaching of skills but also the provision of effective information retrieval tools, including catalogs and indexes, in the school library media center. Through this, information retrieval skills can be learned and reinforced.

Much of the computer software that was available in the past, unfortunately, had been developed to teach traditional library skills rather than more general information skills. Usually the library skills packages focused on using a card catalog, locating books on the shelves (call numbers), using reference books, understanding the Dewey Decimal System. While some of these packages were well produced, many were of relatively poor quality—poorly conceived and organized, lacking in motivational devices, visually unexciting, and without support materials. In addition, almost all these packages were designed with the needs of United States school library media centers in mind. When this was the case, some sections, particularly those on reference skills, had little relevance for school libraries in other countries, where the reference collections did not contain the same basic reference sources. Only a few packages allowed school library media specialists to substitute titles from their own school library media center collections—when looking at encyclopedias, for example—which would have made the material more relevant to local needs in the United States as well as in other places. The author's 1989 directory of *Computer Software for School Libraries* (Clyde, 1989) listed more than 100 library skills packages; by 1993, however, when an updated listing (Clyde, 1993a) was published, the number was smaller, an indication of the change in direction and emphasis within information skills work.

Some current computer-based packages have been developed with the aim of assisting students to acquire and practice information skills, including online information skills. One problem for the developers of this type of software is that the electronic information sources change frequently (something that in any other context might be considered a strength). This means that information skills software based on these sources—or that even mentions them—has to change as well, an expensive process. However, it is now recognized that the prepared commercial databases, news and current-information services, and electronic encyclopedias that are available today are, in themselves, resources for teaching information access and information retrieval skills. Further, many of them contain instructional modules or tutorials or other orientation sections that actually provide guidance and assistance for those who need help in using the resource.

There is now a considerable amount of information skills material on the Internet, too; this includes Web sites for students as well as material for teachers and school library media specialists. "School Libraries Online," the Web site of the International Association of School Librarianship (IASL), has a page of links to information skills resources on the Internet. Among these links is "The Big 6 Skills," the Web site established by Michael Eisenberg and Bob E. Berkowitz to showcase their "information problem-solving approach to library and information skills instruction." Their site is complemented by some associated sites, including one for "The Super 3," an adaptation of "The Big 6" for use with very young children.

RECREATIONAL RESOURCES

It is seldom that a case has to be made for the inclusion of works of creative fiction in the collections of public or school libraries. In fact, it has long been accepted that the school library media center has a responsibility to cater to the recreational, social, and cultural needs of students in the school as well as their need for resources and information to support their classroom studies. Consequently, fiction books as well as learning materials have a place in the school library media center. Not only are fiction materials included in the school library media center collection but school library media specialists implement reading programs designed to promote the reading of fiction and other creative works such as poetry. It is equally accepted that computer-based learning materials have a place in the school library media center alongside other learning resources. It follows, then, that if recreational works in print form are included in the school library media center collection and computer-based learning materials are accepted, then other computer-based materials, such as recreational materials, should either have a place in the school library media center collection or be accessible through the school library media center. These materials could include interactive fiction, disks or CD-ROMs based on books, games, simulations, applications packages, and software and Web sites for personal development. The various resources might be available as computer software on floppy disk or as CD-ROMs or be downloaded from the Internet to the local computer or network system. In addition, there are the interactive resources available through the Internet, such as interactive fiction, role-playing games, and environments such as MUD or MOO. Good computer-based recreational resources enable children to explore a range of settings, experiences, challenges, and emotions just as good fiction books do. In addition, some of them provide an outlet for creativity as well.

Information Technology As a Recreational Medium

Interactive Fiction
Literary Spin-offs ("the disk of the book")
Games
Simulations
Applications Packages
Personal Development Packages

As was the case with computer-based learning resources, there are many ways of categorizing computer-based recreational resources. The following discussion is based on categories developed by the author for a Nordic seminar on "Young People and Information" (held at the University of Iceland in May 1993) and since modified and augmented (see, for instance, Clyde, 1993b) in response to new developments in both information technology and the recreational software industry. As with educational resources, the categories should not be seen as "fixed" or standard; they are simply a useful way of looking at a large group of resources that are enormously varied and becoming even more so. Readers should also bear in mind that the distinctions between these categories are sometimes far from clear, and some resources may well belong in more than one category—for example, a disk based on a classic book but with a considerable amount of interactive game playing included.

Interactive Fiction

The first category is interactive fiction, which is usually seen as a "book" or story written for the computer, rather than for the print medium. It allows the user to become a participant in a story, determining the course of the action and influencing the development of the characters. These stories may be simply computer-based versions of the "Choose Your Own Adventure" stories with which we are all familiar in their book form, or they may be much more complex. The earliest were entirely text based, with words flowing across the screen or filling it and with the user typing questions and commands to explore further or to move the action forward. More recent interactive fiction incorporates graphics, sound effects, and screen action, as well as text. In some of the current interactive fiction, the multimedia is the basis of the presentation of the story rather than just an embellishment to the text as it tended to be earlier.

Many interactive fiction packages are now available, reflecting a range of literary genres and subjects though science fiction and fantasy predominate. Reviews still tend to be mixed, as they were for *Portal—A Computer Novel* (Epyx), a science-fiction adventure set in the year 2106, when the reader/user returns from a 100-year-long space voyage to find a deserted planet. The user/reader searches a Worldnet database for clues, which lead to the sole survivor of the lost world, a biological computer called Homer. *Essex*, by Bill Darrah (Brøderbund), is another science-fiction adventure set in the future. It involves the reader/user in an intergalactic search-and-rescue mission. *Amnesia* (Electronic Arts), an interactive novel by science-fiction writer Thomas M. Disch, re-creates the heart of New York City; the computer package includes a map of Manhattan to guide the reader/user down some 650 streets and through the subway system. *Brimstone,* by James Paul (Brøderbund), is a medieval text adventure in which Sir Gawain, one of the Knights of the Round Table, has to escape from a highly complex underworld or be trapped for eternity.

While some people see interactive fiction as the literature of the future, others see it as a passing fad, something that is popular only because it is on the computer. Some producers of interactive fiction say that their dream is to bring literature to the computer or to change the face of literature. However, much of the current interactive fiction, whether for adults or children, is still very poor as literature—if it can even be labeled as such. It presents none of the hoped-for challenge to printed books. In fact, this is probably an unrealistic idea anyway—it is more likely that interactive fiction will develop as a parallel medium to the printed book, co-existing with it, just as film has developed. Meanwhile, it has to be said that as writers gain experience with this new medium, interactive fiction is improving, and many packages are absorbing and entertaining. With the move from floppy disk to CD-ROM for some interactive fiction, it has been possible to include more sophisticated sound, visuals, animation, and moving sequences in the programs, and some of the CD-ROM-based resources now approach more closely the dreams of those who want to bring a new form of literature or entertainment to the world.

Literary Spin-offs

Literary spin-offs closely resemble interactive fiction, but where interactive fiction stories and packages were originally developed as such, the literary spin-offs are a by-product of another creative endeavor (usually but not always a book). Just as effective films have been produced from books, so have many successful computer packages (and some unsuccessful ones) been created from books. As with the film adaptation of a book, the disk version of a book, or a "book online," presents a book's story and characters through a different medium. Most of these adaptations present the book as interactive fiction, with the reader or user being able to influence the course of the action and play a part in the story. Some of the computer-based adaptations of picture books incorporate new elements that are made possible by the computer, such as three-dimensional animation and interactive sequences. However, others simply present the author's original text on the screen, with the addition of sound, graphics, and perhaps some animation. Sometimes the screen display is actually designed to look like an open book, reinforcing the automated book idea.

One of the earliest and best known of the interactive fiction programs based on books is *The Hitchhiker's Guide to the Galaxy* (Infocom), which has been sold for many different microcomputers and personal computers. Authors whose work has been adapted for the computer range from R. L. Stine to Shakespeare. Stories available on disk include *The Hobbit* by J. R. R. Tolkien (Addison-Wesley), *Journey to the Centre of the Earth* by Jules Verne (Q), *Fahrenheit 451* by Ray Bradbury (Telarium), *Rendezvous with Rama* by Arthur C. Clarke (Telarium), *Goldfinger* by Ian Fleming (Mindscape), *Alice in Wonderland* by Lewis Carroll (Windham Classics), *Treasure Island* by Robert Louis Stevenson (Windham Classics), *The*

Fourth Protocol by Frederick Forsyth (Bantam), *Black Beauty* by Anna Sewell (Sound Source Interactive), and *Macbeth* by William Shakespeare (Strategic). Terry Pratchett's Discworld books have spawned three CD-ROMs (produced by Perfect Entertainment), the most recent being *Discworld Noir.* The children's picture book *The Jolly Postman* by Janet and Allan Ahlberg has become *The Jolly Post Office* on disk (DK). Probably the best known children's picture books on CD-ROM are *Arthur's Teacher Trouble* and *Just Grandma and Me* (Brøderbund), with updated versions of these 1992 classics being produced in 1998 (with words in French, Spanish, and German as well as English). Disney Interactive are active in this market; their Animated Storybook Series includes *101 Dalmatians.* On a different level (but one with a lot of appeal to the target market), Dreamworks Interactive released some of R. L. Stine's Goosebumps books on CD-ROM in 1998, including *Attack of the Mutant* and *Escape from Horrorland.*

Sherlock Holmes provides an illustration of the way in which CD-ROM technology has moved into the leisure and recreation area. *Sherlock Holmes, Consulting Detective* (ICOM Simulations) is "a CD-ROM adventure game cum simulation" based on three of the classic Sherlock Holmes stories ("The Mummy's Curse," "The Mystified Murderess," and "The Tin Soldier"). There are more than 90 minutes of color video sequences on this CD-ROM, with accompanying soundtrack, text, still pictures, music, voice, maps, newspaper pages, and so on. The user/reader/player becomes the legendary detective, faced with solving the three mysteries. All the usual characters and the witnesses in each case can be questioned, library files can be checked, sites associated with the crimes can be visited, and relevant documents can be requested. This disk is attractive, challenging, and surprisingly faithful to the original book version of Holmes. A sequel, *Sherlock Holmes, Consulting Detective, Volume II* (ICOM Simulations), introduces three more Sherlock Holmes mysteries on disk.

Other interactive fiction packages (some indistinguishable from games) have grown out of films or videos: *Star Trek* (Interplay), in which the user is in control of the starship Enterprise; *Star Wars CD-ROM Edition* (Monopoly); *Dune* (Virgin); *The Lost World—Jurassic Park* (Sound Source Interactive); *Babe* (Sound Source Interactive); *The X-Files—Unrestricted Access* (Fox); and *Spice World* (Sony) for fans of the Spice Girls and their movie. Meanwhile, at least three products based on the *Titanic* tragedy—to varying degrees related to the film—appeared in 1998: *Titanic—Adventure out of Time* (Europress); a game called *Titanic Challenge of Discovery* (Mindscape) "endorsed and supported by Dr Robert D. Ballard, the real-life discoverer of the wreck;" and *James Cameron's Titanic Explorer* (Fox

Interactive), which combines graphics and animation with film clips, undersea video sequences, photographs from the time of the tragedy, blueprints for the ship, and an enormous archive of documents. In reviewing this CD-ROM, Alan Copps said that it was "much more than a film spin-off." Endorsing its claim to be the most comprehensive guide to the *Titanic* disaster that had been produced, he commented, "If you've ever wondered what 'edutainment' means, then here's the answer" (Copps, 1998).

Games

Games provide by far the largest group of computer-based resources for recreation; in fact, most of the packages in the other categories also incorporate at least some of the elements of computer games. This latter point is illustrated by products as different as *Titanic Challenge of Discovery* (Mindscape) and *Arthur's Teacher Trouble* (Brøderbund), both of which involve the user through interactive sequences.

The origins of computer-based games are varied. Some have grown out of board games such as chess and snakes and ladders; others have been developed from individual or team sports such as tennis or football. Some are based on television game shows; some are versions of the arcade games that have been so popular with young people; still others have been developed specifically for the personal computer. Some are virtually indistinguishable from interactive fiction or simulations; others are primarily educational in their aims. These computer-based games have moved from floppy disk to CD-ROM and now into the online environment of the Internet as well. Not only can many games be downloaded from the Internet but there are also sites where games can be played interactively, either against a computer or against human opponents.

Games packages based on traditional indoor games or board games include *Chess* (Interplay); *Colossus Bridge 2000* (Dead Good Software); *Monopoly®* (Playstation®); *Trivial Pursuit®* (Hasbro Interactive™); *World Champion Backgammon* (Ninga); *Scrabble®* (Hasbro Interactive™); *Ultimate Yahtzee®*, a dice game (Hasbro Interactive™); *Shanghai II: Dragon's Eye*, based on the ancient Chinese game of Mah Jongg (Activision); *Qubic*, a version of the children's game, ticktacktoe (Micro-Tex).

Many games packages are based on outdoor sports, contact sports, and team games; these include the basketball games *NBA Courtside* (Nintendo) and *Basketball Pro* (Sierra), *Microsoft Golf* (Microsoft), *International Cricket Captain* (Empire Sport), *Earl Weaver Baseball* (Electronic Arts), *Grand Slam Tennis* (Infinity Software), *Championship Boxing* (Sierra), and *Championship Wrestling* (Epyx). Several computer game products were produced to take advantage of the publicity generated by the last Winter Olympic Games; one of these was *The Games,* in which the user became an athlete competing in such events as ski jumping, speed skating, and biathlon (Accolade). Expect similar spin-offs from the Sydney 2000 Summer Olympics. The World Cup (football) in 1998 also resulted in a number of computer games packages, including *World Cup 98* (EA Sports) and *World Cup France 98* (Monopoly), and it is likely that other major sporting championships will have a similar influence. It is worth noting, however, that once the event or tournament is over, the computer game based on it has rather less appeal than in the buildup to the event. One appealing sports game from 1998 was *Backyard Baseball* (Humongous Entertainment™), a CD-ROM game designed for and featuring kids, among them some girls (rare in these kinds of games) and a kid in a wheelchair.

Arcade games that have been developed and adapted for the personal computer environment are common. Typical of these are *Space Invaders* (various versions), *Pac-Man* (also different versions), and *Marble Madness* (Electronic Arts). Computer games based on popular television games and quiz shows include *Jeopardy!* and *Wheel of Fortune* (Gametek); there are now several versions of each, including junior editions. Some early arcade games have come back to haunt us. For example, *Asteroids,* which first appeared in 1979 as an arcade game with minimal graphics, was re-released in 1998 (20 years later) as a personal computer game; intriguingly, however, for people who have been associated with the industry a long time, the current game (from Activision) includes occasional sequences from the classic original version. As a reviewer in London's *Independent on Sunday* said in December 1998, the new game really "differs only in the dimension that has driven the computer industry for 15 years now; the graphics that devour memory" (Kohn, 1998, 40).

Games developed specifically for the personal computer encompass a wide range of types, including adventure games, fantasy, role-playing games, games of skill and chance, and strategy games. Some games, of course, incorporate elements of all these. Among the adventure games are *My Teacher Is an Alien* (Simon & Schuster); *Heart of Darkness* (Amazing Studio); *Riven,* the sequel to *Myst* (Cyan); and *Genewars* (Bullfrog). Among the 1998 fantasy games was *Final Fantasy VII* (Squaresoft), in which an evil and powerful corporation was draining life from the planet. Role-playing games include *Deathtrap Dungeon* (EIDOS) and *Dragon Dice* (Interplay). Among the strategy games are *Capitalist Pig* (a business simulation game from Pluma Software) and *Railroad Tycoon II* (Take 2), which puts participants into the position of running their own railway. Some of these games have become so well-known that they have spawned sequels and look-alikes and, indeed, become the foundation for whole genres of games. Since the release of *Tetris* (Spectrum Holobyte), for instance, we have seen the emergence of *Super Tetris*, *Welltris*, and *Wordtris* (all from Spectrum Holobyte). In addition, there are games such as *Jewelbox* (Varcon Systems) that pay homage to *Tetris* while extending the concept in new directions. *Lode Runner*, as with *Tetris*, had its own sequel, *Championship Lode Runner*, as well as many imitators. Books and articles have been written to assist the frustrated addicts to overcome the many obstacles encountered along the way in this game of search and strategy, not to mention the Internet sites that serve a similar purpose for this and other games.

Some computer games are now sold as part of collections on CD-ROM, including the title, *3 Games in 1 Fun Pack* (Hasbro Interactive™), a disk of games for young children; and *The LucasArts Archives™ Volume III* (LucasArts), a collection of games on one CD-ROM, including *StarWars: Dark Forces*, *The Dig*, and *Monkey Island Madness*.

Internet gaming environments have been categorized in the Yahoo! Directories on the Internet under the following headings:

- interactive Web games;

- games based on IRC (Internet relay chat);

- games based on MUD or MOO;

- multi-user games or MPOG (multi-player online gaming);

- play by electronic mail (PBM); and

- virtual worlds.

This classification gives some indication of the ways in which Internet gaming environments can be accessed: email, telnet, IRC, and the Web. Major gaming sites on the Web, such as the Internet Game Network, Blast Entertainment Network, and Multi-player Online Gaming Central, provide links to a variety of games. School library media specialists are urged to check the gaming sites carefully. Not only do they change their content frequently, but many, particularly but not exclusively in the multi-player online gaming environment, contain graphic adult material and material that is violent; in addition, there may be some unpleasant language from the players themselves in some of these sites. Even more than in the normal IRC channels, care is required here, though not to the point of paranoia. However, there are some multi-player online gaming environments that are safe and suitable for children. Another factor is that while online games such as *Castle Infinity* are fun and teach children to work together to accomplish tasks, there may sometimes be a problem with children playing too long and even staying online to the detriment of schoolwork and other interests.

Participation in many of the online games via the Internet requires the use of *plug-ins* in addition to the standard browser software. Plug-ins are extra pieces of software that work with the standard browser to provide access to such features as sound, radio, video, and 3-D graphics. While some may come built in to some browsers, they can be downloaded from Internet sites if needed. Common plug-ins include *Real Player*, which is needed for access to Webcasts—events that are broadcast only on the Web—and to listen to Web radio, as well as for games; *Shockwave*, which delivers animation; and *Quicktime*, which is used to view video and film clips. All require a fast personal computer with a lot of memory.

In some Internet gaming areas, the user plays against the computer rather than against other people. For example, at Connect 4, the *Forensic Files* game requires that the player solve a mystery while traveling the virtual world. Some networks and electronic bulletin boards provide access to some CD-ROM games as well as true online games, and these are almost always played against the computer. There may be a monthly charge for access to these services. Some, such as Microsoft's Internet Gaming Zone, let players use their own Internet accounts, while America Online has a "members only" area for online gaming. Live competition is an alternative to playing against the computer, as happens with CD-ROM, and playing against live competition often makes the game more fun. For many of the adventure games, a fast modem or network connection is needed; however, for online versions of board games such as Scrabble, chess, checkers, and strategy games such as SimCity, the Internet connection does not have to be as fast.

The multi-player online games on the Internet include *Battlefield Net* (a turn-based strategy game), *Dig Zone* (a multi-user adventure game), *G-NOME* (for up to six players), *Rock* (a role-playing game), *Tanbo* (a strategy game area where players can participate or watch), and *WinBridge* (where players can play against live opponents, watch, or chat to other spectators). *Ultima*, available 24 hours a day seven days a week, is a knightly adventure game in which thousands of players can take part. It is set in a medieval world in which the players, represented by avatars that they create for themselves, either go alone on quests or team up with others. *Castle Infinity* is, like *Ultima,* a "social world" online; in this case, the object of the ongoing game is to find and kill monsters using a range of unlikely ammunition.

Simulations

Computer-based simulations attempt to re-create a real-life situation that the user can explore; some simulations are primarily educational, while others are indistinguishable from games. Early simulation packages were certainly chiefly designed for educational or training purposes—*Flight Simulator* is a striking example. Originally created to train pilots in landing routines or disaster strategies, flight simulators of varying degrees of sophistication are now sold as recreational packages. Examples include *Flight II* (EIDOS), *747 for MS Flight Simulator 98* (Microsoft), *Jet* (Sublogic), and *MiG-29* (Donmark). A natural extension of this type of package has been the development of space flight simulators such as *Shuttle* (Virgin) and *Orbiter* (Spectrum Holobyte).

Other simulations attempt to take the user back in history through the re-creation of historical events. A classic of the genre is *Oregon Trail* (MECC), a simple American-history-based educational simulation that has been on the market for several years and is now available in updated versions. The re-creation of battles or critical historical events has been the focus of some recent leisure-type software for children and adults. Because many of these packages may appear to glorify violence, some schools might want to look closely at those that are purchased for the school library media center. Among these simulations are *Commandos—Behind Enemy Lines* (EIDOS), which follows a squad of elite troopers in World War II; *Battleship CD-ROM* (Hasbro Interactive); *Gunship 2000* (Microprose), a Persian Gulf War helicopter-combat simulation; *NATO's Fighters* (Jane's—Electronic Arts); *Battleground: Waterloo 1815* (Empire Interactive); *Battleground: Bull Run 1861* (Empire Interactive); and *The Great Battles of Hannibal* (Interactive Magic).

Not all recreational activities (for children or adults) revolve around games and entertainment. Like adults, young people write, create artworks, make music, study their family history, follow trends in fashion or cooking, learn a foreign language, collect stamps, take photographs, breed animals, and so on. The final two categories of computer-based recreational resources reflect this situation.

Applications Packages

Applications packages such as database management packages and word processors enable users to carry out activities associated with their own leisure interests or to meet educational needs. For instance, they might use a simple word-processing package to write letters or prepare documents;

an easy database management package to organize a collection of cassettes or coins or postcards; a spreadsheet package for scheduling (perhaps scheduling sporting fixtures or games), forward planning, and budgeting. There are many word processing, database management, and integrated software packages currently on the market that are designed for use by young people; in addition, many young people will be capable of using standard business or personal applications packages such as *WordPerfect* and *Microsoft Office.*

For people who want to create newsletters, greeting cards, signs, banners, or stationery, the packages mentioned earlier in this chapter (applications packages in an educational software context) that are designed with children in mind give a good result for a relatively small financial outlay. *The Children's Writing and Publishing Center* (The Learning Company) is an example of a word processing and desktop publishing package designed for children. It has a range of companion disks that provide clip art, borders, and special fonts that can be incorporated into documents and signs. Another example is *The Print Shop* (Brøderbund), which comes in several different versions, with additional resources included. In many schools (particularly secondary schools), young people are successfully using standard "adult" packages such as *Publish It Easy!* (Timeworks) or *Pagemaker* (Aldus) for these activities. A package called *Instant Greeting Card* (Softkey) is relatively easy for children to use, as is the *Printertainment Software Kit* (Avery Kids). With the latter, children can produce greeting cards, invitations, removable stickers, and other print items. The kit includes printer supplies. *The Print Shop Presswriter* (Brøderbund Software) provides a simplified version of a newspaper editor and page layout program (on CD-ROM) for budding journalists ages 12 and up. It incorporates graphics, photographs, some 100 fonts, and a tutorial to help people get started.

There are specially designed applications packages available for carrying out various tasks associated with recreational interests or schoolwork. People of all ages have become interested in tracing their ancestors and finding out about their family history; thus, genealogy packages such as *Ultimate Family Tree Deluxe* (Palladium Interactive) or *Family Heritage File* (Star*Com Microsystems) or *Family Tree Maker* (Brøderbund) have proved popular. Teenagers are increasingly becoming aware of personal health and fitness, and so packages such as *The Cooking Companion* and *The Diet Balancer* (both from Home Health) have been developed to manage recipe collections and to help people watch their nutrition and plan a balanced diet. For those seeking work, packages such as *Resume Maker* can help prepare the necessary documentation.

Online diaries and address books are popular Internet services that fall under the heading of applications packages. Two of these are *E-Organizer* and *Web Cal.* Both allow users to compile to-do lists and an address book with an appointments schedule. The advantages of using an online organizer are that it is accessible from any computer anywhere in the world (or in your town), it does not take up storage space on your computer, and it is free— assuming that you have an Internet connection from which to use the service.

For people who are interested in computer-realized music or computer-based art, many music and graphics/art packages are now available that suit different skill levels, knowledge, and experience. Most of these packages require special hardware connectors or equipment in addition to the personal computer and software. Both areas are now so highly specialized that there are catalogs and even specialty computer stores, that deal exclusively with hardware and software for art or music. There are also several magazines that provide specialist coverage of both these fields. And while the magazines and the stores are generally aimed at adults, the owners of some of the computer-based art and music stores in London's Tottenham Court Road computer district report that many of the patrons are around 14 or 15 years of age.

While some people are using computers to produce artworks or music, others are beginning to produce their own Web pages, often incorporating multimedia. Web authoring systems and Web page development software can help with this process, as can graphics packages. In addition, there are many resources available on the Internet itself that can be used by anyone who is working on a home page. *Net Explorations with Web Workshop* (Sunburst Communications) is a CD-ROM for children ages 10 and up that takes the user through the process of creating a home page without having to know the HTML mark-up language; patterns, backgrounds, and graphics are provided. Sunburst's Web server will host the completed page free for the first 30 days (after which there is a charge of US $15 every three months to maintain the page).

Personal Development Packages

Software for personal development covers a potentially wide field. It includes packages that young people can use to learn skills that are not related to schoolwork but rather to their recreational or personal interests. Of course, what is a classroom package for one group of young people may well be a package used for personal development by others. An example of this could be the various typing tutor packages that have come onto the market. These are often used in basic secretarial and business classes. However, people who use the computer regularly will recognize the need for typing skills if they are to produce worthwhile output. Some of the packages available include *Typing Tutor* (Softkey), *Slam Dunk Typing* (Creative Wonders—for ages eight and up, with typing drills based on the game of basketball), *Typing Made Easy* (Better Working Software), *Type!* (Brøderbund), *Mastertype* (Mindscape), *Success with Typing* (Scholastic Software), *Type to Learn* (Sunburst), *Ultrakey* (Bytes of Learning), and *Typing Tutor IV* (Simon & Schuster).

Packages for personal development could be related to virtually any subject. Possibilities include *Spanish for Travellers* (Roger Wagner Publishing), *The Right Job* (a job-finding skills package from Sunburst), *Golf Teacher* (FYI Publishing), *Keys to Responsible Driving* (CBS Software), *John Hedgecoe's Guide to Photography* (Anglia Multimedia), and *Rhodes on Rom* (Gary Rhodes' guide to cookery, produced by Anglia Multimedia).

Internet resources are available in these fields among many, many others. Sites such as Homework Helper and Homework Central take young people to a wide range of Internet resources, not all of which relate to schoolwork. For example both have large collections of links related to hobbies and personal development.

CONCLUSION

More schools in different countries are using the new information technologies to enhance the learning experiences of students and to improve access to information in the school for both students and their teachers, as well as school administrators. This should be reflected in the use of information technology in the school library media center. In addition, an increasing emphasis on information skills as essential life skills makes it necessary that school library media centers make appropriate use of information technology so that students leave school with information search skills that are the foundation for lifelong information use.

In Chapters Two through Five, the four major areas of application of information technology in the school library media center have been considered: information technology in school library media center administration, information technology for information access, information technology for communication, and information technology as an educational and recreational resource. The next chapter, Chapter Six, discusses the development of an information technology plan or strategy (based on strategic planning principles) for the school library media center to put into place these applications to best effect in the particular school. Chapters Seven and

Eight deal with planning for and ongoing management of information technology in the school library media center, and issues that will arise when information technology is used in the school library media center.

REFERENCES AND BIBLIOGRAPHY

Bork, Alfred (1981). *Learning with computers.* Bedford, MA: Digital Press.

Clyde, Laurel A. (1985). Computers and school libraries. In Clyde, Laurel A., ed. *School library automation: Proceedings of a second national conference, Western Australian College of Advanced Education, April 1985.* Perth, Western Australia: Western Australian College of Advanced Education, 5–17.

———— (1986). *Computer software for school libraries: A directory.* Wagga Wagga, New South Wales: Alcuin Library Consultants.

———— (1989). *Computer software for school libraries: A directory.* 2nd ed. Adelaide, South Australia: Auslib Press.

———— (1993a). *Computer applications in libraries: A directory of systems and software.* Technology in the Library Series. Melbourne, Victoria: D. W. Thorpe.

———— (1993b). Computer-based resources for young people: An overview. *International Review of Children's Literature and Librarianship.* 8(1), 1–21.

Copps, Alan (1998). Immerse yourself in a great disaster. *Inter//face//software.* 16 December, 12.

Dickinson, Gail K. (1994). *Selection and evaluation of electronic resources.* Englewood, CO: Libraries Unlimited.

Eisenberg, Michael, and Robert Berkowitz (1990). *Information problem-solving: The Big Six skills approach to library and information skills instruction.* Norwood, NJ: Ablex.

Jones, R. (1981). *Microcomputers in primary schools.* London: Council for Educational Technology for the United Kingdom.

Kohn, Mark (1998). Per ardua ad asteroids. *Independent on Sunday.* 20 December, 40.

Shirinian, G., and P. Nicholls (1997). CD-ROM lending at the City of York Public Library: A four-year retrospective. *Computers in Libraries.* 17(1): January, 70–74.

INTERNET SOURCES

Avery Kids
<http://www.avery.com/kids/>

The Big 6 Skills
<http://www.Big6.com/body.html>

Blast Entertainment Network
<http://www.playground.com/>

Brøderbund Education Programs
<http://www.broder.com/education/programs/>

Connect 4
<http://www.luc.ac.be/~hbaerten/vier/vierinit.html>

Homework Central
<http://www.homeworkcentral.com/>

Homework Helpers
<http://www.radix.net/~mschelling/homework.html>

Multi-player Online Gaming Central
<http://central.mpog.com/index.html>

Quicktime
<http://www.quicktime.com/>

RealAudio
<http://www.realaudio.com/>

School Libraries Online (International Association of School Librarianship—IASL),
    Information Skills Resources on the Internet
<http://www.hi.is/~anne/infoskills.html>

Shockwave
<http://www.macromedia.com/Tools/Shockwave/>

The Super3
<http://academic.wsc.edu/redl/classes/Tami/super3.html>

Worlds Without Words
<http://www.argosphere.net/bods/mike.htm>

CHAPTER SIX

An

InfoTech

Plan

INTRODUCTION

The previous four chapters discussed the major applications of information technology in school library media centers: information technology for school library media center administration; information technology for information access; information technology for communication; and information technology as an educational and recreational resource. The potential applications within these broad categories are many and varied, and every school library media center will have many choices to make, both in relation to the applications they implement and the way in which they implement them. An information technology plan provides a framework for analyzing the current school environment and current needs, planning for the future, and documenting decisions so that they can be used as the basis for action. A good information technology plan covers not only equipment and software but also the issues that arise when information technology is used, such as conditions of access, acceptable use, and intellectual property issues.

Some writers distinguish among an *information technology plan,* an *information technology strategy,* and an *information technology policy.* When this is the case, the information technology plan is usually a long-term document that states the aims and objectives for the use of information technology in the school or school library media center and indicates in broad terms how these will be achieved. The information technology strategy is the means by which this happens—a detailed description of the way forward. Both are supported by an information technology policy that covers the issues associated with using information technology. In fact, all three aspects should be dealt with in the planning process and resulting documentation, regardless of the term used.

Alec Gallimore, in his book *Developing an IT Strategy for Your Library* (1997) makes still another set of distinctions among an *information technology strategy* (based on the hardware), an *information systems strategy* (based on the software or systems), and an *information strategy* (based on the idea that information is the most important component of an information system). He says that "there is undoubtedly a relationship between information strategy, IS strategy, and IT strategy" (Gallimore, 1997, 22): he sees them as the three points of one triangle and suggests that at different times in the one organization different aspects might be emphasized, depending on the activities and needs of the organization at the time. However, he says that all three aspects should be considered in developing the strategy (Gallimore, 1997, 22).

Lyn Hay dealt with the *information policy* aspect of planning for information technology in a paper titled "Information Policy Issues: Curse or Cure?" written for the 1997 ITEC Virtual Conference (Hay, 1998). She notes that "the integration of information technologies within the school as a learning community and a workplace in the 1990s is literally forcing schools to develop policies to address problems and issues arising from the school community's increased access to the electronic information environment" (Hay, 1998, 160). Because she deals with the information policy of the school within the context of a planning process that she calls "whole school technology planning" (Hay, 1998, 161), the points she makes are appropriate for people who are developing an information technology plan for a school or a school library media center. She makes a distinction between *macro* issues that affect the information policy (the external environment) and the *micro* issues (the internal environment). Among the macro issues, she includes relevant legislation; regulations imposed by an education or library authority; and legal issues, including copyright and fair use. The micro issues might include information flows within the school, the ways in which information is used in the school, and the ways in which information sources are incorporated into the curriculum at the school level. All of these should be considered as part of a strategic planning process for the development of an information technology plan.

The information technology planning process can take place at a number of levels. In the United States, most of the state departments of education have a published information technology plan; many of these can be accessed through the "State Departments of Education Technology Plans" Web site (see "Internet Sources" at the end of the chapter). The planning process can also take place at the school district level. An example is the technology planning process for school districts, outlined on the North Carolina Public Schools Infoweb on the Internet (see "Internet Sources"at the end of the chapter). The introduction notes that "a comprehensive technology plan is critical as districts, schools, teachers, students and the community attempt to articulate a set of goals that will maximize the learning capabilities of students and prepare them for the twenty-first century," and the document goes on to outline the purposes and components of the plan. While this document is directed toward a district-level planning process, there is much in it that would be appropriate for individual schools to consider. In addition, where state or district information technology plans do exist, they become part of the external environment to be considered by the individual school in developing its plan.

At the individual school level it is most common that a schoolwide information technology plan be developed that covers all aspects of the use of information technology in the school. Sometimes this is required by an education authority or state agency, but it is nevertheless a valuable exercise for a school as a way of working toward more effective use of information technology within the school.

Finally, an information technology plan may be developed at the level of the individual school library media center. This might be done to plan more specifically for information technology in the school library media center as part of a general schoolwide plan. Alternatively, in a school where there is no schoolwide plan, the school library media specialist may develop an information technology plan for the school library media center as the first step in a school plan. It is important that the school library media center should not act in isolation, however; this is not in the interests of either the school library media center or the school. With developments in information technology such as fiber optic cabling and networks, any decision taken by the school as a whole will affect the school library media center. Further, with the implementation of school networks, the school library media center is no longer restricted to a room or set of rooms; the catalog, CD-ROMs, and databases of the school library media center can be made available throughout the school and even outside it. In terms of what the technology offers, the barriers around facilities are coming down. An information technology plan should take advantage of this, and that means that the school library media specialist has to be involved in planning at the school level, even if the school library media specialist has to initiate the school-level planning.

The discussion in this chapter is based at the level of the school or school library media center information technology plan, though reference is made to plans at the district and state levels.

It is important to note (as was discussed in Chapter One) that the planning process for information technology is a cyclical one and one that has to be flexible enough to cope with new and emerging developments in technology and society. The creation of an information technology plan should not be a one-off event; rather, it should be a commitment to a continuing planning process. While most information technology plans are created for a period of three years or five years, the plan should be revised annually by the planning committee to take account of both new developments in information technology and developments that have occurred within the school itself. This annual review also provides an opportunity for the school community to celebrate achievements in terms of meeting the requirements of the plan and to do some public relations work.

WHY HAVE AN INFORMATION TECHNOLOGY PLAN?

The development of an information technology plan involves analyzing the needs of all users of the technology. Each teaching department in the school will tend to see information technology (even in the school library media center) in terms of its own particular current uses or needs and may be quite unaware that other people have different uses and priorities for information technology within their teaching area. The involvement of people from different departments (or teaching areas) and school administrators in a planning process will help everyone involved to appreciate the wide range of potential applications that need to be considered when planning for information technology. It will also help to avoid a situation where the needs of one department or group dominate the development of information technology applications.

The benefits of an information technology plan for the school or school library media center include the following:

- Members of the school community have an opportunity to have input into a decision-making process that helps the school to move into the future with an information technology infrastructure that supports the aims and objectives of the school. If people have been part of the planning process, then they are more likely to be committed to the plan and to support it.

- A clear picture should emerge of the information technology applications that are required to meet the needs of the school now and in the future.

- The financial and human resources that are required to implement the plan are identified and quantified. It may be that this leads to a revision of the plan or to a decision to seek a larger annual budget or alternative sources of funding. The planning process generates the necessary information to support these options.

- In terms of financial resources, the planning process helps the school collect the information that is required to apply for special grants or to seek funding through sponsorships or other forms of support. In addition, it should be noted that many granting bodies require applicants to have a technology plan in place, usually in a form that is approved by the state education authority or other similar organization.

- In terms of human resources, the plan should identify not only the need for new staff but also the continuing education needs of present members of the school staff to ensure the effective implementation of the plan. It is one thing to provide the technology; it is another to have it used effectively. Effective use depends largely on the potential users, who need to feel confident with the various applications that are appropriate in their area of expertise. It may be necessary to either organize training opportunities within the school or fund staff members for training. Thus, the information generated through the planning process can provide information about the budget commitment necessary for staffing if the school is to achieve its goals.

- A written plan should ensure that new information technology purchases and applications are compatible with the hardware and systems already operational in the school and contribute to the overall educational goals of the school.

- The process should ensure value for money in terms of expenditure on information technology. It may be possible to meet the needs of different departments through resource sharing on a school network; an expensive color printer needed by two departments, for instance, can be shared more easily if there is a school network in place. It may also be possible to identify alternative solutions to the technology requirements of departments so that a single strategy meets a range of different needs.

- The identification of stages in the development of the information technology plan should ensure that the school can proceed through logical, agreed-upon stages toward a goal that has been accepted within the school.

- When opportunities arise (such as the availability of special funding or the possibility of sponsorship), then decisions can be made very quickly on the basis of the priorities listed in the plan and the directions that are specified in it. This should also ensure that decisions that are made in these situations will be sensible ones and ones that contribute to the school's capacity to achieve its goals.

- Levels of information technology-related knowledge and skills in the school are built up as people investigate the various options that are available.

- The school library media specialist, as a member of the planning team, will have had an opportunity to articulate both the needs of the school library media center for information technology and the ways in which the school library media center applications of information technology can make a contribution that will benefit the whole school community. This has the potential to promote the function of the school library media center in information management for the whole school and to generate support for the use of information technology in the school library media center.

WHO SHOULD DO THE PLANNING?

As with any policy-making activity, the development of an information technology plan usually requires a great deal of work on the part of many people. Most schools that have such a plan have indicated that a year is the minimum period of time needed to complete the initial planning process. This assumes wide consultation as well as time to explore the options available for each specific application of information technology.

A consultative and inclusive process is likely to result in a more informed school community and one that is committed to the final outcome of the process. Thus, although it can sometimes be frustrating, it is valuable to involve as many people as possible in the development of the plan. In addition, the cooperative development of an information technology plan becomes a professional development activity for all concerned as knowledge and information are shared and new ideas emerge. This means that the school community will have a better knowledge base from which to implement the plan. If a consultant is involved at any stage of the process, then all stakeholders benefit from this contact too.

Given these advantages of a consultative process, planning is most effectively carried out by a planning team comprising representatives from all or most departments plus school administration. If the school has a Technology Committee or other group that is responsible for making decisions about information technology, then this group may form the planning team. Consultants may be employed at any stage of the process; some school districts provide consultant support. The chairpersons or leaders of school committees or teams might be specified in a school policy document; if not, then they might be selected by the team or appointed by the school principal.

The team should include representatives of all the major stakeholders in the school. However, it will also prove useful to take advantage of the expertise of local community members and input from parents. Thus the planning team may include:

- school district representatives,

- school board representatives,

- school administration representatives,

- teachers (from as many subject fields or divisions of the school as possible),

- staff responsible for technology maintenance/support,

- the school business manager,

- community members,

- parents,

- potential business partners or sponsors, and

- the school library media specialist.

In addition, the team should consult as widely as possible with other teachers, parents, local experts, and others, including the students. This consultation can be formalized through meetings, leaflets, questionnaires, focus groups, and other strategies, but there will be opportunities for informal consultation as well. It may also be possible to involve more people through subcommittees set up to work on particular aspects of the plan.

The school library media specialist should be on the planning team, and there have been many schools where the team has been coordinated or chaired by the school library media specialist. In fact, the school library media specialist's knowledge of curriculum and activities throughout the school makes him or her a logical choice for this position.

THE PLANNING PROCESS

Retta B. Patrick defines planning as "a process having to do with determining where you want to go; determining where you are now; and developing ways of getting from here to there" (Patrick, 1989, 88). It has also been said that planning is a way of thinking about the future and doing something about choosing the future that we want. Sandra Naudé has pointed out that "the first step in developing a school IT plan is for the school to accept the need for the plan" (Naudé, 1997, 111); that is, for the school community to accept the need to take charge of its own future. She further says that it may require some lobbying to bring people to this realization and that "chances of success in the implementation stage will be increased if the school community is involved in the planning and decision-making process" (Naudé, 1997, 111). The strategic planning process that is outlined below assumes the involvement of members of the school community in the process. However, it should be noted that this involvement also has to be planned for so that it is, in fact, possible for members of the school community to have input into the process.

The most effective technology plans and those that have the longest "shelf life" focus on people and their needs and the applications that will meet those needs rather than on the specific items of technology. A technology plan that focuses on what school administrators, teachers, and students can do with the technology will be more relevant in the longer term than one that concentrates on machines and cables. With a focus on needs, the plan can be adapted more easily if new developments in technology make it possible to meet the needs in another and more effective way. In addition, the needs-based focus makes it easier to determine the type and amount of hardware and the size of the systems that are required for implementation.

The strategic planning process should not be seen as a rigid set of steps; it is not a straitjacket but a framework to guide logical decision making. In practice, the planning stages will overlap, and it may even be that some people on the planning team have begun work on the final document while others are still collecting information about alternative possibilities for implementing some applications. The vision statement or goals might be revisited and revised several times during the planning process as people become more aware of the possibilities; it is not just something that is written at the beginning of the planning and then put aside. Strategic planning is a tool to assist a process—not something that should dominate the process.

Vision, Goals, and Objectives of the Plan

A plan, by its very nature, is designed to achieve certain goals or objectives. These are usually articulated at the beginning of the planning process so that all people involved understand what the outcomes are expected to be both in terms of the plan itself and as a result of the implementation of the plan. A plan may begin with a *mission statement* or a *vision statement* or a *statement of overarching goals* that makes explicit the assumptions that underlie the planning process. Some have all three. The mission or vision statement should reflect consensus within the school; it should be understandable and acceptable to the people in the school if it is to give them a shared sense of purpose.

An example of a vision statement can be found in the "Technology in Colorado Education Strategic Plan 1994–2004" document (see "Internet Sources" at chapter's end for the URL). It begins with "a vision for technology in Colorado education," stated as: "We envision a lifelong learning environment in which the tools of technology support teaching and learning in all areas for all Colorado citizens, and serve as a catalyst for instructional reform." It is worth noting that this statement incorporates many ideas, among them that education does not end with school, that technology is a tool to support learning rather than an end in itself, that technology will be used throughout the school, and that everyone should have access to the technology. In addition, it is anticipated that technology will be an instrument for curriculum change.

The Colorado strategic plan follows up the broad vision statement with a statement of beliefs (reproduced with permission here) that clarifies and expands on the vision statement:

In order to accomplish this vision, we believe that:

- ¤ students, educators, adult learners, library patrons and other stakeholders must have:
  - – equitable access to the tools of technology;
  - – ongoing training in the skills required to make the best use of these tools

- ¤ the tools of technology will be used in creative and innovative ways to:
  - – access, share and manage information;
  - – maximize building and district resources;
  - – provide access to resources that would otherwise not be available

- ¤ electronic links must be easily accessible and easy to use in order to facilitate communications between and among:
  - – students;
  - – teachers, counselors and library media specialists;
  - – administrators;
  - – school districts;
  - – parents;
  - – universities;
  - – libraries;
  - – local, state and federal agencies;
  - – businesses;
  - – community groups

¤ the State of Colorado (CDE, the Office of the Governor, and the Colorado General Assembly) must take a leadership role in educational technology to promote:

– equitable access regardless of geographic location or demographics;

– adequate funding for acquisition of the tools of technology, ongoing training, ongoing support, repair and maintenance;

– standards for data transfer

¤ effective use of technology in Colorado's schools and libraries is necessary in order to:

– maximize limited financial resources through cooperative innovation;

– enhance the investments that have already been made in technology;

– provide educational equity throughout the state;

– provide the widest possible access to all of the state's information resources.

The Colorado plan goes on to indicate the implications of each of these for the use of information technology in instruction, administration, and networking. It then proceeds with a series of eight general goals, each supported by a number of specific goals for the use of information technology in the schools. The eight general goals are:

1. "Technology should support curriculum and learning"

2. "Technology planning should be an ongoing process"

3. "Technology training should be ongoing and integral to all areas"

4. "A support infrastructure must be created, strengthened and maintained"

5. "The State of Colorado should create, maintain and support an effective statewide electronic network"

6. "Colorado school districts should have management systems in place that facilitate electronic information transfer"

7. "Develop statewide policies for evaluation and purchasing of management hardware and software"

8. "Funding for technology should be adequate, equitable, and stable"

With its supporting documentation, this Colorado plan provides a framework within which school districts and individual schools can develop their information technology plans.

An Analysis of the External Environment

The analysis of the external environment, or *environment audit*, should cover all those factors outside the school that are likely to influence the planning process or its outcomes. The list will be different for each school, though some factors, such as developments in information technology in general, should be on every list. Regardless of how the responsibilities of the planning team members are assigned, the school library media specialist should collect the necessary information on behalf of the school library media center. It would not be wise (or even realistic) to assume that other people will take the library media center needs into account; other planning team members (on a schoolwide basis) may not even be aware that the school library media center has information technology needs. Factors to consider include the following:

- any national or state or provincial policy statements related to "the information society," information policy, information technology, education, libraries, or telecommunications; any statewide information technology plans;

- any relevant school district policies, guidelines, or procedures, including documents relating to technology, information technology, curriculum developments, buildings and facilities, networking;

- evidence from research and published reports that shed light on changes in society that might influence schools and on the changing demands being made on schools;

- information about current developments in information technology in general and predictions of likely future developments;

- information about the options available for all the potential applications of information technology in the school, including, for the school library media specialist, those applications discussed in Chapters Two through Five of this book;

- any potential sources of outside funding or other support for information technology, such as grants, sponsorship, cooperative ventures;

- the availability of consultant support or technical support from an education authority, school district, library authority, or other source;

- community facilities and community resources available to the school that might help the school to achieve its stated goals;

- community expectations of the school (these may be affected by, for instance, the level of computer use in homes and local businesses); and

- community socioeconomic and demographic factors.

Internal Audit or Situation Analysis

The analysis of the internal environment, or *internal audit* or *situation analysis*, provides a comprehensive picture of all those factors in the school or the school library media center that relate to the information technology plan. This analysis should include the mission and goals of the school and the school library media center as a basis; indeed, creating an information technology plan may provide an opportunity to review the mission and goals in the light of the possibilities opened up by new developments. This opportunity to review the plan is particularly helpful in situations where (as in Colorado) there is an expectation that change will occur as one of the outcomes of increased use of information technology. Factors to consider include the following:

- the information technology that is already available in the school (hardware, systems, software), its location, age, and current condition;

- the ways in which information technology is currently being used in the school, the administrative tasks and curriculum applications that it supports;

- curriculum documents for all subject areas and levels and an analysis that will reveal ways in which information technology could enhance the curriculum;

- any special programs in the school, any special school activities or interests;

- the age levels and abilities of the students in the school, any special student needs;

- the financial resources available to the school now and in the future;

- the level of information technology skills possessed by current staff and the likely availability of people with particular skills, including technical skills, software skills, instructional skills, Web page development skills, among others;

- other resources and facilities available, such as space, security, power supply, telephone connections, furniture;

- the identification of all areas where the use of information technology could be expected to be of benefit and to help the school meet its goals;

- the identification of all the different technologies, combinations of technologies, and applications that have the potential to meet the identified needs. Among these technologies and applications might be the following:

  - a schoolwide local area network (LAN) or a school intranet,
  - a link to a wide area network (WAN) maintained by a school district or library authority,
  - CD-ROM access,
  - access to other optical disk media,
  - access to online information services,
  - access to the Internet,
  - electronic mail,

- access to an electronic bulletin board,
- electronic publishing (including use of the World Wide Web),
- electronic conferencing,
- a library media center management system,
- a school management system,
- access to computer-based curriculum resources,
- access to computer-based recreational resources,
- broadcasts received via a school satellite dish,
- robotics equipment and software, and
- virtual reality resources.

In conjunction with this, the school library media specialist should be conducting an internal audit or situation analysis of the school library media center so that the information becomes part of the whole-school planning process. This school library media center audit should cover the goals and objectives of the school library media center, the users of the library media center and their needs, the programs of the school library media center and the extent to which they are meeting current needs, current levels of use of the facilities and requirements for optimal use, the current applications of information technology in the school library media center and the extent to which they are meeting needs. It should also cover the aspects listed previously for the school audit but from a library media center perspective, including, for instance, an analysis of the school's curriculum information resources in terms of access through the library media center and an analysis of information management needs.

A matrix used by the Western Australian School Library Association (WASLA) for planning professional workshops provides a useful tool for school library media specialists who want to identify where their library media center stands in relation to the implementation of various technologies such as library automation, CD-ROM, and Internet access (see Figure 6.1, p. 182). It could be extended even further. For example, a Stage 5 could cover access to the school network and information systems from outside the school, while a new line across all stages could cover the use of the Internet for providing information and publishing (in addition to the line that relates to Internet access).

	Stage 1	Stage 2	Stage 3	Stage 4
IT Plan	School has no IT plan	IT planning started	IT plan implemented	IT plan being revised
Access to Equipment	Minimal access for staff and students	Some access by roster, does not meet need	Satisfactory access with some flexibility	All staff & students have ready access to IT
Curriculum	IT awareness program	IT specialist programs	IT integrated into some learning areas	IT integrated across all learning areas
Networks	No networked computers	Some computers networked	Network goes beyond a single room or library	Major school-wide network
Library Software	Library software on single workstation only	Catalogue on an independent network	Catalogue linked to school network but accessed in library only	Catalogue accessed across schoolwide network
CDROM	Stand alone CDROM drive in workstation	CDROM stacker serving a few workstations	A few CDROMs installed on network	Access to multiple CDROMs on network
Internet	No student Internet access	Single line dial up access	Several work-stations sharing modem	Schoolwide ISDN access across network
Support	Not in any staff member's duty statement	Individual(s) released to provide support	Technician or consultant available	IT support team is meeting school needs

Figure 6.1   Matrix for identifying the basic current information technology situation in the school library media center. Reprinted with permission from the President of WASLA on behalf of the professional development activity organizing committee.

This kind of matrix allows the school library media specialist to identify possible stages in the implementation of the various technologies, suggests relationships between them, and relates them to the rest of the school.

Identification of the Strategic Alternatives

If the situation analysis is carried out in terms of the needs of the school and the requirements for technology if these needs are to be met rather than in terms of numbers and types of computers, then it is almost certain that there will be different paths to achieving what is needed in the school. With information about the external and internal environments of the school and the school library media center and information about the needs of the school community, the planning group can turn its attention to investigating the *strategic alternatives*—all the possible ways in which the needs and goals of the school can be met through information technology.

The process usually begins with an expansion of one of the activities of the previous stage; that is, the identification of all the different technologies, combinations of technologies, and applications that have the potential to meet the identified needs. At this stage, however, the investigation will be much more detailed and will cover hardware, systems, and software options for each. Information should be collected about how other schools have attempted to meet similar needs or to solve similar problems using information technology. The planning team should focus on the different ways of implementing each application and the most effective ways of implementing each application in the school setting.

This investigation should be followed by an analysis of the ways in which the various needs of the school can be met most effectively through a process of rationalization—using the same network, for instance, and the same hardware to support multiple applications. This means balancing the demands of one application against the others to develop a system or network that is flexible and meets more of the school's needs than is possible through separate, stand-alone applications. As the jigsaw puzzle of potential applications is put together, it is important to make sure that potential future applications are not made more difficult to implement by current decisions.

Selecting the Course of Action

The final decision may be based on a process of achieving the *best fit*, that is, a system that meets the largest number of needs and requirements, given financial, staffing, and other constraints. Or it may be based on a process of *ranking* all needs and requirements and then finding the best way to implement those that have been ranked highest. However, this stage does provide an opportunity to look at ways in which the needs of all subject departments or areas in the school can be met through schoolwide planning.

The following elements should all be considered in defining the course of action to be taken over the period of time that is covered by the plan:

- a broad time line covering the lifetime of the plan and indicating phases or stages in the implementation process, with the anticipated outcomes for the school and the community as a whole as a result of the completion of each stage;

- a description of the tasks and activities to be carried out by school staff and others (such as consultants) during each stage of the plan. This may include planning time, consultations, preparing documentation, training, user education, data entry, lobbying, technician time, changes to existing facilities;

- an indication of any new staffing requirements or new skills that will be needed for the implementation of each stage of the plan. In the first case, this may mean on-site technical support personnel; in the second, it may mean professional development opportunities for teachers;

- the information technology purchases that will be required at each stage. These may include hardware, software, cabling, telephone connections. Special consideration may need to be given to establishing the number of computer workstations that will be needed for the school population and their location on the basis of the applications to be implemented and likely usage;

- any other expenditures that will be required to support the implementation—for example, ergonomic furniture, structural alterations, security facilities, additional electrical outlets, changes to the lighting or ventilation systems; and

- school policies and procedures that will be necessary to support the implementation of the technology plan—for instance, a policy for the acceptable use of information technology resources, user agreements, and procedures for scheduling use.

Implementation and Evaluation

A good information technology plan includes information necessary for its implementation and for ongoing monitoring and evaluation of the implementation. Activities associated with the implementation of the plan include the following:

- purchase of hardware, systems, and software;

- installation of hardware, systems, and software;

- setting up workstations for the various user groups and applications;

- any necessary data input;

- establishing security for equipment, data, and system access;

- developing school policies and procedures related to the use of the information technology;

- staff and user training;

- ongoing job design and revision of role statements to take account of the new information technology;

- monitoring of the impact of automation on procedures (including school library media center procedures) and adapting as necessary;

- creation of a maintenance schedule for the equipment and a replacement schedule for equipment, systems, and software;

- evaluation of hardware/systems/software performance in relation to the needs that they were purchased to meet; and

- ongoing planning for future developments, and establishing ongoing strategies to assess future needs and to incorporate them into the information technology plan as time goes on.

THE PLANNING DOCUMENT

The information technology plan should be committed to print and distributed widely; it should also be made available through the school network if one is in place. If people in the school are unaware of the plan, then it will not be implemented. Instead, decisions will be made without reference to it, thus wasting the planning effort and possibly bringing about some of the problems of duplication and incompatibility of equipment and applications that the plan was developed to avoid.

The information in a planning document might be presented in a variety of ways; however, time lines are a particularly useful way of indicating stages of implementation and relating them to budget stages and staffing reviews. Implementation schedules or matrices can also be used to show the inter-relatedness of the different aspects of the plan and the links to funding and staffing. Other techniques include flowcharts, checklists, tabulations, visuals (diagrams and other graphics), lists of resources, and ordinary prose descriptions.

The Arizona Department of Education Local Educational Agency Strategic Long Range Technology Plan (see "Internet Sources" at the end of the chapter) asks for the plan to be presented according to the following broad sections:

- information about the school and its technology committee;

- a technology needs assessment (administrative needs, student and program needs);

- vision, mission, goals (with goals related to connectivity, curriculum and instruction, and professional development, in keeping with the department's stated goals);

- hardware and software acquisition (in the form of a five-year time line);

- a technical design for the school's information infrastructure (to support compatibility, inter-operability, and inter-connectedness of the technologies);

- a description of what will be needed to develop the infrastructure;

- a curriculum integration time line (covering five years) to show how the "acquired technologies will be integrated into the curriculum to enhance instruction and assist students in meeting the Arizona State Standards";

- a professional development time line (covering five years) showing "sustained, ongoing professional development for teachers, administrators and school library media personnel which will ensure the effective use of technology in curriculum and instruction";

- support resources required and a five-year time line;

- a statement showing how the technologies will promote equity for students;

- a statement describing the ways in which the information technology will provide improved access for teachers, students, and parents to "the best teaching practice and curriculum resources";

- costs and funding sources (a five-year time line) and a budget summary; and

- an evaluation plan.

The Arizona Local Educational Agency Strategic Long Range Technology Plan relates to a particular program in that state (the Technology Literacy Challenge Fund), and parts of the template refer specifically to the requirements of that program. It would not be possible for a school outside the state of Arizona to use the template as it stands, but it does provide a useful guide to the features that are normally expected in an information technology planning document.

THE NETWORK OR INTRANET

Increasingly, schools and school library media centers are choosing a local area network (LAN) or intranet as a way of making available a range of information resources and communications tools. This means that in the information technology planning process, special consideration should be given to planning related to the school's local area network or intranet. It is the network or intranet that links all the other information technology applications; the success of applications such as access to the Internet, access to information on CD-ROM, or the provision of computer-based educational or recreational resources depends in part on the successful implementation of the network. In addition, a considerable financial investment is required to set up an effective network, and it is, therefore, imperative that the school reap all possible benefits from this investment. Thus, the planning for the network should be at the heart of the information technology plan.

At the most basic level, a network is simply a collection of computer hardware and software that is linked together in some way so that files, information, or equipment can be shared. Thus two personal computers in one room might be networked to share one printer or one modem, or a local area network might link several hundred computers of different kinds in various locations around the school. Any computer network consists of hardware (computers, printers, CD-ROM towers, and so on), software (network software such as Novell or LANtastic or Windows NT), and a communications carrier of some kind (usually cabling) to link the hardware. A local area network (LAN) is usually restricted to one building or one organization, and a local area network might comprise a number of subnetworks. A wide area network (WAN), however, links multiple sites in a town or a region or a country. Thus, a school library media center might have a local area network linked into a school local area network, which is in turn linked into a school district or statewide area network. The school network might be linked to the Internet directly through a local Internet service provider, or it might be linked into the Internet through a district or statewide area network.

One of the main advantages of a school network is that expensive equipment such as color printers or expensive resources such as a news database on CD-ROM can be shared and used by people throughout the school. In addition, many users can access software or resources such as an encyclopedia on CD-ROM at the same time. Further, the network can be used to provide schoolwide access to school resources such as the school library media center catalog and the school schedule and to schoolwide communication tools such as electronic mail. A school network helps to ensure equity of access to resources throughout the school and provides a tool through which access and use can be monitored for future planning. Finally, it is easier and more efficient for a system administrator to maintain equipment that is networked than to maintain stand-alone items of equipment that are scattered throughout the school. On the other hand, a network is costly to set up. Considerable expertise is required for its installation and maintenance, and if security is not done well, then hackers and even minor misdemeanors or user mistakes can cause major problems. Generally speaking, if the installation was done well and maintenance is good, then the educational and administrative benefits far outweigh the disadvantages.

While there are many different ways to put a local area network together, the two basic configurations are a peer-to-peer network and a client-server network. On a peer-to-peer network, all computers are of equal status; while these networks are relatively easy and relatively inexpensive to set up, they tend to be slower than other options, and the number of machines that can be connected is limited. In a client-server network, one machine (usually more powerful than the others) acts as the server, controlling the network and providing storage space for users' work, while the workstations linked to the network are clients, accessing the server for software and resources. A workstation is simply a computer that uses the resources (processing power, storage space, information, and data) of another. These client-server networks are faster, security can be more reliable, and different levels of access to different resources can be set by the system administrator. This means that students, logging on with a password that gives them limited access, see only those network resources that they are authorized to use, while teachers, logging on with a faculty password, will see many more resources and services. Increasingly, library automation systems are being designed to operate on client-server networks; even when they can be installed on both peer-to-peer and client-server networks, they will operate better and faster on the client-server networks. The trend is quite clear. However, a great deal more expertise is required to install and maintain a client-server network than a peer-to-peer network.

The basic components of the network are computer hardware and software and the cabling or linkages between them, as noted previously. However, it is not quite that simple. In most cases, a network card (with associated software) will be needed for each computer. The type of network card depends on the type of network being set up. The network operating system is a complex series of programs that includes the protocols and standards required to establish communication between the components of the network and to provide access to the resources on the hardware. There are a number of network operating systems available, most of which allow the system administrator to connect a range of hardware. A number of different *topologies* can be used as the basis of a network. A topology describes the pattern in which the computers and other equipment are linked. Topologies used today include the "star" (with each machine linked to a central "hub"), a "bus" (with machines linked in a long line), and a "ring" (with machines linked in a circle). Each topology has its particular strengths and limitations. The wiring or cabling that holds the hardware together in the network is also not simple. Basically, the higher the number of bits per second (bps) transmitted, the faster the network will be. Wiring currently on the market operates at a range of different megabits per second, while fiber optic cabling (based on silicon rather than wire) allows much faster speeds. In addition, infrared and radio-frequency connections offer other options that do not require a physical link between the pieces of hardware. As John Fracasso (1996, 37) indicates, this area of network development "is generally best left to professionals," because bad choices at this stage can have a significant effect on network performance.

While the term *intranet* is sometimes used to describe any local area network that is linked to the Internet, in fact an intranet is a local area network with some special characteristics. An intranet is a private network within an organization that is based on Internet network *architecture* (the wires, the technology, hardware, and the software behind the system), on Internet *protocols* (standard ways of doing things), and on Internet software. Just as the Internet is often defined as a network of networks based on TCP/IP (Transmission Control Protocol/Internet Protocol) that allows all the machines linked to the net to function together, so intranets are sometimes defined as local area networks based on TCP/IP. This means that the increasingly familiar and easy-to-use Web browsers such as *Netscape* and *Microsoft Internet Explorer* can be used to locate information on the local system in the same way that they are used on the wider Internet. Students and teachers do not have to learn different sets of skills for using resources on the local area network and the Internet. In addition, documents are made available on the intranet in the same HTML (hypertext markup language) format that is used for the creation of Web pages, and there is now a range of software available to assist with this. The intranet is usually linked to the Internet for external communication—for instance, by electronic mail—and for information searching via the World Wide Web and commercial online information services. However, it is also normally separated from the Internet by a *firewall* or security system, so that people from outside the organization cannot access the organization's own internal information.

"Intranets can be used for anything that existing networks are used for—and more," says Preston Gralla (1996, 5). The school intranet can be used to provide teachers and school administrators with access to the school's databases, including the student information system, the schedule, course information, and other databases maintained by the school. Password protection can be used to restrict access to those databases that should be used only by particular groups of people. Programming languages such as Java allow common Web-type interfaces to be developed for these databases even though they may have been created using different software or systems. Web browser software can then be used to access the databases—and all the other material on the intranet. The school library media center catalog might be made available via the school intranet; already, many of the automated library systems on the market today are providing this facility as an option. School documents of all kinds, including curriculum information, might be made available throughout the school via the intranet. This process is made easier by the latest versions of the major word processing packages (such as *Word)* allowing the user to save documents in HTML format. Material on the intranet can include documents with hypertext links (as on the World Wide Web), interactive materials, and materials in multimedia formats. Students might use the intranet to publish their own work within the school community without the fear that this material will be misused by strangers. Because the school can control the content of the documents and databases on the intranet, teachers can be sure that the material to which the students have access is appropriate, considering the values of the school community and the age levels of the students.

The development of networks or intranets in schools and school library media centers raises a number of issues, particularly related to personnel. A library media center network or school network is not something that can be managed effectively by an untrained person in their spare time. However, there are relatively few people who do have real skills in this field. The new document *Information Power: Building Partnerships for Learning* (American Association of School Librarians and the Association for Educational Communications and Technology, 1998) recommends the provision of adequate, trained technical support for the implementation of facilities such as networks. Often this means that someone already in the school will be trained to manage the network: this will usually be satisfactory if they are interested and if they are given the time in which to do the job. Sometimes the school library media specialist is expected to add a sysop role to other school library media center duties, without training and without an allocation of time. For the school, this is usually a recipe for disaster; for the school library media specialist concerned, it is certainly not a recipe for a good life. Once a network is extended beyond a small number of computers, then its management requires expertise and considerable attention on a day-to-day basis—that is, on-site technical support. Training for information technology management is another issue. Information technology can be managed just as other resources and services are managed, but it does require a good—but not necessarily technical—knowledge of current information technology.

For more information about school networks and intranets, see Becky R. Mather's 1997 book, *Creating a Local Area Network in the School*

Library Media Center or (on the Web) the California Department of Education's K-12 Network Technology Planning Guide. Further resources are listed in the bibliography and in the list of "Internet Sources" at the end of this chapter.

REFERENCES AND BIBLIOGRAPHY

American Association of School Librarians and the Association for Educational Communications and Technology (1998*). Information power: Building partnerships for learning.* Chicago: American Library Association.

Bannan, Joan (1997). *Intranet document management: A guide for Webmasters and content providers.* Reading, MA: Addison-Wesley.

Bernard, Ryan (1996). *The corporate intranet: Create and manage an internal Web for your organization.* New York: John Wiley.

Blodgett, Teresa, and Judi Repman (1995). The electronic school library resource center: Facilities planning for the new information technologies. *Emergency Librarian.* 22(3): January-February, 26–30.

Cimino, James D. (1997). *Intranets: The surf within.* Rockland, MA: Charles River Media.

Clyde, Laurel A. (1998). The school intranet: An opportunity.... *Emergency Librarian.* 25(3): January-February, 36–38.

Corrall, Sheila (1994). *Strategic planning for library and information services.* An Aslib Know How Guide. London: Aslib.

Fracasso, John (1996). An introduction to local area networks: A lesson in construction and renovation. *Feliciter.* October, 35–38.

Gallimore, Alec (1997). *Developing an IT strategy for your library.* London: Library Association Publishing.

Gralla, Preston (1996). *How intranets work.* Emeryville, CA: Ziff-Davis.

Hay, Lyn (1998). Information policy issues: Curse or cure? In Hay, Lyn, and James Henri, eds. *A meeting of the minds 2: ITEC virtual conference, 97 proceedings.* Belconnen, Australian Capital Territory: Australian School Library Association, 160–74.

Manczuk, Suzanne, and R. J. Pasco (1994). Planning for technology: A newcomer's guide. *Journal of Youth Services in Libraries.* Winter, 199–206.

Mather, Becky R. (1997). *Creating a local area network in the school library media center.* Westport, CT: Greenwood Press.

Naudé, Sandra (1997). Establishing an IT plan for a school. In Butterworth, Margaret, ed. *Information technology in schools: Implications for teacher librarians.* 3rd ed. Perth, Western Australia: Australian Library and Information Association, School Libraries Section (WA Group), 109–34.

Nott, Sue (1997). LAN at Lanyon: Information services at Lanyon High School, ACT. *Access.* 11(1): March, 23–25.

Patrick, Retta B. (1989). Information power: The planning process. *School Library Media Quarterly.* 17(2): Winter, 88a–k.

Research Machines (1994). *Planning IT in schools: A strategy for schools IT development.* Abingdon, Oxfordshire: Research Machines.

See, John (1992). Ten criteria for effective technology plans. *The Computing Teacher.* May, 34–35.

Vaughan-Nichols, Stephen J. (1997). Planning your intranet. *Internet World.* 8(4): April, 52–54.

INTERNET SOURCES

California Department of Education, Electronic Information Resources, Acceptable Use Policy, District Guidelines
<http://www.cde.ca.gov/ftpbranch/retdiv/ed_tech/programs/Policy.html>

California Department of Education, K–12 Network Technology Planning Guide
<http://www.cde.ca.gov/ftpbranch/retdiv/k12/ntpg/>

Critical Issue: Developing a School or District Technology Plan
<http://www.ncrel.org/sdrs/areas/issues/methods/technlgy/te300.htm>

North Carolina Public Schools Infoweb
<http://www.dpi.state.nc.us/>

State Departments of Education Technology Plans (USA)
<http://www.milkenexchange.org/s3/s3c/state_list.shtml>

State of Illinois K–12 Information Technology Plan
<http://www.isbe.state.il.us/learn-technology/technopages/ncsa/k12.htm>

Technology in Colorado Education Strategic Plan 1994–2004
<http://www.cde.state.co.us/download/pdf/et_strat.pdf>

CHAPTER SEVEN

Implementing

in the
School Library Media Center

INTRODUCTION

The development of the information technology plan provides guidelines for the implementation of information technology in the school and the school library media center. This chapter discusses aspects of the implementation of the major applications of information technology within the school library media center itself. The applications are those that have been the subject of Chapters Two through Five of this book—that is, an automated library system, access to online information services and CD-ROMs and the use of the Internet for communication, and computer-based educational and recreational resources.

In each case, the discussion highlights the planning and implementation issues that are particularly related to that application. There is also some discussion of selection issues associated with that application. Each section concludes with references to resources and services that can provide the school library media specialist with more detailed information or reviews. In Chapter Eight, some ongoing administrative issues that are common across all the applications—such as staff training, budgeting, facilities, and ergonomics—are discussed in more detail.

IMPLEMENTING LIBRARY AUTOMATION

Library automation (automating the administrative functions of the school library media center, as in Chapter Two of this book) should be seen as a process involving a number of stages, each of which makes an important contribution to the final outcome. The first major decision is the decision to automate. This decision changes the nature of the school library media center forever. It implies a commitment to efficiency and effectiveness in administration and to better information access for library media center users. It results in changes in the way the library media center is used, in the way in which it is perceived, and in the way in which it is operated. The jobs of the people who work in the school library media center also change. The appearance of the facility changes. The way the budget is managed changes. It opens up new possibilities for service, for information skills instruction, and for outreach into the school community. When a school library media center is already automated, the decision to update an old system or to move to a new or second generation system may begin the process again (though in a changed environment and with changed expectations).

System Selection

Once the decision to automate is made, then the process of selecting an automated system for a school library media center should begin with the collection of background information, a process that may already have started with the development of an information technology plan. Information should be collected on current trends in information technology generally and library automation in particular, on the systems that are available for school library media center automation, on developments in education at the district and state level that impinge on the school library media center, and on the school library resource center and the school. A preliminary analysis of the school library media center situation is important, because this helps to determine the areas in which automation might be expected to assist the library media center to meet the needs of users and to contribute to school goals. Such an analysis should cover the strengths and limitations of the systems currently in operation, the aims and goals of the library media center, the needs of users, the extent to which those needs are being met, the demands of changing curricula and school restructuring, likely future developments in the school and the education authority that affects the library media center, and the resources available to the library media center (staff, expertise, space, money, and so on).

This analysis should give an indication of the directions that should be taken in relation to library automation—the areas in which library automation could be expected to be of most benefit and the resources available to implement a library automation project. The introduction of library automation provides a school library media center with an opportunity, not just to automate its current systems, but also to move in new directions, to set new goals for service, and to do things in a different way. Simply automating old manual systems so that they work faster or better may not really meet the current and future needs of the school library resource center. Without this planning audit process, the risk is that this is all that will happen. The computer industry dictum, "If you automate a mess, you'll get an automated mess," is one that school library media specialists should heed.

At this point, it is appropriate to decide whether to use a consultant in the system selection and implementation process. If a decision is made to use a consultant, a list of possible consultants must be prepared through discussion with people in the school district or the education authority, with other school library media specialists, and through other channels (such as directories). Sometimes it is appropriate to advertise for a consultant; then an advertisement will need to be prepared as well as a brief for the consultant. From the resulting list of possible consultants, a "shortlist" of people with the greatest knowledge and expertise for the job should emerge. As much attention should be given to the selection of a consultant as would be given to any other major decision made by the school. People on the shortlist should be interviewed, and it is appropriate to contact other organizations for which the consultant has worked. Steps should be taken to ensure that the consultant does not have a vested interest in any particular approach to library automation (or that this vested interest is declared) so that the school library media center has some assurance that its needs are paramount in the selection process. In addition, it is important that school and school library media center staff are able to work comfortably with the consultant and that the consultant appreciates the goals of the school library media center and the school. It is worth noting that, as with the library automation systems themselves, the cheapest consultant may not necessarily be the best for the particular school library media center. Whether or not a consultant is employed, the following steps should normally be part of the system selection process.

The options for library automation that would be most appropriate in the particular school library media center setting should be identified: whether membership of a network should be considered, for instance; whether the school library media center should be looking at library automation as part of a total school administration system; whether the school library media center should be looking at integrated, multi-function library automation systems or software to automate just some of the library functions; and so on. In relation to this, an analysis should be made of the hardware and software already available within the school, the computer and networking expertise available in the school or available to the school, the financial support that is likely to be available, and the likelihood that the school library media center will be able to hire new staff or to take advantage of locally sponsored employment projects to augment the staff for the implementation of a library automation project.

The question of adherence to standards should also be considered at this stage. For example, the use of MARC format for catalog records (discussed in Chapter Two) is important. If the school library media center wishes to use an outside source of catalog records (online or on CD-ROM), then the library automation system has to be able to import MARC records; if participating in a union catalog project among a group of libraries, it will be necessary to export MARC records. In addition, it is easier to move to a new "second-generation" system or upgrade later if the catalog database is in a standard form. In this situation, the catalog database is loaded from the old system to the new, and the vendor's ability to do this becomes one of the selection criteria for a second-generation system.

Another standard that is predicted to become more important for libraries in general is the Z39.50 standard officially known as the "Information Retrieval Service Definition and Protocol Specifications for Library Applications" (Nickerson, 1998; Lunau, 1997). It is an American national standard approved in 1988 by the National Information Standards Organization (NISO) and widely accepted internationally. It defines conditions for automated networking of libraries of all types at a time when networking and access to information held in other locations is becoming more important. It particularly relates to client-server architecture (see Chapter Six), and its purpose is to enable one computer, that acts as a client, to access and search for information on another computer acting as a server. Because the World Wide Web is based on the client-server model, the Z39.50 standard will be important in making library catalogs available for searching via the Web. At the moment, Z39.50 is gaining acceptance only very slowly, but already some library automation vendors in the school library media center market are announcing Z39.50 compliance plans.

Once the needs of the school library media center have been identified, a specification document or a request for proposal or a tender document should be prepared, or a list of selection criteria should be drawn up that is based on the identified needs. Sometimes (usually depending on the size of the project and the location) a bidding process is a legal requirement. One of the first three options is normally used when a large library or a state education authority or a large school district is considering a system. The specification document describes the features of the desired system in detail and describes the way in which the library would like its system to operate. The specification should provide both technical information about the desired system and information about what the system should do for the library. It should also contain information about implementation, a time line, budget, training, insurance, any hardware and cabling that will be supplied with the system, and any other relevant information. The specification would normally form the basis of an advertisement asking library automation system vendors to tender for the library automation project; it then forms the basis for testing and evaluation of the systems that have been offered by the vendors in response to the advertisement. The request for proposal is similar: vendors are provided with a request for proposal that contains the specification and other related documentation and are asked to submit a proposal for the project, usually within a specified period of time. The Request for Proposal document for the Minnesota statewide library information system (which includes school library media centers) is available on the Web; it provides an example of this approach. The specification and other project documentation should be written in such a way that the library is not forced to simply accept the lowest bidder but can go through a process of evaluating the responses in terms of what they can do for the amount of money involved.

Individual school library media centers that are automating alone would normally prepare a list of selection criteria for selecting an automated library system rather than preparing a large specification document. The criteria may vary from one school library media center to another, though the majority of lists of criteria will have many things in common. Since most school library automation systems currently on the market perform the basic library management functions of cataloging and circulation, the list of criteria should concentrate on particular features that the school library media specialist wants to see in the system or ways in which the functions are to be implemented. The list of criteria might take the form of a checklist or a weighted checklist.

A checklist simply lists all the features that the school library media center feels that a library automation system must have to meet its needs. As each library automation system is tested, the evaluator simply checks off features on the checklist. The system that is chosen would be the one that had all the required features (or most of the required features if no system had them all). Figure 7.1 shows a small section of a checklist created to compare automated systems for school library media centers. An "Evaluation Checklist for Full Bibliographic Displays in Web Catalogs" is available on the Web; this provides another example of a simple checklist (with the addition of a column for evaluator comments).

Some vendors have themselves produced checklists that, to quote one from Data Research, are "designed to allow librarians to compare various vendors' systems." The Data Research checklist is divided into seven

EVALUATION CHECKLIST AUTOMATED LIBRARY SYSTEM		
Name of system: _____		
Date of assessment: _____		
FEATURE	**YES**	**NO**
Cataloging		
Import full MARC records from CD-ROM		
Import full MARC records from online source		
Export full MARC records to disk		
Guided data entry for original cataloging		
Web resources can be cataloged		
Images can be added to catalog record		
Subject authority control		
Author authority control		

Figure 7.1   A small section of a simple checklist for evaluating automated library systems for school library media centers.

categories of items under the following headings: adherence to standards, integration of the functions, software functionality, hardware, networking, service, and "corporate financial viability." All these are important, of course, and should be noted. Columbia, a vendor whose system has been popular in schools, produced a more comprehensive "Comparison Checklist for Library Automation Systems" of 18 pages, with the information about Columbia already inserted and space for the school library media specialist to insert information about two other systems. Of course, Columbia scored yes on every item on the checklist, but again the general headings are useful: the company, general features of the system, training and support, the catalog module, the circulation module, MARC record interface module, acquisitions, and serials. However, the school library media specialist needs to be aware that checklists can be compiled to highlight the features of a particular system; in other words, there is a possibility of bias.

While the use of a simple checklist (based on the school library media center's own needs) can be helpful in compiling a shortlist of the systems that have all or most of the features required, for many school library media centers the situation is a little more complex. There may be features that they feel their new system simply *must* have, and features that they would very much like to have and some things that would be nice but are not really important in comparison with other features. A weighted checklist allows the school library media center to give more emphasis to those features that are deemed essential and a lower weighting to those that are just desirable or simply nice to have. In using the weighted checklist to evaluate systems, three points might be given when a system has an essential feature, two points when it has a desirable feature, and one point when it has a useful or nice feature. Other weighted checklists use separate columns to distinguish essential features from desirable ones, and the system selected would then be the one that had all the essential features and most of the desirable ones. Weighted checklists have an advantage in the selection process in that they can more accurately reflect the priorities of the school library media center in relation to library automation. However, if they are allowed to become too complex, they will hinder the work of system selection rather than help it.

Figure 7.2, page 202, shows a weighted checklist that works in both directions; that is, the essential, desirable, and useful features are listed downward, and the evaluator can indicate whether each feature—if it exists—is excellent, good, or poor. A rating scale (ratings of one to five or one to seven) could be given for each feature if greater precision were required. Figure 7.3, page 203, shows a simple, comparative checklist, with provision to compare the features of three systems.

AUTOMATED LIBRARY SYSTEM EVALUATION CHECKLIST

System name: _____

OPAC—Required features:

SYSTEM FEATURE	Excellent	Good	Poor
Graphical user interface			
Icons for all major functions			
Graphics that appeal to ages 6-12			
Instructions use language suitable for ages 6-12			
High level of tolerance for searcher spelling errors			
Short and long display of results			
Item status available			
Ability to print search results as bibliography			
Keyword searching on subject and title			
Boolean searching on subject and title			

OPAC—Desirable features

SYSTEM FEATURE	Excellent	Good	Poor
Relevance-ranked display of search results			
Images of book covers can be displayed			
Higher-level search and display for teachers			
Links to Web resources			
Ability to place "holds" from OPAC			

OPAC—Other useful features:

SYSTEM FEATURE	Excellent	Good	Poor
Library news can be displayed on OPAC screen			
New books highlighted in search results			

Figure 7.2   A small section of a weighted checklist for evaluating integrated library automation systems for school library media centers.

EVALUATION OF LIBRARY AUTOMATION SYSTEMS

Student Search Features

Essential Features	Function Description	System A	System B	System C	System D
x	Author search accepts given name or family name first				
x	Title search accepts full title or keyword in title				
x	Subject search by keyword				
x	Boolean search on title or subject				
x	Automatic spelling correction on student input				
x	Automatic search for both singular and plural of terms				
x	Graphical user interface for different levels of students				
	Error messages provide search guidance....				

Figure 7.3   A small section of a simple comparative checklist for evaluating integrated library automation systems for school library media centers.

The development of selection criteria or an evaluation checklist is not easy, but it should be done by each individual library to ensure that the needs of the library and its clients are met. It involves an analysis of current services and desirable future services, current library practices and desirable future practices, and current user needs and likely future needs. While a published specification document or checklist might be used as a basis, this will need to be adapted to take account of the requirements of the particular school library media center and of its institutional and budget constraints.

The documentation should include realistic information about the budget that will be available to the school library media center for initial system purchase (and development) and installation and for ongoing maintenance and development costs. If a selection checklist is used, it should include an item related to budget limits or costs. This will ensure that personnel involved in the selection process have realistic expectations. By the same token, if it emerges that the expectations of the school library media center cannot possibly be met within the budget, then the school library media specialist will have information on which to base a submission for increased funding for the automation project.

The next step is the identification of systems for further testing and evaluation that are likely to meet the needs of the school library media center as outlined in the checklist or specification. The sources of information listed in "Sources of Information About Automated Library Systems" will be useful at this stage as will consultation with other school library media specialists who have been through the automation process. Even in a situation where the school library media specialist is working in isolation, monitoring professional listservs such as LM_NET and OZTL_NET can lead to online contacts with people who are at about the same stage of the process as well as with people who have completed it. In addition, the select bibliography at the end of this book gives some references to useful reading on the topic. All vendors should be contacted for current brochures and other information about their systems (including, if possible, a list of local users who can be contacted).

On the basis of this work, a shortlist of systems that seem most likely to meet the needs of the school library media center should be compiled. If possible, this list should be kept fairly short—no more than three to five systems. If the shortlist turns out to be relatively long, the number of systems on the list can be reduced through a preliminary viewing of the systems so those that seem least likely to meet the needs of the school library media center can be eliminated. This preliminary viewing might be done with an abridged checklist—a checklist that contains only the lead items from each category on the list, or only those items that are of critical importance for the school library media center, or specifies only how the major functions of the system are to operate. A consideration of costs and budget would be important at this stage, as would consideration of the size and capabilities of each system relative to the size of the task. Systems that are obviously too expensive for the school library media center or too small for its present and projected future needs should be eliminated from the list before the remaining systems are examined in detail.

The systems on the shortlist should be subjected to more rigorous assessment of their ability to meet the identified needs as outlined in the checklist or specification document. The assessment procedures should include demonstrations of the system in operation (including "hands on" sessions), visits to libraries or school library media centers where the system is in use (or correspondence or telephone contact with such libraries or school library media centers), and reading reviews of the system and articles about the system in operation. Contact with a user group, if there is one, would be useful.

Sometimes, the hardware and software for the automated library system is purchased as a unit or *turnkey system* (the idea being that the hardware arrives with the software already installed, and all the school library media specialist has to do is "turn the key"—though nothing is really quite that simple). For other school library media centers, the system will be purchased to operate on equipment that is already available within the school or that is being purchased to meet a range of school needs. Where the hardware and software are being purchased together, then there should be an assessment of the capability of the hardware to run the system efficiently and to provide a growth path for the system and the library media center in line with the needs assessment. Where the software is to be mounted on hardware that is already available in the school, then during the selection process it would be wise to visit a school library media center that has the system running on similar hardware or to contact such library media centers. In fact, wherever possible, the system should be assessed when running on the same hardware as that on which it is to be used or on the hardware that the vendor is recommending. Going for hardware or a network configuration that is less powerful than the vendor is recommending is pointless. With vendors regularly releasing system upgrades—some of which require the newest or most powerful hardware and system software—the school library media center with a minimum hardware or network configuration will soon find itself locked out of the upgrade cycle.

Vendor support is critically important for the maintenance and on-going development of an efficient system. It is easy to be swayed by a pleasant vendor's representative who seems sympathetic to the school library media center and its aims. Remember though, that the school library media center will be entering into an ongoing business relationship with the vendor of the system, thus the vendor must be assessed in this light, as personnel may change over time. It would be a mistake, however, to regard the system vendors as the opposition in this process—it is in the vendor's best interests, as well as those of the school library media center, that the system chosen be appropriate and work well. The following should be considered when assessing the capability of the vendor to provide support for installation and for the ongoing development of the system:

- reports from school library media centers and libraries that have the system installed;

- experience and knowledge of the personnel involved in the maintenance and development of the system;

- long-term viability of the firm or company (in as much as this can be assessed);

- support offered for installation (in person or by telephone or online), the timeline for installation, costs associated with installation;

- training for the school library media center staff, both at the time of installation, and ongoing training and the costs associated with these items;

- the quality of any manuals, training documents, and system documentation;

- warranties and guarantees, and the legal enforceability of any such warranties and guarantees (this is the time for expert legal advice);

- the annual maintenance fee (if any) and the services that it covers;

- the availability of enhancements to the system over time, and system updates, and the costs of these (if any) to the school library media center (some vendors provide system updates free to those school library media centers that pay the normal annual maintenance fee); and

- user groups, newsletters, and other sources of information and support.

The purchase agreement should be given close attention, and a sample contract or purchase agreement should be requested as part of the system evaluation process. Any contract or purchase agreement drawn up with a system vendor should be approved by legal personnel representing the school or the school district. If the school does not have access to legal assistance through the school district or education authority, then a lawyer should be retained to check the contract and to provide a report on it. System vendors will be accustomed to such checks and, indeed, will anticipate them.

Sources of Information
About Automated Library Systems

Automated library systems are changing rapidly in response to developments in information technology and to changing expectations on the part of libraries and school library media centers. This means that sources of information about automated library systems also become outdated quickly. Consequently, only the most recent sources should be used to collect information about the automated library systems on the market. Sources of information about automated library systems include the following:

- published directories of library and information system software, such as the *Directory of Library Automation Software, Systems and Services 1998,* edited by Pamela R. Cibbarelli and Shawn E. Cibbarelli;

- articles about library and school library media center automation projects in journals such as *Computers in Libraries, The Electronic Library, School Library Journal, Access* (Australian School Library Association), *Teacher Librarian* (formerly *Emergency Librarian), Library Journal, Feliciter* (Canadian Library Association), *School Libraries in Canada,* among others;

- reviews of automated library systems in journals such as *Library Technology Reports, The Electronic Library, Computers in Libraries, Database, Library HiTech,* and *VINE;*

- articles in free electronic journals on the Web, including *D-lib* and *PACS-P* (the BUBL directory on the Web has the best guide to these journals);

- searches of online databases such as LISA, Library Literature, and IAC Computer Database on Dialog, and Library Literature and ArticleFirst on OCLC for articles about library automation and for system reviews;

- attendance at conferences and exhibitions devoted to the use of information technology in libraries and school library media centers, including the annual "Computers in Libraries" conferences in the United Kingdom and the United States, the American Library Association and American Association of School Librarians annual conferences, the Canadian Library Association and Canadian School Library Association conferences, state/provincial school library media conferences, among others;

- the proceedings of the various annual international, national, and major state conferences related to library automation where there may be a record of presentations by system vendors or developers and by school library media specialists and librarians who are using the systems. The Inside Conferences database on Dialog and the PapersFirst database on OCLC, among others, index papers presented at major librarianship and education conferences. In addition, many professional conferences are now making papers available via the Web;

- World Wide Web directories of automated library system vendor home pages, including the directory of automated library system vendors provided on "School Libraries Online" (the International Association of School Librarianship), "Vendors of Automated Library Systems with Web Pages" (CSU School of Library and Information Science), and "Library Automation Systems on the Web" (created by Ian Piggot for the European Commission Directorate General XXIII/E-4);

- the searchable archives of listservs for school library media specialists, particularly LM_NET and OZTL_NET (these archives can be a rich source of opinion and comment about systems by people who are using them or considering them);

- informal discussion with fellow school library media specialists at conferences, meetings, and exhibitions;

- where an automated library system has a Web interface, testing out the online public access catalog (OPAC) by going to the Web pages of libraries or school library media centers that are using it and carrying out test searches; and

- visits to school library media centers and libraries where automated library systems are being used.

In addition, a select list of vendors of automated systems for school library media centers is provided at the end of this book as Appendix One.

Implementation Issues

The selection of an automated library system is only the beginning of the library automation process. An implementation plan will need to be developed covering all aspects of system implementation, from staff training to data security and the purchase of appropriate and ergonomically correct workstation furniture. The implementation schedule should be agreed upon with the system vendor before work commences, and it should be discussed with the school administration and any personnel associated with the management of systems and networks in the school. System implementation includes, among other things, the following:

- scheduling of software and hardware installation;

- finding appropriate locations for all the equipment, considering security, the need for special conditions (such as air conditioning and cabling), and servicing;

- installation of cabling and any necessary additional electrical outlets;

- workstation design and location (workstations for staff and library media center users);

- training of school library media center staff;

- system and data security, plans for back-up of data and software;

- barcoding the library collection for the circulation system;

- data input, whether done manually or through downloading from other sources (such as MARC records from online sources for the school library media center catalog, student data from the school administration system for the circulation system);

- user training (teachers, students, and others), development of user guides to the system;

- a review of the impact of library automation on school library media center functions and procedures, and any necessary changes to procedures, manuals, and job descriptions;

- monitor the process of installation and adapt the implementation plan as necessary as the implementation proceeds;

- development of a maintenance schedule for hardware and software based on requirements and performance;

- establishment of procedures to evaluate system performance (according to the criteria used to select the system and bearing in mind emerging user needs) and relating performance to emerging needs;

- ongoing monitoring of developments in library automation and relating these to the procedures for evaluating system performance so that when the time comes to select a new or second-generation system, the process of collecting information will already be in hand.

Two major tasks associated with the implementation of an integrated library automation system are data entry (for the catalog and circulation system) and barcoding the library collection (for circulation). If a security system is being installed at the same time, then a third task is putting the security system targets into all the items in the collection as well. These are all major tasks, but all can be commenced well before the automated library system hardware and software even arrives and can continue through the installation process. However, even before this work is begun, the school library media center staff need to undertake two other tasks. An inventory of the collection is necessary as a basis for both of these. The first task is weeding obsolete items and items in poor condition. There is no point in spending money and time on creating catalog records for and barcoding items that will have a short shelf life. The second task is checking the integrity of the current shelf list as a record of the items in the collection and as a basis for creating the computer-based catalog.

Retrospective conversion is the process through which a computer-based library catalog database is created when a library moves from a manual system to a new library automation system. Regardless of the way it is done, database creation will not be cheap; it may be more expensive than the hardware on which the automated library system will be running, and (depending on the size of the collection) it could be the most expensive component of the school library media center's automated system. However, the catalog database is critically important for the efficient operation of other aspects of the integrated automated library system, such as the public access catalog (OPAC) for library media center users and the circulation system. There are a number of options for retrospective conversion, among them the following:

- manual data entry, copying from the shelf list cards (if available);

- loading catalog records into the automated system from an external cataloging source, such as a CD-ROM database or an online source;

- data entry outsourced or contracted to a bureau which will usually work from the shelf list;

- catalog records available from a local centralized cataloging unit; and

- catalog records supplied by the vendor of the automated library system as part of the service.

Manual data entry of MARC (MAchine Readable Cataloging) records is usually the most expensive option. It requires accuracy and some expertise. It also takes time, and time is needed to check and proofread the records once entered. It is recommended only for those items in the school library media center collection for which a catalog record cannot be found through a commercial service.

The cost of purchasing catalog records varies from service to service, but the school library media center will be able to create a database quickly using this method, and the catalog records are usually of good quality. MARC records are available on CD-ROM (such as Brodart's *Precision One* or Follett's *Alliance Plus*) or from online sources (such as Marcive's *WebSelect* or OCLC). Apart from price and record quality, a consideration for selecting a service is the likelihood of a high percentage of matches or "hits" in the database; that is, that the service will have catalog records for a large proportion of the items in the school library media center collection. A list of sources of MARC records can be found in Chapter Two. The ISBN (International Standard Book Number) is usually the best way to search for catalog records on a CD-ROM or online service. If the shelf list does not include the ISBN for each item, then this information may need to be added to each shelf list card during the preautomation inventory check so that it is possible to use the shelf list as the basis for finding MARC records through these sources.

As with the online and CD-ROM services, bureau services vary in price and in the length of time they require for the job. Where catalog records are provided by the vendor of a library automation system, this is usually an incentive to choose the system. Some system vendors also provide an on-going catalog update service as part of their service package. Where a school library media center has access to a centralized cataloging service, retrospective conversion may not be an issue at all—though if the service charges, then it might be wise to investigate all options.

Once the catalog database has been created with the records in MARC format, then this database can be *ported* to a new automated system that the school library media center may move to in the years ahead. Thus, retrospective conversion is a job that should be done only once for any school library media center; it is important that it be done well, because if the basic catalog data is of poor quality, then this will affect information retrieval through the catalog.

The catalog database is not the only database that will have to be created when an integrated, multi-function library system is first installed. The second-largest database will probably be the database of borrower information. In a school, it may be possible to load this information from the school administration system. In addition, borrower cards will have to be created, or some other system be used for maintaining the user numbers or barcodes (such as keeping a file with class lists and barcodes at the circulation desk). If acquisitions/ordering functions are automated, then there will be a small database of book and media vendors. If the school library media center wishes to keep track of expenditures from multiple sources of funds, then there will also be fund accounting files to be created.

The second major task associated with preparing the school library media center for automation is barcoding all the items in the collection for the circulation system. There are two aspects to this. First, there is the work of actually placing the barcode labels on the items. This procedure might be done at the time of the preautomation inventory, or it might be done later. The second aspect is recording the barcode number as part of the catalog record for the item. If items are barcoded before the catalog database is created, then the barcode reader can be used to read in the barcode number as an addition to the catalog record. If the catalog database is created first, then each item is taken from the shelves, matched to the catalog record, a barcode label is placed on the item, and the barcode number is read into the catalog record. In designing this stage of the library media center automation process, the aim should be to reduce the number of times that each item in the collection has to be handled.

As soon as the new automated library system is operational, planning should begin for the second-generation system through evaluation of the system in place and ongoing monitoring of industry trends. *System migration* is the term used for the act of moving from one automated library system to another or of moving from one version of an automated library system to another. There are many reasons why a school library media center might move from one automated library system to another, including the following:

- the vendor of the system currently in use decides to discontinue development of the system;

- the current system is based on an operating system such as DOS that is no longer being supported, and the school library media center has to make a change to a system that is compatible with newer operating systems such as Windows (or, alternatively, a move from PICK to UNIX) and so investigates all options;

- the current system (in 1999) is not Y2K (year 2000) compliant, and the school library media center has the option of either upgrading or changing to a new system;

- the vendor goes out of business, or the system is taken over by a new vendor;

- the school decides to upgrade its network hardware, and the library automation system in use is not compatible with the newer hardware;

- an increasing interest in resource sharing among libraries or school library media centers in a region may mean that new systems are considered to facilitate this;

- changes in the school environment (such as changes in enrollments or changes in school specialization) may mean that the original system no longer meets the needs of the school; and

- because of changes in information technology, the system is no longer an appropriate vehicle for information skills instruction.

In an editorial in *The Electronic Library* in June 1997, Pamela R. Cibbarelli indicated that automated library system vendors were then concentrating their development efforts in four main areas: a movement toward client/server system architecture (and away from mainframes and terminals on the one hand and peer-to-peer networks on the other); graphical user interfaces to the systems for library users and librarians; "embracing the Internet" (Cibbarelli, 1997, 167); and a migration toward the Windows NT and other Windows operating systems. All these trends are very much in evidence in the library automation systems that are currently on the market for school library media centers. All these features offer some advantages in the school setting, and it is worth keeping them in mind when evaluation criteria are being developed to select a new system or when an operational system is being monitored with a view to updating it. Other "growth areas" in the automated library system market (that is, areas in which vendors are concentrating their development resources) include systems aimed at libraries that are choosing a second-generation system, multilingual systems, the incorporation of multimedia and Web resources into library media center catalogs and other databases, and online public access catalogs based on Web browsers.

IMPLEMENTING ONLINE AND INTERNET ACCESS

Providing access to online information services and the Internet through the school library media center (as in Chapters Three and Four of this book) involves planning, evaluation and selection of equipment and resources, and a number of implementation stages, some of which may have to be coordinated with school network developments. The first major decision is the decision to provide access to information and information services outside the school. This decision may be made on the basis of the information needs of the school community or on the need for resources for information skills instruction. The range of external resources available to the school and the school library media center is wide and varied, and decisions will need to be made about the kind of access, the kinds of information services that are needed and the purposes for which they are needed, and the information content that the school requires. Because most online information services are now accessed via the Internet, the Internet predominates in the discussion that follows.

Service and Resource Selection

Evaluation and selection of external information sources, including online information services and the Internet, takes place at several levels. Four of these will be discussed in this section. The first is selecting the Internet service provider (ISP) who will provide the school or school library media center with Internet access (and therefore with access to online information services via the Internet as well). The second is selecting the commercial online information services provider (or utilities or hosts) to which the school or the school library media center will subscribe. The third is selecting the individual databases and services on the online information services and the Internet that will be used for particular applications or purposes in the school or the school library media center. The fourth is selecting individual Web pages either for use as resources in the educational process or for links from the school library media center's own Web pages.

Selecting an Internet service provider is very important as this service will provide the gateway to the Internet and to the online information services. For some schools and school library media centers, this will not be an issue, because the school district or the education authority will have a recommended or contracted Internet service provider. Schools in remote locations may find that they have very little choice, because there may be only one or two Internet service providers with a local point of presence. For others, a choice may have to be made between competing providers. The following criteria can be used to select an Internet service provider:

- a local point of presence so that connections can be made at local telephone call rates or through a high-speed line;

- a system that allows a large number of users to be online at any one time, so that very few attempted connections result in a busy signal;

- speed of access to Web pages and speed of downloading files;

- services provided as part of the basic charge and services available for an additional charge;

- a telephone help desk that is open for a large number of hours a day and that provides sensible and appropriate help; and

- cost and value for money.

The last—cost and value for money—is very important for schools, but working out true comparative costs can be quite difficult. Some Internet service providers will quote rates by the month; others by the quarter or as an annual fee. Some will quote for a total package of services; others will provide a basic quote with a number of extras priced separately. Some will set up the system on site as part of the basic service; some will do it for an additional fee; others will not do it at all. Some have strict limits on the amount of email that can be sent, received, or stored as part of the basic service. Some provide free space for Web pages, while others charge for this (and use different measures to assess the space used). The best solution may be drawing up a matrix so that the information about all providers can be reduced to a common format and compared.

There are two main aspects of the selection of online information services and databases. The first relates to the selection of an online source over a source in another format (such as CD-ROM or print); the second relates to the choice of a particular online information service over another online service. With Internet access available in more schools, online is increasingly becoming the preferred option, partly because no other hardware is required beyond the Internet connection and all that goes with it and partly because it offers the potential for access to the most current information. It helps that the interface provided by the standard Web browsers is easy to use and provides a consistent interface to the Internet and online information services.

Many information sources are now available in two or more formats. For example, the ERIC education database from the United States federal Department of Education was originally available in print form and online through online information service providers like Dialog. It is now available on CD-ROM and via the Internet (on the AskERIC Web site). To also make the situation more complex, the online version is currently available through several online information services, the database is available on some North American campus networks, and there is more than one CD-ROM version. In each of these versions, the database is searched in different ways. The costs are different for each, as are the procedures used to calculate the costs. On the Web, searches of the database are free but document delivery incurs a charge. The version of ERIC the school uses might be determined by factors such as whether Dialog or OCLC (both of which have

ERIC) are already used in the school for other purposes, the willingness of school library media center staff (or the time available to them) to learn the new search techniques necessary to use another online information service, and the relative importance of document delivery.

In choosing one online information service over another (given that most school library media centers will be able to afford only one or two), the following criteria should be considered:

- the number of databases made available through the online information service and the value of at least a significant number of them in the school setting (while Dialog has more than 900 databases early in 1999, for instance, only 100 to 200 may have any relevance for the school, yet this may still be more than on any other online information service provider);

- timeliness of the information on the service, including frequency of updating key databases of interest to the school;

- accuracy and authority of the content of the databases on the service that are of interest to the school, for example, the quality of the full-text newspapers that are available and the reputation of the information providers who are responsible for other key databases on the service;

- the quality of data input and indexing;

- any national or political or cultural bias in the databases available on the service or in the sources selected for inclusion in individual databases on the service;

- the ease of use and user-friendliness of the service, including the quality of the printed manuals and online help screens, the instructions on the screen, and simple and easy-to-remember procedures;

- the availability of support from the online information service;

- whether it is necessary for the school library media specialist to attend a special course before the service can be used effectively and the nature, cost, and location of those courses;

- the overall cost, including any monthly or annual subscription or minimum charge, any charges for online time, charges for particular databases, charges for viewing or downloading particular records, and charges for any other services or facilities such as documentation or software; and

- the availability of special rates, services, and facilities for schools.

The picture that emerges is a rather complex one, but school library media specialists will find that they are able to effect considerable savings while increasing access to information in the school library media center by considering carefully the options available to them.

World Wide Web resources are currently selected and evaluated by a number of organizations for different purposes, though not many of these take the needs of libraries and school library media centers into account in their processes. Some search engines rank Web pages according to the number of hits they receive, and/or by other measures that also take into account the value and usefulness of the content or the design of the pages. The Lycos search engine, for example, has its "Top 5% Sites;" reviewers use a rating scale of zero to 100 and take into account content, presentation, and the overall "experience" of the page, though they say that "excellence is our only criterion" for each, which gives little real guidance for the reviewers. The Magellan directory of Internet resources has taken a different approach; it uses a system of stars to rate its reviewed sites on completeness of the content presented in the resource, organization of the resource, currency of the information presented, ease of access to the resource, and "net appeal." This directory has covered newsgroups, listservs, FTP sites, Gophers, and telnet sites as well as Web pages. Other sites that evaluate and list Web pages include Luckman Best of the Web and SelectSurf.

Some specialist Web directories state the criteria they use to select resources for listing, though the criteria used in these situations are usually related to the aims and objectives of the organization and the needs of the users of the directory rather than specifically to the needs of school library media centers and their users. However, there are exceptions, particularly in the field of education. Blue Web'n, "a searchable library of Blue Ribbon Web sites categorized by grade level, content area, and type," has been created by the Pacific Bell Education First Fellows at San Diego State University's Department of Educational Technology as a service for teachers and schools. An evaluation rubric is used to assess all resources listed in the weekly Blue Web'n electronic newsletter and added to the database. This rubric is available on the Blue Web'n Web site (see "Internet Sources" at the end of this chapter) and could be used by school library media centers—perhaps with some adaptations for the local setting.

Criteria that have been developed specifically for the evaluation and selection of Internet resources for libraries and school library media centers (usually as the basis for links on the Web pages maintained by the library or school library media center) often reflect the collection development and/or resource selection/evaluation criteria traditionally used by them for the selection of print and audiovisual resources—though with adaptations for the Internet environment. Lisa Janicke Hinchcliffe provides an example of this approach on her page dealing with "Evaluation of Information." She lists the standard criteria used to evaluate print resources (such as format, scope, relation to other works, authority, treatment, arrangement, and cost) and shows how they can also be applied to Internet resources. Other lists of criteria that also rely on this approach include "Evaluating Internet Resources" from the University at Albany (New York) Libraries and "Thinking Critically About World Wide Web Resources" by Esther Grassian. The Internet Public Library (a virtual library on the Web) has a collection policy statement for ready reference resources that, while being "net oriented," is still to some extent based on the traditional criteria covering content, updating, the function of the graphics, evidence of proofreading, and whether the source is a primary one. These kinds of criteria have served libraries and school library media centers well over the years; it is therefore understandable that they should be applied in dealing with a new medium. This means that the selection and evaluation criteria currently specified in the school library media center's selection policy or collection development policy could be used with some modifications to cover Web resources.

In 1996, Nancy Everhart worked with some 40 members of LM_NET (the listserv for school library media people) to develop a "Web Page Evaluation Sheet" specifically for use by school library media specialists. See Figure 7.4, pages 220–21. The idea is that it can be used to assign a score to Web pages based on criteria that are important for school library media centers. The general criteria include currency, content and information, authority, and ease of navigation, among others. Under each of these broad headings are more specific points for consideration. The worksheet is provided as a Web page (on the "Schrockguide for Educators," see "Internet Sources" at the end of this chapter) so that it is available to as many potential users as possible.

 **WEB PAGE EVALUATION WORKSHEET**

Title of Web Site: _____

URL: _____

Directions: *Use your judgment in allotting points for the various categories.
Total the points for the final score.*

Currency (0 to 15 Points)   _____
    The site posts the date of the last revision.
    The site has been updated recently.
    The frequency of planned updates and revisions is stated.

Content (0 to 15 Points)
    The information will be useful to our curriculum or will meet   _____
        student interest.
    This information is not available in any other format elsewhere
        in my library.
    The information on the topic is thorough.
    The information is accurate.
    The purpose of the page is obvious.
    The information is in good taste.
    The page uses correct spelling and grammar.

Authority (0 to 10 Points)   _____
    The authors are clearly identified.
    The authors and maintainers of the site are authorities in their field.
    There is a way to contact the authors via e-mail or traditional mail.
    You can easily tell from the domain name where the page originates.

Navigation (0 to 10 Points)   _____
    You can tell from the first page how the site is organized and what
        options are available.
    The type styles and background make the page clear and readable.
    The links are easy to identify.
    The links are logically grouped.
    The layout is consistent from page to page.
    There is a link back to the home page on each supporting page.
    The links are relevant to the subject.
    The icons clearly represent what is intended.

**Figure 7.4   Web Page Evaluation Worksheet. Reproduced with permission
from Dr. Nancy Everhart <nancy@ptd.net>.**

Experience (0 to 10 Points) _____

The page fulfills its intended purpose.

The page is worth the time.

The page's presentation is eye-catching.

The site engages the visitor to spend time there.

Multimedia (0 to 10 Points) _____

Sound, graphics, or video enhance the site's message.

Treatment (0 to 10 Points) _____

Any biases towards the subject matter can be easily identified.

The page is free from stereotyping.

The content and vocabulary of the page is appropriate for its
intended audience.

Access (0 to 5 Points) _____

You can connect quickly to the page.

The page is available through search engines.

The page loads quickly.

You can choose whether to download smaller images, text-only,
or nonframe versions.

Miscellaneous (0 to 15 Points) _____

The page has received one or more awards.

There are no per-use costs involved.

Interactions asking for private information are secured.

Information can be printed without the need to change your
system configuration.

Information is presented in short enough segments so it can be
printed out without backing up the system for other users.

The page has its own search engine for searching within the page.

TOTAL: _____

Scoring

90 - 100	Excellent
80 - 89	Good
70 - 79	Average
60 - 69	Borderline Acceptable
Below 60	Unacceptable

Comments:

At least two Web sites provide useful guidelines to support the work of school library media specialists in information skills development, specifically in teaching students to evaluate the information that they locate through their Internet searches. The Web site of Loogootee Community Schools has three "Evaluation Rubrics for Websites," developed by Tammy Paynton. These are designed for use by students. The "Web Evaluation for Primary Grades" form is for young children to "begin learning how to assess the content of Internet information." A rating scale is used to lead them through a process of assigning up to 25 points for each site on the basis of design, content, technical elements, and credibility. The form for intermediate grades is a little more sophisticated—the students can assign up to 50 points for each site, while the form for secondary grades provides for up to 100 points to be allocated for each site. On the Cyberbee Web site for educators, school library media specialist Karen McLachlan has two cyberguides or Web page evaluation tools for "teachers and students to evaluate content and graphic design of home pages." One, called "WWW Cyberguide Ratings for Content Evaluation," provides "a guide for rating curriculum content on Web sites," while the other, called "WWW Cyberguide Ratings for Web Site Design," covers the presentation of the information and particularly those aspects of presentation that are related to the medium itself, such as speed of downloading, ease of navigation, and use of graphics, sound, and video.

The number of sets of criteria that have been developed for the evaluation of Web pages reflects the problems associated with evaluating Web sources. They include the transitory nature of some of the material on the Web and changes in location of the material, the mutability of Web pages and sites (a site that is appropriate for a curriculum unit one semester may be quite different and quite unsuitable the next semester), the different ways in which the same Web site can appear via different Web browsers, and the different levels of audience that may be targeted in different sections of the same Web site. In addition, many Web sites use more than one language, and even where English is used throughout, the English spelling and usage may not be standard American English.

It is important that a hands-on approach be adopted in dealing with online and Internet-based resources. There is no substitute for actually using the service; in fact, this is the only way that most resources really can be evaluated. While it is relatively easy to gain hands-on experience with Internet resources, commercial online information services present a greater problem, because most school library media specialists do not want to pay for a subscription until they have tried the service. In this case, the options include testing the online service at an exhibition associated with a professional conference and perhaps using the trial databases or trial subscriptions that some providers offer through their Web sites.

Sources of Information About Online Information Services and the Internet

Both the online information industry and the Internet are changing rapidly. In addition, the two are becoming more closely intertwined. There are two main implications of this: sources of information tend to become outdated very quickly, and sources of information about the two are gradually merging. Only the most recent sources of information about the Internet and online information services should be used.

Some of the print journals and magazines related to the Internet provide reports and assessments of Internet service providers. One of these is *Internet Magazine,* which each month publishes the results of ongoing "performance tests" that the staff have devised for Internet service providers in the United Kingdom. Tests include availability (how often the busy signal comes when an attempt is made to connect), Web page speeds, and download speeds. However, prices and technical support are not tested.

Sources of information about online information services include the following:

- the Web sites of the various online information service providers; these can be accessed, for instance, from the Web page of "Online Information Services" created by the author at the University of Iceland;

- directories of online databases and services, such as the annual *Gale Directory of Databases: Online Databases* (Gale Research, 1998);

- print periodicals such as *Database, Online, Online and CD-ROM Review,* and *Information World Review* provide current information on the online information services industry plus reviews of individual databases and services;

- print periodicals devoted to the use of online information services and other information technologies in schools, including *Classroom Connect, Information Searcher,* and *CMC News*; and

- the proceedings of the regular online information industry conferences, such as the international "Online Information" conferences held in London each December and in New York each April or May, and the Australian "Information Online and On-Disc" conferences held in Sydney each January.

It is often said that the Internet itself is the best source of information about the Internet. However, this is not much help to those who are new to the Internet and still trying to find the information that they need among the hundreds of millions of Web pages and other resources available on the net. The list below, therefore, includes both print and Internet-based resources:

- printed books about the Internet and its use in education and school libraries (see the "References and Bibliography" at the end of this chapter and the "Bibliography" at the end of this book for further information);

- print magazines about the Internet (and their associated Web sites), including *Internet World, Internet Magazine, .net, Online Access,* and *Boardwatch*;

- print magazines devoted to the use of the Internet and other information technologies in schools, including *Classroom Connect, Information Searcher,* and *CMC News*;

- general computer magazines (and their associated Web sites) that also provide some coverage of the Internet, including *MacWorld, PC World, Windows,* and *Byte*;

- professional print journals in the field of library and information science and school librarianship that have some coverage of the use of the Internet in libraries and school library media centers, including *Library Journal, School Library Journal, School Libraries in Canada, Access* (Australian School Library Association), *Scan* (New South Wales Department of Education, which published Web site evaluations), and *Teacher Librarian* (formerly *Emergency Librarian,* which has a regular column about the Internet);

- the proceedings of the regular "Internet World" conferences held in different locations around the world, with several being held each year;

- Web sites designed specifically for school library media specialists, including "School Libraries Online" (the International Association of School Librarianship), LION (Librarians Online Network, School District of Philadelphia), "School Librarian Links," and "The Library Spot;" and

- the directories and searchable databases provided by services such as Yahoo! AskERIC, Blue Web'n, Encyclopaedia Britannica Internet Guide (BIG), BUBL (Bulletin Board for Libraries), and the NetFirst database on OCLC (see "Internet Resources" at the end of this chapter).

Implementation Issues

Given the likely demand for Internet access once it is available in a school, a major issue will be finding a way of providing such access in a cost-effective way. For many schools, this will be providing access for a number of users at a time through a school or school library media center network. In setting this up, the needs of users of other applications through the network (such as CD-ROMs or the school library media center catalog) will also have to be considered. It may be that access to the Internet is restricted to particular times or to particular groups.

Most schools will find it necessary to establish schoolwide policies and procedures related to the Internet and its use within the school. These policies and procedures may need to address issues such as who will have access, under what conditions and for what purposes—especially given that few schools or school library media centers will be able to afford the facilities to provide unlimited access for all. The policy may also need to address the strategies to be used to supervise student access and the problem of the availability of material on the Internet that many parents consider undesirable for children. It may be that students and parents are asked to sign an "Acceptable Use Agreement" or other form, and, if so, this should be stated as part of the school policy. This issue of policy making in relation to Internet use was taken up in the discussion of email access in Chapter Four. In addition, the use of filtering software and other strategies to restrict access to undesirable Web sites is discussed in Chapter Eight.

A plan will need to be developed to ensure that all people in the school who will need to use the Internet or online information services do have the necessary skills to do so. This may involve working cooperatively with classroom teachers to ensure that they and their classes can use the facilities available to them. It might involve short orientation sessions for teachers, school administrators, and others. It may be necessary to create posters or guides that are placed where users of the system can see them and refer to them. In addition, simple user manuals may be necessary so that users can refer to them as necessary, including those times when they are planning searches at home.

The Internet is different from most information sources made available through the school library media center in that, apart from links to specific sites, the information is not selected by the school library resource center staff. Further, as a communications system, the Internet can be used in many different ways, not all of which could be considered appropriate by the school. When access to the Internet is made available to faculty and students, the development of an acceptable use policy for the Internet will be a necessity for most schools. In addition, it may be necessary to have separate policies and procedures for staff and students. As with all school policies, this should have the support of the whole school community, and this may require considerable discussion with all stakeholders—including parents. The acceptable use policy recognizes that, while supervision will be provided, it will be almost impossible to closely supervise every school user all the time. It gives parents an indication of their responsibilities and those of the student and indicates the responsibilities of the staff of the school or the school library media center. The acceptable use policy usually has two aspects: the kind of material that the student will access via the Internet and the student's own behavior as an Internet user.

An acceptable use policy is usually supported by a user agreement, which, depending on the age of the student, may be signed by the parent, by parent and student, or by the student. In addition, some schools have a user agreement for teachers. Many schools withdraw student Internet privileges for breaches of the conditions of a user agreement.

IMPLEMENTING CD-ROM ACCESS

Providing access to information on CD-ROM in the school library media center or throughout the school (as discussed in Chapter Three of this book) involves a number of decisions, including decisions about hardware and networking. There may also be decisions about whether to use Internet-linked CD-ROMs such as encyclopedias and indexes that are updated via the Internet or that incorporate interactive links to Internet resources. There will also be evaluative decisions to be made about the CD-ROMs themselves, such as choosing one electronic encyclopedia from among those available or choosing one curriculum-related CD-ROM for a particular school subject such as American History.

Selection Issues

The first selection issue that arises relates to the selection of a CD-ROM resource over a resource in another format that covers the same topic or contains similar information (such as an online database or an Internet resource or printed materials). The second major issue is the selection of a specific CD-ROM over other CD-ROMs dealing with the same topic. The evaluation of CD-ROMs itself has two aspects: the information and resources that are available on the CD-ROM and the ease of use of that information and the resources; and the technical aspects of the CD-ROM, such as the ease with which it can be installed. The criteria for the former will have much in common with evaluating similar resources in print format, with some extensions to cover the electronic environment. The technical criteria, however, will be similar across the range of CD-ROM types.

The general selection criteria that are applied to library media center resources should also be applied to CD-ROMs, with the addition of criteria specific to the medium as mentioned previously. The general criteria may relate to users and their needs and to the school curriculum and curriculum resources already available in the school. Other general criteria such as timeliness (or currency of the information), accuracy, arrangement or organization of the information, purpose, and bias (if any) will be relevant. Depending on the CD-ROM, other criteria might also be relevant. For example, when evaluating a database on CD-ROM, some, if not all, of the criteria normally used to evaluate online databases will be appropriate. The criteria normally used to evaluate a print encyclopedia can be applied to an encyclopedia on CD-ROM, along with some extra criteria related to the CD-ROM as the means of delivery, while criteria used to evaluate directories in print form could be applied to a directory on CD-ROM, with the addition of extra criteria related to the new medium.

Special criteria related to the CD-ROM medium itself include user-friendliness and ease of use, the quality of the instructions (on screen and in the manual), the visual appeal and design of the screen displays, the effectiveness of any navigation tools to guide the user through the material on the disk, and the quality of any support materials. In addition, the CD-ROM must be compatible with the school library media center hardware; while there are cross-platform disks that will operate on both Windows machines and Macintoshes, others are designed for particular hardware and operating systems and will work on no other. While not covering all the possible CD-ROM selection issues, the following shortlist of selection criteria will be useful as a guide in most settings:

- compatibility with the CD-ROM equipment available in the school or school library media center;

- relationship to the school curriculum or other identified need within the school and appropriateness for the age and maturity level of the intended users;

- the user-friendliness of the CD-ROM and the quality of any instructions and help screens;

- the quality of any accompanying documentation;

- the amount of service and support users are likely to need in the school library media center setting;

- the necessity for any technical support and maintenance;

- cost considerations, particularly related to value.

As was the case with evaluating online information services, there is no substitute for hands-on experience when evaluating CD-ROMs—it is, in fact, essential. It is useful to have the CD-ROM available in the school for a trial period so the reactions of teachers and students can be assessed. If this is not possible, then the school library media specialist may be able to test the CD-ROM in a local computer store or an exhibition associated with a professional conference. In addition, some CD-ROM vendors have a free trial available via their Web site.

Sources of Information About CD-ROMs

As was the case with automated library systems and online information services, the CD-ROM industry is changing rapidly—only the most recent sources of information about CD-ROMs should be used. Sources of information and reviews include the following:

- print and CD-ROM directories of CD-ROMs in print, including *CD-ROMs in Print: An International Guide* (Meckler);

- professional print magazines that are general in focus but nevertheless often publish reviews of CD-ROMs include *Teacher Librarian* (formerly *Emergency Librarian), School Library Journal,* and *Library Journal*;

- professional print magazines related to information technology, including *Online and CD-ROM Review, Computers in Libraries, CD-ROM Professional,* and *CMC (Computers in the Media Center) News*;

- computer magazines such as *PC World* and *MacWorld* often review both CD-ROM disks and the hardware needed to run them;

- online databases such as Microcomputer Abstracts on Dialog and OCLC's FirstSearch, Computer News Fulltext on Dialog, IAC Computer Database on Dialog, Library Literature on Dialog, and OCLC's FirstSearch;

- review sites on the Internet, including the California Instructional Technology Clearinghouse and the Web site of the New South Wales (Australia) Department of Education, both of which have reviews of CD-ROMs (among other resources); and

- the archives of professional listservs such as LM_NET and OZTL_NET, which may contain comment about particular CD-ROMs, including comparative comment.

Implementation Issues

Access can be provided to the information on CD-ROMs in a number of different ways in the school setting. The options include the following:

- a CD-ROM drive on a stand-alone workstation, whether internal drive or external;

- a CD-ROM drive on a local area network (LAN). The drive will play only one CD-ROM;

- a CD-ROM "stacker" on a local area network. A stacker contains multiple CD-ROMs but plays only one CD-ROM at one time and switches from one to another as users select CD-ROMs from a menu system on the network;

- a CD-ROM tower on a local area network. The tower contains multiple CD-ROMs and allows people using the network to access different CD-ROMs at one time (thus it is faster than the stacker);

- loading the CD-ROMs to a large hard drive on the network, which increases access speed still further but is far from being a simple procedure and is one that cannot be used with all CD-ROMs; and

- lending the CD-ROMs to users for use on their own computers through the school library media center circulation system.

There are still other options, too, and some work better than others in different settings. Some schools use a mixture of these options. The reasons for this are varied and depend on the license terms (and the additional cost of a network license) for the CD-ROM, the search software that each CD-ROM uses, the amount and type of use of the particular CD-ROM title, the need for an Internet connection for the CD-ROM to function effectively, and because some disks do not function well over a network. Some CD-ROMs can be installed within a few minutes with simple procedures; others require many hours of work to install. CD-ROM technology is undergoing a great deal of change at present, and new forms are likely to emerge. While this brings advantages, it also means that there is considerable diversity among the disks that schools might want to purchase and install.

Making CD-ROMs available over a network means that the users never handle the disks, so disks cannot be stolen or damaged by users. When CD-ROMs are made available on a stand-alone machine, security becomes a concern for the machine that has either an internal or an external CD-ROM drive. If the drive is lockable, then either it can be used for just the one CD-ROM, or a staff member has to change the disk for the user. One is a security risk; the other is inconvenient and discourages use of CD-ROMs. If more than one CD-ROM is to be used on a stand-alone machine, then additional security measures should be considered. These might include placing the machine where its use can be supervised easily, checking out the CD-ROMs to users through the circulation system, and keeping the CD-ROMs at the main desk and recording all users. This additional supervision can have positive effects in that the school library media center staff will be aware of any problems that the users are having and will be able to offer assistance as soon as the need for it is apparent.

Lending CD-ROMs through the normal circulation procedures has been successful in some libraries. An advantage is that, since most CD-ROMs contain large amounts of data, users want to spend a lot of time working through the disk. It is often more convenient for them and the school library media center if they are able to do this on their own computer and CD-ROM drive. Because many current desktop and laptop computers come with a CD-ROM drive built in, this is becoming possible for more home computer users, and people want to take advantage of the hardware that they have at their disposal. It helps that the CD-ROM disks are reasonably durable (certainly as durable as books), and they cannot transmit computer viruses from one machine to another (as floppy disks can when moved from machine to machine).

Although CD-ROMs are becoming more user-friendly, many school library media center users will still need help in using reference works and databases on CD-ROM. The options for organizing and providing this include the following:

- cooperative planning with the classroom teacher when the CD-ROM is appropriate for a particular curriculum unit so that instruction in the use of the CD-ROM can be built into the work for the unit;

- individual and small-group instruction carried out by the school library media specialist at point of need—when people are using the CD-ROM;

- a chart or "crib sheet" posted beside the workstations, giving a summary of the basic commands and other things that people need to know to use the resource;

- the creation of small manuals suitable for the users of the school library media center; and

- storing any manuals that came with the CD-ROM, either with the disk or in a place where they are accessible to users of the system.

Much of the information in this section relating to CD-ROMs as information sources in the school library media center collection and to their selection and evaluation is also applicable to educational and recreational resources on floppy disk and CD-ROM, which will be discussed briefly in the following section.

IMPLEMENTING EDUCATIONAL AND RECREATIONAL APPLICATIONS OF INFOTECH

When computer-based educational and recreational resources (on floppy disk or on CD-ROM) are incorporated into the collection of the school library media center or made available through it (as in Chapter Five of this book), then decisions will have to be made about such matters as how the resources are to be selected, how they are to be stored, and how they are to be made available or circulated. The first major decision is, in fact, to add this kind of material to the school library media center collection or to provide access to it. The reasons for this decision will influence the procedures that are adopted.

The provision of curriculum-related resources on disk is more widely accepted and more common in school library media centers than the provision of recreational resources. It is easier to justify, particularly to those who provide the budget and to those who are waiting to get access to a computer for real work while someone else is playing a computer game. For this reason, when recreational resources are made available on floppy disk (or students use them via the Internet), their use may be restricted to times of the day when other users will not be competing for access to the machines. In addition the playing of games that require sound (and many do) might have to be restricted to particular locations or particular times to avoid disturbing other users.

Another problem associated with making computer-based recreational resources available on floppy disk or CD-ROM is that fashions come and go so quickly in this field. Computer-based curriculum resources can usually be used for a few years, but, apart from the books on disk, computer-based recreational resources tend to have a very limited life span. There is nothing quite so dead as last year's hot computer game. When money is scarce, the school library media specialist may have to weigh, among other factors, the expenditure on computer-based recreational resources against the length of time that they will be used.

Selection Issues

The selection of curriculum-related resources on floppy disk will be governed by the same criteria that are used to select curriculum-related resources in other formats (such as books or videos) for the school library media center, with the addition of some criteria specific to the computer-based medium. The general criteria for curriculum-related resources include:

- authority or the reputation and knowledge of the person or people responsible for the resource;

- the scope, coverage, and learning objectives of the resource and its relationship to the school curriculum;

- accuracy, reliability, and currency of the information, including visual information as well as text content;

- any evidence of bias or reinforcement of particular attitudes or opinions (and the appropriateness of these in context);

- the suitability of the resource given the age level and prior knowledge of the students who will be using it;

- the quality of the accompanying documentation, including instructional support materials;

- the appropriateness of any activities, including assessment activities, that are incorporated into the resource; and

- price and value.

Criteria that are related to the computer-based medium include the following:

- compatibility with the hardware and systems available in the school;

- the availability of networked versions at a reasonable additional price;

- user-friendliness, ease of use, any help facilities; and

- the amount of preparation time that is required of the teacher and school library media specialist if the resource is to be used effectively.

Most of the selection criteria listed previously can be applied, to some extent, to computer-based recreational resources. The disks should be compatible with the hardware and systems available (and in particular, any program extensions or plug-ins that are needed to support the resource should be noted). The resources should be suitable for the age level and interests of the intended users. The screen displays and sound should be of good quality. A check should be made for evidence of bias or prejudice. The documentation should be clear and comprehensive enough to install the disk and get it working. Apart from the obvious requirements that a recreational resource be attractive, fun to use, and appealing to the users for whom it is intended, there are few other general guidelines that will help. In the case of games and simulations, so much depends on the latest fashion and student interests. With computer-based literature, the situation is clearer; after all, school library media specialists have been selecting fiction books for a long time. However, it needs to be kept in mind that a good book does not necessarily translate well to the computer-based medium, while some mediocre printed books have become very successful as a book on a disk. In other words, where a book is available in print and in a computer-based version, both the book and the disk should be evaluated on their own merits.

As was the case with other computer-based resources such as online information services and the Internet, it is important that the person undertaking the selection have some hands-on time with the resource before making a selection decision. Reviews will help, but there is no substitute for seeing the program in action and testing it.

Sources of Information

As with the other technologies discussed in this chapter, it is important to use the most recent sources of information when considering computer-based educational and recreational resources. This is particularly the case when dealing with recreational resources such as computer-based simulations and games, where fashions change so very quickly. Sources of information about curriculum-related resources include the following:

- review sites on the Internet, including the California Instructional Technology Clearinghouse and the New South Wales (Australia) Department of Education Web site;

- reviews of software in professional print periodicals such as *Teacher Librarian* (formerly *Emergency Librarian), Booklist, School Library Journal, Media and Methods, The Computing Teacher*, and *Electronic Learning*;

- reviews of computer software in periodicals for teachers across all subject areas and age levels—for example, periodicals for history teachers, science teachers, or teachers of kindergarten classes; and

- print and online directories of computer software, including the Bowker annual *Educational Software Directory* and *Only the Best: The Annual Guide to the Highest Rated Educational Software and Multimedia* (Association for Supervision and Curriculum Development).

It is rather more difficult to find reliable sources of information about computer-based recreational resources, and it may be necessary to take a less formal approach here. In fact, the best single source of information will be the staff and the shelves of the largest store in the district that sells computer games. Watch the games that people are trying out; talk to the people who are buying games. Other sources of information include the following:

- reviews in the major newspapers—many of which can be searched online on Dialog;

- magazines dealing with computer games, including *Computer Gaming World, PC GameGuide,* and *Electronic Gaming Monthly*;

- the many game sites on the Internet—the Yahoo! Directories provide the best point of access to these.

Implementation Issues

For the school library media specialist, there are a number of issues to be considered if computer-based educational and recreational resources are added to the school library media center collection. Among them are the following, not all of which will be applicable in every school library media center:

- storage of the disks, either on the open shelves or in a secure location, with any accompanying material;

- making the resources available to users via the school or school library media center network and providing access at the workstations to any necessary supporting material;

- if the resources are to be lent, then establishing procedures for this (unless the normal circulation procedures are to be used);

- periodic checking of the disks for damage;

- recording details of the school's site license (some automated library systems make provision for this as part of a catalog record for computer software and CD-ROMs);

- if floppy disks are loaned for use outside the school library media center, making sure that appropriate virus protection software is installed on the school library media center machines and that disks are checked for viruses before being used in the school library media center; and

- ensuring that all members of the school community are aware of the copyright conditions related to the use of these resources.

The next chapter deals with the ongoing administration of information technology in the school library resource center, including evaluation, as stages in the strategic planning process. The implementation issues discussed in this chapter in relation to automated library systems, access to online information services and the Internet, access to information on CD-ROMs, and the incorporation of computer-based educational and recreational resources into the school library media center collection will also be relevant to the discussion in the next chapter.

REFERENCES AND BIBLIOGRAPHY

Alexander, Jan, and Marsha Tate (1996). Teaching critical evaluation skills for World Wide Web resources. *Computers in Libraries.* 16(10): November-December, 49–55.

Berger, Pam, and Susan Kinnell (1994). *CD-ROM for schools: A directory and practical handbook for media specialists.* Wilton, CT: Eight Bit Books.

Bosch, Stephen, Patricia Promis, and Chris Sugnet (1994). *Guide to selecting and acquiring CD-ROMs, software, and other electronic publications.* Chicago and London: American Library Association.

Butterworth, Margaret (1991). *Preparing for automation in the school library.* SLA Guidelines. Swindon: School Library Association.

Butterworth, Margaret, ed. (1997). *Information technology in schools: Implications for teacher librarians.* 3rd ed. Perth, Western Australia: Australian Library and Information Association, School Libraries Section (WA Group).

Cibbarelli, Pamela R. (1997). Library automation vendors: Today's perspective. *The Electronic Library.* 15(3): June, 167–68.

Cibbarelli, Pamela R., and Shawn E. Cibbarelli (1998). *Directory of library automation software, systems and services 1998.* San Jose, CA: Information Today Inc.

Del Vecchio, Stephen (1997). Out for a spin: A school librarian test drives 14 CD-ROM encyclopedias. *School Library Journal.* September, 118–24.

Dickinson, Gail K. (1994). *Selection and evaluation of electronic resources.* Englewood, CO: Libraries Unlimited.

Fitzgerald, Mary Ann (1997). Misinformation on the Internet: Applying evaluative skills to online information. *Emergency Librarian.* 24(3): January-February, 9–14.

Furrie, Betty (1991). *Understanding MARC (MAchine Readable Cataloging).* McHenry, IL: Follett.

Glogoff, Stuart (1994). Reflections on dealing with vendors. *American Libraries.* April, 313–15.

Head, Alison (1997). A question of interface design: How do online services GUIs measure up? *Online.* May-June, 20–29.

Jacobson, Frances F. (1990). Evaluating commercial databases. *Journal of Youth Services in Libraries.* 3(3): Spring, 239–41.

Johnson, Claire, Pru Mitchell, and Robin Wake (1997). School library automation: Migrating to second generation systems. In Butterworth, Margaret, ed. *Information technology in schools: Implications for teacher librarians.* 3rd ed. Perth, Western Australia: Australian Library and Information Association, School Libraries Section (WA Group), 79–90.

Kemeny, Linley (1988). The process of automation. *Access.* 2(4): November, 21–23.

Kirkwood, Hal P. (1998). Beyond evaluation: A model for cooperative evaluation of Internet resources. *Online.* July-August. 66–72.

Knight, Jon (1996). From the trenches: Networking (notworking?) CD-ROMs. *Ariadne,* 3, 20 May. <http://www.ariadne.ac.uk/issue3/trenches/>. (Accessed 9 February 1998).

Lighthall, Lynne (1989). A planning and implementation guide for automating school libraries: Selecting a system. *School Libraries in Canada.* 8(2): Winter, 27–36.

Lunau, Carroll D. (1997). Implementation of Z39.50 in Canadian libraries. *Feliciter.* October, 40–44.

Manczuk, Suzanne, and R. J. Pasco (1994). Planning for technology: A newcomer's guide. *Journal of Youth Services in Libraries.* Winter, 199–206.

Meghabghab, Dania Bilal (1997). *Automating media centers and small libraries: A microcomputer-based approach.* Englewood, CO: Libraries Unlimited.

Murphy, Catherine (1990). Questions to guide retrospective conversion choices for school library media centers. *School Library Media Quarterly.* Winter, 79–81.

Nicholls, Paul (1995). CD-ROM to go: Circulating CD-ROM collections in the public library. *Computers in Libraries.* October, 55–58.

Nickerson, Scott (1998). The application of Z39.50 in your library. *Feliciter.* June, 47–50.

Nordgren, Layne (1993). Evaluating multimedia CD-ROM discware: Of bells, whistles and value. *CD-ROM Professional.* January, 99–105.

Notess, Greg R. (1998). Tips for evaluating Web databases. *Database.* April-May, 69–72.

Piontek, Sherry, and Kristen Garlock (1995). Creating a World Wide Web resource collection. *Collection Building.* 14(3): 12–18.

Piternick, Anne B. (1990). Decision factors favoring the use of online sources for providing information. *RQ.* 29(4): Summer, 534–44.

Pratt, Gregory, Patrick Flannery, and Cassandra I. D. Perkins (1996). Guidelines for Internet resource selection. *College and Research Libraries News.* 57, March, 134–35.

Riner, Hank (1995). On the information highway, take your eyes off the road: Evaluating database content. In Williams, Martha E., ed. *16th national online meeting proceedings, 1995.* Medford, NJ: Learned Information, 333–38.

Schlegl, Karen (1998). The reference experience expands: New options for getting answers. *Computers in Libraries.* May, 62–65.

Schrock, Kathy (1998-1999). The ABCs of Website evaluation. *Classroom Connect.* December-January, 4–6.

Schwartz, Candy (1993). Evaluating CD-ROM products: Yet another checklist. *CD-ROM Professional.* January, 87–91.

Shrewsbury, Lynn D. (1994). The request for proposal: Basics for the beginner. In Day, Teresa Thurman, Bruce Flanders, and Gregory Zuck, eds. *Automation for school libraries: How to do it from those who have done it.* Chicago: American Library Association, 79–97. (Includes a sample request for proposal.)

Smith, Alastair G. (1997). Testing the surf: Criteria for evaluating Internet information resources. *The Public-Access Computer Systems Review.* 8(3): 5–23.

Sowards, S. W. (1997). Save the time of the surfer. *Library HiTech.* 15(3/4): 155–58.

Thiessen, Hal (1994). *Systems for automating school libraries: A comparative study with checklists.* Occasional Papers Series. Ottawa: Canadian Library Association.

Valenza, Joyce Kasman (1997). How to choose an encyclopedia. *Electronic Learning.* 16(6): May-June, 50–53.

INTERNET SOURCES

AskERIC
<http://ericir.syr.edu/>

Bibliography on Evaluating Internet Resources
<http://www.networx.on.ca/~jwalker/educat2.htm>

Bibliography on Evaluating Internet Resources—Nicole Auer
<http://www.lib.vt.edu/research/libinst/evaluating.html>

Blue Web'n
    <http://www.kn.pacbell.com/wired/bluewebn/>
Blue Web'n Rubric
    <http://www.kn.pacbell.com/wired/bluewebn/rubric.html>

BUBL (Bulletin Board for Libraries)
    <http://bubl.ac.uk>

California Instructional Technology Clearinghouse
    <http://clearinghouse.k12.ca.us/>

Cyberguides (Cyberbee)—Karen McLachlan
    <http://www.cyberbee.com/guides.html>

Dialog
    <http://www.dialog.com/>

D-lib
    <http://mirrored.ukoln.ac.uk/lis-journals/dlib/>

Encyclopaedia Britannica Internet Guide (BIG)
    <http://www.britannica.com/>

Evaluating Internet Resources—Trudi Jacobson and Laura Cohen (University
    at Albany, New York, Libraries)
    <http://www.albany.edu/library/internet/evaluate.html>

Evaluating Quality on the Net—Hope Tillman
    <http://www.tiac.net/users/hope/findqual.html>

Evaluation Checklist for Full Bibliographic Displays in Web Catalogs
    <http://www.fis.utoronto.ca/research/programs/displays/juliana.htm>

Evaluation of Information—Lisa Janicke Hinchcliffe
    <http://alexia.lis.uiuc.edu/~janicke/Evaluate.html>

Evaluation Rubrics for Websites (Loogootee Community Schools)
    <http://www.siec.k12.in.us/~west/online/eval.htm>

Internet Public Library Selection Policy
    <http://www.ipl.org/ref/RR/Rabt.html#policy>

Library Automation Systems on the Web—Ian Piggot (for the European
    Commission Directorate General XXIII/E-4)
    <http://www2.echo.lu/libraries/en/systems.html>

Library Selection Criteria for WWW Resources—Carolyn Caywood
    <http://www6.pilot.infi.net/~carolyn/criteria.html>

The Library Spot
    <http://www.libraryspot.com/>

LION (Librarians Online Network, School District of Philadelphia)
    <http://www.libertynet.org/lion/lion.html>

LM_NET
    <http://ericir.syr.edu/lm_net/>

Lycos
    <http://www.lycos.com/>

Magellan
    <http://magellan.excite.com/>
    <http://www.mckinley.com/>

Minnesota State-wide Library Information System Request for Proposal
    <http://www.mnlink.org/vendor-select/vendor-select.htm>

New South Wales Department of Education (Australia)
    <http://www.dse.nsw.edu.au/>

OCLC
    <http://www.oclc.org/>

Online Information Services—Anne Clyde
    <http://www.hi.is/~anne/online_services.html>

OZTL_NET
    <http://www.csu.edu.au/research/cstl/oztl_net/>

School Librarian Links
    <http://www.nyx.net/~rbarry/>

School Libraries Online (International Association of School Librarianship)
    <http://www.hi.is/~anne/iasl.html>
    For the interactive list of automated library system vendors on School
    Libraries Online, see <http://www.hi.is/~anne/libaut.html>

Schrockguide for Educators—Kathy Schrock
    <http://discoveryschool.com/schrockguide/>

SelectSurf
    <http://www.selectsurf.com/>

Thinking Critically About World Wide Web Resources—Esther Grassian
    <http://www.library.ucla.edu/libraries/college/instruct/web/critical.htm>

Vendors of Automated Library Systems with Web Pages (CSU School of Library
and Information Science)
<http://witloof.sjsu.edu/peo/alsvend.html>

Yahoo!
<http://www.yahoo.com/>

CHAPTER EIGHT

Administering

in the
School Library Media Center

INTRODUCTION

This chapter deals with the later stages of the strategic planning process as applied to information technology in school library media centers, that is, ongoing administration and evaluation. It covers ongoing management and administration of information technology, including personnel, budgeting, buildings and facilities, maintenance, user education, staff development, and ongoing evaluation. Some issues and concerns associated with the use of information technology are discussed, and the chapter ends with some comments about future directions.

When any form of information technology is introduced into the school library media center, it changes more than just the appearance of the place. It changes the way things are done, the way the budget is spent, the way staff work, the way students and teachers get information, even the image of the school library media center. The users' expectations will change. The relationship between the collection of the school library media center and access to information in the school changes. The teaching of information skills changes. The resources available for teaching all school subjects are extended and enhanced, perhaps leading to changes in instructional methods within the school. Both school library media center policies and on-going school library media center management should reflect these changes.

PERSONNEL

When information technology is introduced into any work environment, the nature of the jobs change and the skills that people need to do those jobs change. This is true, for instance, of operating a circulation system, entering cataloging data into an automated library system, or using an online information service to answer reference questions from teachers and students. This new reality should be reflected in the job specification from the time that the change occurs, not just at the time new staff are hired. The changed job specification becomes the basis for negotiating time release for training and for possible salary increases to reflect new skills.

Where the school library media specialist is assisted by other staff in the school library media center, the personnel planning or human resource management becomes part of the role and responsibility of the school library media specialist. In this case, it is the school library media specialist who is responsible for ensuring that role statements, job specifications, policies and procedures are reviewed and updated when new information technology is introduced into the school library media center.

The training needs of the school library media center staff are particularly important, because appropriate training is vital if the technology is to be used effectively. Even where the staff already have a high level of skills, it is probable that training related to the specific system to be introduced will be needed. Further training will be needed when a new version of the automated library system is installed or when the school library media center subscribes to a new online information service or when the network is upgraded—or when any other major changes are made. Training is an aspect of the introduction of information technology that is often neglected in budgeting for the project, yet it should be a part of any school information technology plan.

The costs of training depend in part on the existing level of skills possessed by the staff and on the training opportunities available locally or by distance education. If distance education is the best option, then it needs to be recognized that people still have to have release time to take advantage of distance education opportunities. It is easy for administrators to understand that a school library media specialist needs release time to attend a three-day course in the next town; it is sometimes more difficult for them to accept that release time is necessary for a distance education course. Distance education should not be seen as the cheap alternative to "real training" through on-site or local courses. Where a school library media specialist works alone in the school library media center without any clerical or other support, leave for training can be difficult to organize, but this neither affects the entitlement of the school library media specialist to such leave nor the advisability of making it possible.

It is not only the skills needed to do the job that change—the way in which people use their time on the job also changes. Tasks that took a long time to do manually (like sending out notices for overdue books or creating bibliographies) can be done very quickly with an automated system. However, at the same time there are new tasks to be performed when information technology is introduced (like system backups or clearing paper jams in the printer). The changes in the ways staff spend their time should be documented and work schedules and procedure manuals updated to reflect these changes. If this is not done, then school library media center staff will be under additional stress in the new situation, because the old expectations of the way they should be spending their time will not match the realities of the new situation.

One of the most frequently reported changes in the work of the school library media specialist as a result of the introduction of information technology—specifically a library automation system—is a reduction in the amount of clerical work (Wolfgram, 1996, 389), since tasks such as following up on overdues, creating mailing lists, preparing orders for booksellers, and creating reading lists can all be handled much more quickly using the computer. However, this does not mean that the job has been simplified or made easier. Many school library media specialists have assumed new responsibilities related to information technology in the school, sometimes as a result of the new knowledge and skills they acquired through automating the school library media center. Many have noted that they have been able to expand their curriculum role in the school by working more closely with teachers and students (Wolfgram, 1996, 389). Others, including Betty Costa (one of the first school library media specialists to have a microcomputer-based library system), have noted that although automation did not necessarily save the time of the school library media specialist, "the payoffs come in the form of expanded and high-quality patron services" (Costa & Costa, 1991, 3).

Not all reported changes have been positive. A study by Jean Donham van Deusen (1996) showed that school library media specialists in elementary schools were spending more of their time providing technical support with an automated system than they had with a manual system. Another study by Nancy P. Zimmerman (1993) showed that the amount of time that school library media specialists were spending on troubleshooting their hardware and software reduced the amount of time they could spend helping library users. These examples illustrate the problems that can arise when proper provision is not made for the specialist tasks associated with the use of information technology. They seem to be good arguments for the provision of adequate technical support rather than examples of the disadvantages of automation.

BUDGET

When any form of information technology is introduced into the school library media center, there are long-term and short-term budget implications over and above the initial cost of the hardware, software, and installation. There are several aspects of budgeting that need to be considered on an ongoing basis. Some budget changes are necessary not so much as a direct consequence of the introduction of the information technology but because of the changes that will be set in motion by the introduction of the technology.

One important consequence of the introduction of information technology in a school library media center is a change in emphasis from ownership of books and other resources as part of the library media center collection to access to resources via the computer networks. When the Internet or commercial online information services are used for access to information, the costs are ongoing and usually depend at least partly on use, whereas an item such as a book or a videotape that is purchased for the library media center collection is usually paid for on purchase and the total cost is known from the beginning. It is much easier to justify or explain known, once-only costs. An emphasis on resource and information access rather than resource ownership requires a different approach to budgeting and planning.

Another aspect of the "access" versus "ownership" dichotomy is the way in which resources and systems based on information technology are purchased. Many of the automated library systems on the market today are not actually "sold" to the school library media center; rather the school purchases a license for the system; at the same time, it may be committed to an ongoing fee of some kind (whether a license fee or a maintenance fee) and to system upgrades, as well as system support. When the school library media center purchases a current information source on CD-ROM, it may be purchasing a site license that is valid only as long as the subscription is paid for updates. What the school is buying in these cases is not the system itself but the right to use it. This affects both the budget and how the school views its assets.

Many CD-ROM disks, like electronic encyclopedias and newspaper databases, need to be updated regularly so that the information on them is current and relevant. The vendor may provide for updates by sending a new disk, or by using the Internet. Sometimes an ongoing subscription has to be purchased in order to get the updates; sometimes the new version has to be purchased when one is published. Other vendors include a certain amount of updating in the original price for the disk. With some of the automated library systems, it is possible to use the catalog module or the serials module to keep track of all the various license and subscription arrangements and agreements that are entered into by the library media center.

The ongoing costs associated with the use of information technology are sometimes either neglected or underestimated in budgeting, but if appropriate provision is not made, then the technology will not be used as effectively as it could be. With an automated library system, for instance, ongoing costs include the barcode labels, paper for the printer, printer cartridges, floppy disks, backup disks or tapes, the purchase of MARC (MAchine Readable Cataloging) records, hardware and software maintenance and support (perhaps including the cost of a maintenance contract), system updates (if not included in the original purchase price), any necessary hardware repairs, plus staff costs. With a CD-ROM system, ongoing costs include printer paper and printer cartridges, hardware maintenance and support, and any necessary repairs. With access to the Internet, there are also going to be costs associated with printer paper and cartridges, maintenance and support, and personnel costs, as well as any charges payable to the Internet service provider (which may be a flat monthly or annual fee or a fee based on hours of usage or disk space or bandwidth used or a combination of these) and any telephone and data line charges. There are also some minor costs across all these applications, such as mouse balls (they do wear out, particularly if computer games are allowed), cleaning products for keyboards and screens and mouse balls, and replacements for keys that disappear from the keyboards.

As well as the current costs, it will be necessary to budget for future costs, such as future hardware expansion and replacement—any computer hardware has a limited useful life span, as does any piece of software.

BUILDINGS AND FACILITIES

The introduction of new information technology in a school library media center will almost certainly result in physical changes to the building and facilities unless the library media center is housed in a relatively new building that was designed for the use of technology. Even then, the speed of developments in information technology in recent years has been such that changes may be necessary beyond those provided for by the architects. When the school library media center is housed in a building that is more than ten years old, then changes to the facility are almost inevitable. Aspects that will need to be considered include the building itself, the use of space in the school library media center, the furniture and its arrangement, and the placement of equipment and hardware.

Space planning and furniture layout is more than just finding a convenient and sensible place for everything. The aim of space planning is to ensure that the new information technology will perform well and contribute to the efficiency and effectiveness of the school library resource center through careful arrangement of furniture and fittings to support the activities and programs of the library media center. Space planning and design include making best use of the space available, ensuring that traffic flows work well and that related activities take place near one another, that the environment is an attractive one in which to work, and that electrical power and network connections are satisfactory (bearing in mind that power and connectivity can be supplied to workstations from the walls, from the floor, or from the ceiling).

The use of information technology will change traffic patterns in the school library media center, and this may mean changes in the arrangement of permanent furniture, room dividers, and other basic features of the library media center design. For example, in the days of the card catalog, it was necessary to have a cabinet of catalog card drawers in a reasonably central place in the library media center, with space around it for users. However, if users have already searched the catalog via the school network before they even come to the library media center, then they do not need to see catalog terminals in a central position as they walk in. When a security system is introduced, it may mean changes to the location and layout of the circulation desk, which, with some of the systems, will need to be located near the exit doors. The need for supervision of users of the computers may also dictate room arrangement to a certain extent.

Computers need an environment that is relatively free of dust (including chalk dust) and where air can circulate freely around them (they generate a lot of heat when operating). They should neither be situated near heaters nor exposed to direct sunlight. However, lighting is important: users should have adequate light, but there should be no reflected light on the screens. If the room has a nylon carpet or other flooring that could cause a build-up of static electricity then both the tables or desks and the chairs of computer users should be on a rubber mat. There should be space around the workstations for the various manuals, instruction sheets, and other tools that are provided to assist users of the computers.

Where the school library media center has multiple computers, some thought will need to be given to their arrangement, bearing in mind the above points plus the necessity to consider cabling and power source constraints. However, if potential usage of the computers is not kept in mind during planning, then the arrangement of the computers may come to dictate usage. For example, if the computers are arranged in a long line with very little space between them, then it will not be possible for groups of students to work together at one computer without restricting the use of the nearby machines. The use of the computers should be monitored on an ongoing basis to ensure that the arrangement really does contribute to the goals that people have in using them. Possible arrangements of computers include a *horseshoe* (appropriate when all the users need to be able to see an instructor), *clusters* and *ranks* (see Figure 8.1, page 250).

Furniture is another consideration when information technology is introduced into a school library media center (or any other workplace). Staff may be working on the computer for relatively long periods of time—for instance, when doing catalog data input or when checking books in and out at the circulation desk. They should be working at a desk that is designed for computer use and sitting on a chair that can be adjusted for computer use so that the risks of eye strain or repetitive strain injuries (occupational overuse syndrome) are minimized. Workstations that are to be used by students require some considerable thought, especially in schools where there is a wide age range. While students seldom use the library catalog for long periods of time, they may spend a lot of time with a CD-ROM or an educational simulation, and so the furniture must be appropriate for them. In addition, in a school library media center setting, selection of ergonomically correct furniture for computers that are used by students and teachers, provides an example of good practice in an educational setting where students are learning about computers and their applications as well as using them in the school library media center.

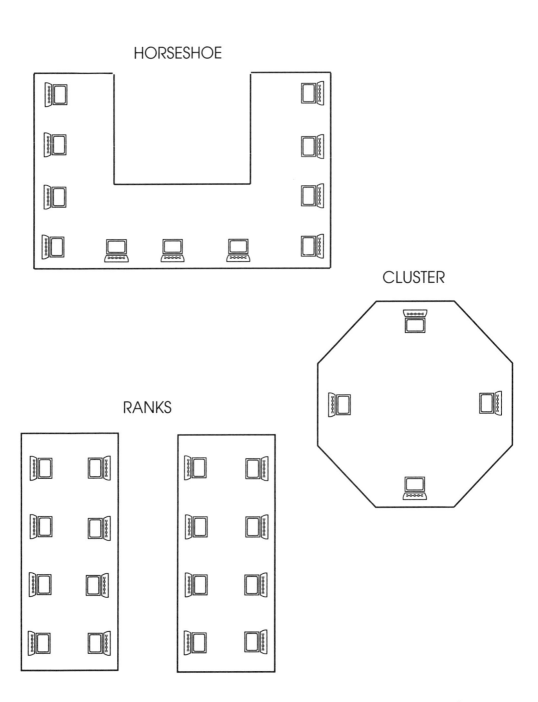

Figure 8.1   Some possible arrangement patterns for multiple computers in a school library media center.

When planning for the use of information technology in a school library media center, future developments and needs should also be considered in as much as this is possible so that any changes made to the building and furniture are appropriate for future needs. If this is not done, then *ad hoc* changes will be necessary later in response to emerging conditions or problems, and these *ad hoc* solutions may need to be reversed or modified at a future time, leading to more inconvenience and expense.

In their article "The Electronic School Library Resource Center: Facilities Planning for the New Information Technologies," published in *Emergency Librarian* in 1995, Teresa Blodgett and Judi Repman provide a series of checklists to help school library media specialists evaluate their current floor plan, assess their current equipment and furniture, and analyze the organization of their equipment. This is a useful starting point for ongoing monitoring and evaluation of the school library media center facilities.

ERGONOMIC CONSIDERATIONS

The importance of ergonomics has already been alluded to. Despite numerous articles in newspapers, popular magazines, and professional journals about ergonomics-related issues, ergonomics is still, as Lee Inkster has noted, "a neglected aspect of library automation," particularly in small libraries and school library media centers (Inkster, 1992, 40). This is illustrated by a letter to the editor of London's *Daily Telegraph* in June 1998 that comments on a photograph published in a previous issue. The writer, Alan Raison, notes that the students in the photograph "look suitably uncomfortable with their mouse mats in front of their keyboards. If anyone were to use those computers for a lengthy period, they would surely find it painful." He further says, "It's a shame that while so much money is being poured into equipping schools with computers, ergonomics are being ignored," and because few people realize its importance, "there is no attempt to encourage good ergonomics" in schools (Raison, 1998, 4). Another letter to the editor in the same issue—this one from David Ruegg—makes the point that children should be given not only a "practical appreciation of the potential" of information technology, but also a knowledge of "safe working practices—something that is often forgotten" (Ruegg, 1998, 4). For educational reasons, as well as for reasons of staff and user efficiency and safety, ergonomic issues have to be taken seriously in school library media centers.

The term "ergonomics" was coined by researchers in 1949. Although a more recent term, "human factors engineering," is sometimes used instead, ergonomics is now a generally accepted term for an area of study that "addresses human performance and well-being in relation to the job, the equipment, and the environment" (Weisberg, 1993) and that embraces three main fields: the safety and health of workers, their comfort and well-being, and their productivity and efficiency. These fields indicate clearly that the well-being of the worker is crucial to the productivity of the organization—something of which education authorities and schools should be aware.

Ergonomics is obviously a wide field. However, an understanding of ergonomics and its application to the school library media center as a workplace is important not only for the success of any projects related to information technology but also to ensure that the library media center environment is one that promotes the safety and well-being of staff and users and enhances productivity and efficiency. In many school library media centers, there may be only one paid worker—the school library media specialist—and it is in this setting that ergonomic considerations are most likely to be overlooked. However, school library media specialists owe it to themselves and to their users to ensure that their own work environment is as ergonomically sound as possible and that any workplace risks are minimized.

Disabling workplace injuries date back much further than the introduction of computers. In the Middle Ages, monks working in the scriptoria of monasteries suffered a range of conditions that have since been traced to their equipment, to the poisonous substances with which they sometimes worked to produce their beautiful manuscripts, and to the poor lighting conditions in the monasteries of the time. In the seventeenth and eighteenth centuries, lace-makers and other craft workers seem to have been susceptible to disabling conditions of the hands and arms. With the industrial revolution, more workers were employed in repetitive, stressful production line work, and some experienced problems as a result. The introduction of computers, however, coming at a time when ergonomics was developing as an area of study and involving repetitive work carried out under special conditions, led to an emphasis on computer ergonomics as a special field within ergonomics as a whole.

In libraries and school library media centers, as in other workplaces where computers are used, research has shown that problems can result from a range of activities, including long periods spent looking at a monitor (particularly if this is done under adverse lighting conditions); using input devices such as keyboard, mouse, trackball, touch screen or handheld barcode reader; sitting for long periods in an inappropriate position while using the computer; and performing tasks under stress. When sensible precautions are taken, however, any risks are minimized and personal efficiency is increased.

Repetitive strain injury (RSI), also known as occupational overuse syndrome (OOS) or cumulative trauma disorder (CTD) or reversible fatigue syndrome or work-related upper limb disorders (WRULD), is one of the better-known (but not necessarily well understood) conditions that have been associated with the use of computers. However, it is by no means restricted to users of computers. This condition affects both the musculo-skeletal system and the nervous system. According to a 1991 Occupational Safety and Health report, it "may be caused or aggravated by repetitive motions, forceful exertions, vibration, mechanical compression (hard and sharp edges), sustained or awkward postures, or by exposure to noise over extended periods of time" (Bryant, 1993). One type of repetitive strain injury that may affect people who work with computers is the condition known as carpal tunnel syndrome (CTS). This condition involves the median nerve and the flexor tendons that extend from the arm into the hand through a "carpal tunnel" made up of the wrist bones, or carpals, and the transverse carpal ligament. When the hand or fingers are moved, the flexor tendons rub against the sides of the tunnel; this rubbing, particularly when it is prolonged or occurs under stress, can cause irritation of the tendons, which then swell and exert pressure on the median nerve. The result can be tingling, then numbness, then debilitating pain. The causes of carpal tunnel syndrome are complex but a common factor in the workplace where computers are used is repetitive motion at the keyboard. Other factors, such as workstation design, posture, job stress, and general health, are also involved.

School library media center staff can take precautions to reduce their chances of developing either carpal tunnel syndrome or some other repetitive motion conditions. Proper seating is important—chairs should be on wheels, and have adjustable seat and backrest. Table height should be appropriate for the worker, and allow for the proper placing of computer monitor, keyboard, mouse, and other equipment. The table height should be such that the elbows form a 90 degree angle when the hands are on the keyboard. The keyboard should be positioned so that the wrists are not bent up or down when the fingers are on the keys; some people find that a wrist rest in front of the keyboard helps to maintain the correct wrist position.

Monitoring work routine can also help library workers to avoid repetitive strain injury. It is particularly important that care be taken when working under stress (for example under the pressure of an impending deadline or the need to finish a major data input project quickly). Some researchers advise taking a 10 to 15 minute break from the keyboard every hour, though this does not necessarily mean a break from productive activity! This may be the time to open the mail, make telephone calls, or show a teacher how to work the computer projection unit. It appears that small hand exercises, carried out regularly while at the keyboard, can also help.

While computer users can take some steps to protect themselves, the problem is also being tackled from the other side, by some of the computer manufacturers, who are attempting to design more ergonomically favorable computer equipment. New input devices that have been designed to reduce the risk of carpal tunnel syndrome and other conditions include new versions of the keyboard, the mouse, and the trackball. In the early 1990s, Apple had a split and adjustable keyboard on the market, with an optional curved wrist rest. In 1998, Microsoft was marketing a natural keyboard, designed for ergonomic comfort, with an angled keyboard and wrist rest. However, as with the Apple keyboard, many reviewers found the Microsoft product difficult to use—people who have learned to type using a standard keyboard don't want to retrain themselves unless they have to (Murphy, 1998, 8). Other manufacturers with ergonomic keyboards on the market include Logitech and Dick Smith Electronics. Different types of keyboards that have been market-tested over the last six or seven years include the Bat keypad (in which the user's hands rest while creating the letters and numbers with combinations of just seven keys), and the Ullman keyboard (an inverted V shape board designed to be held in the user's lap).

Manufacturers have also been experimenting with ergonomic designs for the mouse and trackball. In part, this is a response to problems experienced by some users of the standard mouse—for example, people who have experienced tendinitis in the elbow as a result of the repetitive motion of excessive clicking of the computer mouse, a condition popularly known as mouse elbow. As with carpal tunnel syndrome, however, there is more behind this condition than just the clicking of the mouse. Other things that contribute to the problem include stress, poor posture, the seating arrangement, the angle at which the hand holds the mouse, and the grip on the mouse.

While repetitive strain injuries have had considerable publicity, they are not the only problems associated with the use of computers. Eye problems, including eyestrain, headaches, and blurred vision, have been identified in research studies. However, as with the two conditions discussed previously, causes are complex and relate not only to the use of a computer monitor but also to the work environment as a whole, the design of the workstation, and the general health of the worker. Environmental problems include lighting, glare from the screen caused by bright lights in the peripheral vision, reflections on the screen, and screen height. Problems can be alleviated by appropriate placing of the computer equipment, reduction of harsh overhead lighting, using blinds or shades on the windows, using hoods or antireflection screens, and careful choice of screen display colors (Weisberg, 1993; Robertson, 1998).

While research evidence is not clear, many people believe that there are other potential hazards associated with information technology in libraries and school library media centers. In Chapter Two, there was mention of the reservations that some school library media specialists have about the electromagnetic waves used by some of the library security systems. Others have questioned the low-frequency magnetic fields produced by computer monitors (but not by the screens of portable computers, which use a different technology), though these concerns are not supported by work of the United States National Institute for Occupational Safety and Health (NIOSH), or by the results of a survey carried out by the National Safety Council of Australia (NSCA). Yet the idea persists that electromagnetic fields may cause long-term problems (McKimmie, 1994). This being the case, prudent avoidance or risk minimization is the advice generally given. Among other things, this means ensuring that each workstation is sufficiently far from any other to avoid the magnetic fields that are strongest at the back and sides of desktop computers.

MAINTENANCE

Although school library media specialists will not usually be acting as the systems operators (though some do), they nevertheless need to be aware of the basic activities necessary to support an automated library system and other school library media center applications of information technology. Ongoing maintenance of information technology covers internal and external support for the systems, regular maintenance checks, security (system security and data security and backups), and a disaster recovery plan. Issues associated with security include such things as virus protection and system misuse. A maintenance schedule will help to ensure that work is done as necessary to keep the hardware and software operating efficiently.

There are basically two types of maintenance carried out on computer systems: preventive maintenance and remedial or corrective maintenance. Preventive maintenance is carried out regularly regardless of the current state of the system. It involves tests of equipment and software, adjustments as necessary, replacement of parts, and any necessary repairs. The aim is to keep the system operating effectively without any inconvenient down time, in other words, to prevent future malfunctions from occurring. Corrective maintenance is carried out at point of need, when a system malfunction occurs. Both preventive maintenance and corrective maintenance may be carried out by the hardware or software vendor through a maintenance contract or by a local contractor, or they may be done in-house. Some automated library systems require the school library media center to sign an annual maintenance contract as part of the purchase; for others, this is optional. In the latter case, the type and quality of the maintenance support available locally might be considered before a decision is made to sign a maintenance contract for hardware and software.

Regular system backups of the automated library system (and any other databases and systems) are necessary if the library is to survive disasters ranging from a power failure to a fire. Other causes of loss of data from the system include software failures, hardware failures, human error, and vandalism. A backup is a copy of the files supporting an automated system. Some files do not change very often, and these will not have to be backed up as often as files, such as the loan files, that change a great deal within a short space of time. A catalog backup might be done whenever a number of catalog records are added to the database, while a backup of the acquisitions/ordering system might be done whenever a number of orders are sent to vendors. A backup schedule should be developed to ensure that regular backups are done of the files that change a lot. Backups are usually made to magnetic tape or disk (such as a Zip disk). There should always be more than one copy of backups; any new backup should not be done immediately over the most recent backup but over an earlier one. This means that in the event of a problem with the most recent backup, another copy (though less recent) is available. The backups should never be stored in the same location as the computer.

A disaster plan goes hand in hand with backups. Disasters that might affect the computer systems include internal system disasters such as disk crashes and external disasters such as fire, flood, a severe storm, a lightning strike, malicious damage, and theft. In relation to the automated system, there are two aspects to disaster planning. The first relates to the recovery of the system so that it can be made operational again in the shortest possible time. This is where backups are so important—it may be possible to mount the latest backup of the system on a machine that has been hired for use while a hardware problem is dealt with, for instance. The second aspect relates to keeping the school library media center functioning without the automated system. This might mean having borrowers write their name, borrower number, and the barcode numbers of the items they are borrowing in a book at the circulation desk and keying this information into the automated circulation system when it is back up again.

The power supply is one of the more common sources of problems. To minimize risks, the computer systems should not share a circuit with such power-hungry devices as photocopiers or air conditioners. A surge protector or surge suppressor or power source adapter may be necessary in areas where the power supply fluctuates and is actually a good idea in any setting to protect the computers against any high-voltage variations in power supply. This will not, however, be much help in the event of a blackout. The best protection against computer damage and data loss in this situation is an uninterruptible power supply (UPS). This combines the features of surge protection, line conditioning, and battery backup. It means that in the event of a power failure, there will be time to save work and close the system down. The amount of time will depend on the UPS that is chosen. Some UPSs can even shut down a system with the help of software extensions

Another source of potential problems is computer viruses. It is almost impossible to make a system virusproof, but there are some measures that will help, including restricting students' use of floppy disks from other sources. However, the most effective measure is to install good virus protection software that is invoked automatically when a program is loaded from a floppy disk or downloaded from the Internet.

PUBLICITY AND USER EDUCATION

It is one thing to make information technology available—it is another for it to be used well. Some forms of user education will be necessary whenever new information technologies are introduced or whenever there is a major upgrade to an existing system. In addition, there will be a need for an ongoing program of publicity and promotion of the resources that are available to users of the school library media center. In most school library media centers, user education will have two main areas of focus: system orientation and professional development for teachers and other school staff and instruction for students (usually as part of an information skills program).

Promotion of the information technology-based resources of the school library media center should be undertaken on a systematic basis. In promoting these resources, emphasis should be placed on the potential benefits to the user, and this presupposes an awareness of the educational programs of the school and the needs of users of the school library media center. Possible avenues for promoting information technology include:

- displays, not only in the school library media center but outside it, in locations where they will be seen by as many people as possible;

- talks and demonstrations at school meetings;

- small-group demonstrations and hands-on sessions arranged for people with common interests or needs;

- working cooperatively with teachers on curriculum units that incorporate resources based on information technology;

- library newsletters;

- posters in locations outside the school library media center; and

- information provided on a school electronic bulletin board or Web site.

As with promotion, user education for teachers and students should be undertaken on a planned basis. Teachers are unlikely to use new technology unless they feel comfortable with it and unless they are convinced of its benefits for them and their classes. While some will be confident with the new technology and welcome its use in the school library media center, others will see it as a threat. This means that the school library media specialist will need to be able to show them applications of information technology that make sense to them in terms of the way they teach and the way they structure learning experiences for their students. Research suggests that good technology training for teachers has certain characteristics:

- the training should be supported and recognized by the school and the education authority;

- it should be provided using the equipment and software that the teachers will actually be using in the school;

- there should be a strong hands-on component;

- there should also be a strong demonstration component (using a large screen and projector) so that teachers have the opportunity to see how the system works before they use it themselves;

- there should be time for teachers to share ideas and experiences with others;

- at the end of the training period, teachers should have developed resources or lesson plans or strategies that they can implement immediately in their classrooms;

- teachers should leave the training session with strategies to implement what they have learned;

- there should be some form of follow-up after the training so that the new learning is reinforced; and

- there should be some form of provision for on-the-job coaching afterwards and opportunities for teachers to work cooperatively with the school library media specialist or the technology coordinator on curriculum units.

In addition, outside speakers can be used at various stages to generate enthusiasm, to provide information about what is being done in other places, to lead group discussion sessions in which ideas are shared, and to provide outside evaluation.

Ideally, user education for students should be undertaken at the point of need within the context of the school curriculum. This will usually be best done through cooperative teaching strategies developed by the school library media specialist and the teacher working together. Information search skills and information use skills should be taught in the context of meaningful classroom work, they should involve the use of information in a variety of formats, students should be required to develop and exercise critical thinking skills so that their use of information sources involves more than copying material and creating a bibliography, and the resulting work should be subjected to authentic assessment. The use of information technology is integrated across the curriculum, and students' exposure to new information technologies should not depend on the enthusiasm of their teacher. The "Nine Information Literacy Standards for Student Learning," from *Information Power: Building Partnerships for Learning* (American Library Association and Association for Educational Communications and Technology, 1998), available on the Web (see "Internet Sources" at the end of the chapter), provide a conceptual framework for this, as does the "Policy Statement—Electronic Information Literacy" of the Australian School Library Association (also available on the Web—see "Internet Sources" at the end of the chapter).

At the same time, however, individual students and small groups will need help and support in using information technology in the school library media center. This will mean that the school library media specialist responds to individual inquiries and requests for help. It will also mean creating guides or posters or "help sheets" that are available at workstations to assist users who are carrying out their own searches or working on their own projects.

ISSUES AND CONCERNS

Throughout this book, there have been allusions to a number of issues and concerns related to the use of information technology that need to be addressed by school library media specialists. These include:

- equity of access to information and information technology;

- information overload and information anxiety—the downside of the information age;

- the ongoing arguments about Internet filtering and censorship;

- copyright and intellectual property issues in an electronic environment;

- the right to privacy and its implications in a networked environment;

- computer crime;

- the development of techniques for organizing information on the Internet;

- "Internet addiction"—a real condition or figment of the imagination?; and

- the changing nature of the information skills that will be necessary for people in the future.

Just two of the more important issues will be discussed here: equity of access to information and information technology and the Internet filtering and censorship debate (which also has implications for other information technologies).

Equity of access is a concern in developed and developing countries. Access to information technology, including Internet access, can be affected by factors such as age, sex, geographic location, and economic status. According to a 1998 study, 78 percent of the public schools in the United States had an Internet connection somewhere in the building, but only a little over a quarter of all K–12 classrooms (27%) were connected to the Internet. However, these figures do not give a clear picture of the actual use of the Internet in public schools, which "is estimated to be much lower" (Online-Class, 1998), nor do they shed any light on the use of the Internet in school library media centers in the United States. The overall situation is also very different from state to state within the United States. In California, there is a Digital High School Grant, the aim of which is to have all high schools in the state connected. In a few states, all schools (as distinct from school library media centers) are connected; in other states, there are whole school districts that have no connection at all.

In Australia, the New South Wales Department of Education achieved its goal to have all 10,000 public schools connected to the Internet two years ago. The Canadian province of Alberta achieved the same goal at about the same time. In Iceland, the Icelandic Education Network (ISMENNT) has been connecting more than 95 percent of schools to the Internet for more than five years; only Finland has a higher rate of connectivity. However, even in Iceland, where all the schools had the option of joining ISMENNT and most had done so, overall a minority of the school libraries were using the Internet at the time of the most recent national survey (Clyde, 1996). Further, the rate of school library connectivity varied among the eight educational regions into which the country was then divided, with 37.5 percent of school libraries in Reykjavík (the capital) having an Internet connection but only ten percent of the school libraries in the remote Western Fjords region having access. Clearly, if true equity is to be achieved, then national and international planning will be important.

However, while these examples provide illustrations of inequity at international, national, and regional levels, the same kind of inequity can also be found at the individual school level. There are many schools where some classes have a lot of opportunities to learn to use new information technologies because they have teachers who are interested and willing to try new methods and ideas, while other classes have little access because their teachers are not interested or not aware of developments.

The issue of Internet filtering and censorship is also an equity-of-access issue. Behind all attempts at censorship or filtering of content is a belief that certain groups of people have the right to decide what other people should read, see, or access. These attempts also reflect an ambivalent attitude to the Internet. At the same time as it is being promoted as an important educational resource, there is considerable evidence of the widespread endorsement of a seemingly contradictory belief: the Internet is an environment from which children must be protected. Popular magazine articles, such as the notorious *Time* magazine cover article (Elmer-Dewitt, 1995) about pornography on the Internet (an article based on research that has since been discredited) have helped to confirm this view. Its proponents see the Internet as a place filled with evils such as pornography and formulas for drugs or bombs, a place where pedophiles and rapists prey on the unwary, where disorder and even lawlessness reign. In one sense, whether this view is valid or justified is beside the point. Simply because it is a view that is held by many people, it will influence what happens at the school level. Regardless of the educational programs available through the Internet, regardless of the amount of valuable current information that is provided on the Internet by governments and other organizations, regardless of the information skills that children can learn through use of the Internet, all children in some schools will be denied access unless these views and concerns are addressed by schools and school library media specialists.

This concern then creates a dilemma for school library media specialists and others in the school. Professional values associated with support for freedom of access to information for children as well as adults are enshrined in professional statements such as the American Library Association's statement on "Access to Resources and Services in the School Library Media Program" (see the "Internet Sources" section):

> The school library media program plays a unique role in promoting intellectual freedom. It serves as a point of voluntary access to information and ideas and as a learning laboratory for students as they acquire critical thinking and problem solving skills needed in a pluralistic society. Although the educational level and program of the school necessarily shape the resources and services of a school library media program, the principles of the Library Bill of Rights apply equally to all libraries, including school library media programs. School library media professionals assume a leadership role in promoting the principles of intellectual freedom within the school by providing resources and services that create and sustain an atmosphere of free enquiry.

The "Library Bill of Rights" affirms that libraries are "forums for information and ideas," and states that they should challenge censorship and that they should "cooperate with all persons and groups concerned with resisting abridgment of ... free access to ideas"; it further states that a person's rights should not be denied or abridged because of age.

In reality, professional views about access to the Internet in schools and current practice cover the range from unfettered license (free access for students and staff, without supervision) to a total ban on access to the Internet within the school. Most schools fall somewhere in between the two, with Internet access available under certain conditions. One approach to providing limited access is a negative one: strategies include requiring parental permission, requiring teacher supervision, installing blocking or filtering software to restrict students to approved Internet sites, or providing students with access only to printouts of information from the Internet rather than online access. On the other hand, the conditions of limited access may be positive, that is, they make take the form of strategies to ensure that students take responsibility for their own Internet access and behavior online, or the provision of guides to good Internet resources for young people, sometimes through a Web home page. Two particularly useful Web sites support this approach—one is an online brochure, "Child Safety on the Information Highway;" the other is a site called "Australian Families' Guide to the Internet" from the Australian Broadcasting Authority (see "Internet Sources" at the end of the chapter).

Above and beyond the issue of censorship, there are many problems associated with the use of Internet filters or blocking programs to control access. One is that, as Karen Schneider's work has shown, they simply do not work very well (Schneider, 1997, *passim*). Most blocking or screening software relies on some combination of two basic concepts:

- the school library media specialist or teacher or parent decides what words, phrases, or specific Internet sites will be excluded. This may first require extensive Internet searching through a range of pornographic and otherwise unpleasant sites and the typing of lots of swearwords in Internet search screens to establish what will be barred;

- the vendor of the software or system produces lists of sites and keywords to be excluded and updates those lists regularly. Mostly, these lists can also be customized by the parent or teacher or school library media specialist; however, some filtering program vendors regard their list of sites as confidential and do not even supply a list to people who purchase the program.

These points hint at some of the limitations of the use of filtering software. First, a school library media specialist using a program that comes with a list of sites has handed control of resource selection and information access in the school to someone else, whose views may be unknown and who may not have any professional qualifications or experience on which the base the decisions. Secondly, the lists of blocked sites become dated very quickly. Thirdly, because working through the many Web sites on some servers takes a great deal of time, the programs tend to block whole servers when just one or two pages might be considered objectionable. Some take "easy" decisions—for example, blocking all sites with a tilde (~) in the URL, on the dubious grounds that these are likely to be personal sites. Filtering programs that block sites on the basis of keywords or combinations of words also present problems, especially where a word can have more than one meaning—this has led to the blocking of sites dealing with breast cancer, the Easter Bunny, travel information about Lesbos, and children's stories about pussy cats. This means that much useful material is filtered out, while the programs are not always effective in blocking undesirable material.

What are the alternatives? Rather than restricting children's access in order to avoid harm, another approach is to take the initiative to point children in the direction of resources that they should be exploring, resources selected for their interest and educational or creative value. Acceptable use policies and user agreements encourage children to become self-managing Internet users. A learning environment in which the use of the Internet for curriculum-related activities is encouraged, and young people are given advice, guidance, and support in their use of it, will help. Information skills programs should include segments on online netiquette and appropriate online behavior; guidance should be given in "safe surfing." In addition, parents and other members of the school community need information about issues associated with Internet use, so that they understand what is involved. But in the end, as Doug Johnson says, "we have to ask ourselves if we are living in a filterable world" (1998, 13)—can people really be protected by being denied access to information and resources?

There are no easy solutions to the problems of equity of access to information technology, censorship and filtering, or any one of a number of issues facing schools. School library media specialists need to be aware of the issues and the arguments, and to find opportunities to discuss them with school staff and parents. Further, this discussion should be ongoing as one of the aspects of administering information technology in the school library media center.

EVALUATION

Evaluation is the final stage of the strategic planning process and an ongoing process that stimulates new planning cycles. Evaluation can take many forms. It can be formal or informal. It can be formative (contributing to a process or project while the project is being implemented) or summative (assessing what has been achieved through an initiative). All forms are necessary and have value at different stages of the process of implementing and administering information technology and for different purposes.

Ongoing, realistic, and documented evaluation of any information technology initiative is important. Without a commitment to measuring and assessing progress on the project and evaluating the project in terms of its aims, then the project may simply drift into the backwaters of irrelevance, wasting the investment of money and time involved. Realistic and relevant assessment can help to keep a project on course and ensure that it continues to be related to the needs of the users for whom it was developed. Ongoing assessment also helps to relate the project to new and emerging needs.

Evaluation should be related to the goals that the information technology implementation was to support but not restricted to them. After all, goals can change over time. However, when information technology is introduced into a school library media center with the aim of increasing library media center efficiency or supporting student learning or both, then the information collected as part of the evaluation process should reflect this and provide a basis for showing how efficiency has increased (more loans processed by the same staff in the same amount of time, perhaps, indicating more efficient circulation of resources in the collection) and how the implementation of information technology has contributed to student learning (better overall student scores in a curriculum unit, perhaps).

There are a number of strategies for collecting information about the technical performance of an automated library system or other information technology implementation. The reliability of the system might be measured in terms of a specified level of effectiveness over a stated period—for example, the automated library system is required to operate reliably over the school term with less than four percent downtime. This measure should have been part of the specification for the original system and should have been agreed to by the system vendor. There are also strategies available for measuring response time of a system and performance over a range of tasks, among other things. Sometimes features such as response time of the system (the time it takes to process, say, a catalog enquiry or a loan transaction) become critical only if they begin to deteriorate. If measures have not been done over time, then it will be difficult to show that response time has, in fact, deteriorated, yet it would be useful to be able to provide this evidence as part of a case for a new second-generation automated library system.

The school library media specialist should keep records of loan transactions through the automated library system, the rate of return of overdue items, the number of catalog searches, the usage of different parts of the library collection and the relationship of this to user education programs. Most automated library systems currently on the market can provide these kinds of statistics and many others. This will help the school library media specialist assess the contribution of the automated library system to resource use within the school. Statistics kept over time will indicate areas for collection development or further user education. Usage reports should be compiled for the CD-ROMs and other electronic information resources and for Internet access, again with a view to identifying those resources that seem to be making the largest contribution to the school's program and those areas where promotion and user education are necessary. The security system can be used to keep a record of the people who actually use the school library resource center—as distinct from those who do a catalog search or borrow a book—to analyze patterns of use over time.

While these kinds of quantitative measures have their place in evaluation, there is also a need for more qualitative information that addresses questions such as user perceptions of the information systems (as well as the number of users of the systems). This kind of information might be obtained through formal and informal discussions with users, through response forms on the school library media center Web site, through student evaluations of the information sources they used for a curriculum-related project, and through simple qualitative questionnaires. An illustration of the latter would be a postcard-size questionnaire beside the CD-ROM terminal, with a closed box in which students can deposit the completed questionnaire form. The questionnaire could simply ask students for their age and grade and then ask them to complete one of two sentences: either "I like using the electronic encyclopedia to search for information because. . . ." or "I don't like using the electronic encyclopedia to search for information because. . . ."

On a broader level, a useful form of evaluation is measuring the achievements of the school in relation to information technology against accepted national and state standards, such as the *Indicators of Schools of Quality, Volume 1: Schoolwide Indicators of Quality* (developed through a collaboration among several organizations, including the American Association of School Librarians and the National Study of School Evaluation). The second volume of the series will cover *Program Level Indicators of Quality*. Another similar form of evaluation is benchmarking, that is, measuring the performance of the school against the performance of schools that are recognized as national or state leaders in the implementation of information technology.

Both of these forms of evaluation and others can be regarded as strategies for school improvement. They should feed back into the strategic planning process so that the cycle continues. This takes us back to the beginning of the book. School library media specialists should be monitoring new developments in information technology with a view to assessing their applicability for the school library media center; they should be monitoring the external environment (related to changed community expectations of schools, for instance); and they should be evaluating their current use of information technology as a basis for ongoing information technology planning.

REFERENCES AND BIBLIOGRAPHY

Blodgett, Teresa, and Judi Repman (1995). The electronic school library resource center: Facilities planning for the new information technologies. *Emergency Librarian*. 22(3): January-February, 26–30.

Bruce, Harry (1994). Media center automation: A watershed for the school library media specialist. *School Library Media Quarterly*. 22(4): Summer, 206–12.

Bryant, Barbara (1993). Ergonomics: LC workers risk injury. *Library of Congress Gazette*. 19 November.

Butterworth, Margaret (1990). *The school library: Annual report and statistics*. SLA Guidelines. Swindon: School Library Association.

Caffarella, Edward P. (1996). Planning for the automation of school library media centers. *TechTrends*. 41, October, 33–37.

Clyde, Laurel A. (1994). Ergonomics and school library automation. *Emergency Librarian*. 22(1): September-October, 52–54.

——— (1996). State of the Art of Information Technologies in Nordic Libraries: Iceland, Country Report for a NORDINFO/European Community Study. Reykjavík: Félagsvísindastofnun/Social Science Research Institute, Háskóli Íslands/University of Iceland.

Costa, Betty, and Marie Costa (1991). *A micro handbook for small libraries and media centers*. 3rd ed. Englewood, CO: Libraries Unlimited, 85–92.

Donham van Deusen, Jean (1996). An analysis of the time use of elementary school library media specialists and factors that influence it. *School Library Media Quarterly.* 24(2): Winter, 85–92.

Elmer-Dewitt, Philip (1995). "On a screen near you: cyberporn," *Time,* 3 July.

England, Claire, and Karen Evans (1988). *Disaster management for libraries: Planning and process.* Ottawa: Canadian Library Association.

Everhart, Nancy (1994). How high school library media specialists in automated and nonautomated media centers spend their time. *Journal of Education for Library and Information Science.* 35, Winter, 3–19.

Haycock, Ken (1998). Appropriate use and Internet filters. *Emergency Librarian.* 25(3): January-February, 7.

——— (1998). *The indicators of schools of quality, Volume 1: Schoolwide indicators of quality.* Schaumburg, IL: National Study of School Evaluation.

Inkster, Lee (1992). Ergonomics and computers, a neglected aspect of automation. *The Bookmark.* December, 40–41.

Johnson, Doug (1998). Internet filters: Censorship by any other name? *Emergency Librarian.* 25(5): May-June, 11–13.

Kentwell, Rosalind (1997). Changing human resource management. *FYI.* Spring, 7–9.

McKimmie, Tim (1994). The ELF in your library. *Computers in Libraries.* 14(8): September, 16–20.

Morris, Anne, and Hilary Dyer (1998). *Human aspects of library automation.* 2nd ed. Aldershot, Hampshire: Gower.

Murphy, Kerrie, *et al.* (1998). Standard choice. *The Weekend Australian.* 7–8 February, "Buy IT" 8.

Nicholson, Fay (1997). Looking to the future. *FYI.* Spring, 3–6.

OnlineClass (1998). Message posted to the Net-Happenings listserv, 1 April <http://www.onlineclass.com/>.

Raison, Alan (1998). Untitled (Letter to the Editor). *The Daily Telegraph.* Connected. 4 June, 4.

Robertson, Guy (1998). Our vision of things: Basic eye care for librarians. *Feliciter.* 44(4): April, 26–28.

Ruegg, David (1998). Untitled (Letter to the Editor). *The Daily Telegraph.* Connected, 4 June, 4.

Schneider, Karen A. (1997). *A practical guide to Internet filters.* Neal-Schuman Net-Guide Series. New York: Neal-Schuman.

———— (1996). "Talking to parents about the Internet," *Classroom Connect*, 2 (6), March, 1, 4–5.

Waters, David (1994). New technology and the image of the school library media center. *School Library Media Quarterly.* 22(4): Summer, 213–20.

Weisberg, Michael (1993). Guidelines for designing effective and healthy learning environments for interactive technologies. *Interpersonal Computing and Technology: An Electronic Journal for the 21st Century.* 1(2): April.

Wolfgram, Linda M. (1996). The effects of automation on school library media centers. *Journal of Youth Services in Libraries.* 9: Summer, 387–94.

Wright, Kieth (1993). *The challenge of technology: Action strategies for the school library media specialist.* Chicago: American Library Association.

Zimmerman, Nancy P. (1993). Compromise in the information age: The attitudes of school library media specialists toward technology. *Journal of Youth Services in Libraries.* 6(3): Spring, 305–11.

INTERNET SOURCES

Access to Resources and Services in the School Library Media Program—
American Library Association, American Association of School Librarians
<http://www.ala.org/aasl/positions/ps_billofrights.html>

Child Safety on the Information Highway
<http://www.4j.lane.edu/safety/childtoc.html>

Emerging from the Smog: Making Technology Assessment Work in Schools—
Jamie McKenzie
<http://www.fromnowon.org/>

Internet Filters—Karen Schneider
<http://www.bluehighways.com/tifap/>

K–12 Acceptable Use Policies—Nancy Willard
<http://www.erehwon.com/k12aup/>

Mankato Public Schools—Information Literacy Curriculum
<http://www.isd77.k12.mn.us/resources/dougwri/ImpLit.html>

The Nine Information Literacy Standards for Student Learning—Information
Power (American Library Association and Association for Educational
Communications and Technology)
<http://www.ala.org/aasl/ip_nine.html>

Policy Statement—Electronic Information Literacy (Australian School Library
Association)
<http://www.w3c2.com.au/asla/p_eilit.htm>

InfoTech

Bibliography

This bibliography provides a list of recommended reading on topics related to the coverage of this book, including information technology in schools and school library media centers, specific applications of information technology, and management of libraries and school library media centers. Readers should also note the "References and Bibliography" at the end of each chapter. In addition, there is a list of relevant "Internet Sources" at the end of each chapter.

American Library Trustees Association, Association for Library Services to Children, and Public Library Association (1998). *Children and the Internet: Guidelines for developing public library policy.* Chicago: The Associations.

Anderson, Judith (1996). Internet use—A primary perspective. *Scan.* 15(4): November, 27–29.

Andronik, Catherine, ed. (1998). *School library management notebook.* New York: Linworth.

Barker, Roz (1996). The Internet and information skills—A primary school perspective. *Scan.* 15(1): February, 14–15.

Berger, Pam (1998). *Internet for active learners: Curriculum-based strategies for K-12.* (ICONnect Publication Series). Chicago: American Library Association.

Berry, David (1996). What lurks in cyberspace? *Orana.* 32(1): February, 4–17.

Breeding, Marshall (1997). Library software: A guide to the current commercial products: 1997 update. *Library Software Review.* 16(4): December, 261–76.

Bruce, David (1999). Filtering the Internet for young people: Products and problems. *Teacher Librarian*, 26(5): May-June, 13–17.

Bruce, Harry (1994). Media center automation: A watershed for the school library media specialist. *School Library Media Quarterly.* 22(4): Summer, 206–12.

Bryson, Jo (1997). *Managing information services: An integrated approach.* Aldershot, Hampshire: Gower.

Bucher, Katherine (1997). *Information technology for schools.* 2nd ed. Worthington, OH: Linworth.

Butterworth, Margaret, ed. (1997). *Information technology in schools: Implications for teacher librarians.* 3rd ed. Perth, Western Australia: Australian Library and Information Association, School Libraries Section.

Clyde, Laurel A. (1996). School libraries: At home on the World Wide Web? *Scan.* 15(4): November, 23–26.

———. (1996). The library as information provider: The home page. *The Electronic Library.* 14(6): December, 549–58.

Cohn, John M., Ann L. Kelsey, and Keith Michael Fiels (Revised and adapted by Graeme Muirhead) (1998). *Planning for library automation: A Practical handbook.* London: The Library Association.

Cooke, Alison (1998). *Finding quality on the Internet: A Guide for library and information professionals.* London: The Library Association.

Craver, Kathleen W. (1997). *Teaching electronic literacy: A concepts-based approach for school library media specialists.* Westport, CT: Greenwood Press.

Day, Teresa Thurman, Bruce Flanders, and Gregory Zuck, eds. (1994). *Automation for school libraries: How to do it from those who have done it.* Chicago: American Library Association.

Dillon, Ken (1996). Management of student access to the Internet: Issues and responsibilities. *Scan.* 15(4): November, 32–35.

Dillon, Ken, ed. (1997). *School library automation in Australia.* 2nd ed. Wagga Wagga, New South Wales: Centre for Information Studies.

Ensor, Pat, ed. (1996). *The cybrarian's manual.* Chicago: American Library Association.

Gallimore, Alec (1997). *Developing an IT strategy for your library.* London: The Library Association.

Hanson, Terry, and Joan Day (1998). *Managing the electronic library.* East Grinstead, West Sussex: Bowker Saur.

Harbour, Robin T. (1994). *Managing library automation*. An Aslib Know How Guide. London: Aslib.

Hay, Lyn, and James Henri, eds. (1999). *The Net effect: School library media centers and the Internet*. Lanham, MD: Scarecrow.

Herring, James (1999*). Exploiting the Internet as an information resource in schools*. London: The Library Association.

Herring, James E. (1998). *Exploiting the Internet as an information resource in schools*. London: The Library Association.

Junion-Metz, Gail (1996). *K–12 resources on the Internet: An instructional guide*. Berkeley, CA: Library Solutions Press.

Kuhlthau, Carol Collier, ed. (1996*). The virtual school library: Gateway to the information superhighway*. Englewood, CO: Libraries Unlimited.

Lancaster, F. W., and Beth Sandore (1997*). Technology and management in library and information services*. London: The Library Association.

Lighthall, Lynne (1996). The sixth Canadian school library automation survey. *Feliciter*. 42(5): May, 34–51.

Loertscher, David V. (1997). *Reinvent your school library in the age of technology: A handbook for principals and superintendents*. San Jose, CA: Hi Willow Research and Publishing.

Mabey, Mary (1997). School libraries in the UK: Towards the millennium. *Online and CDROM Review*. 21(6): 366–68.

Martinez, Michael E. (1994). Access to information technologies among school-age children: Implications for a democratic society. *JASIS: Journal of the American Society for Information Science*. 45(6): July, 395–400.

Mather, Becky R. (1997). *Creating a local area network in the school library media center*. Greenwood Professional Guides in School Librarianship. Westport, CT: Greenwood Press.

Mayo, Diane, and Sandra Nelson (1999). *Wired for the future: Developing your library technology plan*. Chicago: American Library Association.

Meghabghab, Dania Bilal (1997*). Automating media centers and small libraries: A microcomputer-based approach*. Englewood, CO: Libraries Unlimited.

Minkel, Walter, and Roxanne Hsu Feldman (1998). *Delivering Web reference services to young people*. Chicago: American Library Association.

Moore, Penny (1995). Information problem solving: A wider view of library skills. *Contemporary Educational Psychology*. 20: 1–31.

Muirhead, Graeme, ed. (1997). *Planning and implementing a successful system migration.* London: The Library Association.

Owens, Genevieve S. (1996). *Electronic resources, implications for collection management.* New York: The Haworth Press.

Paling, Stephen (1999). *A hardware and software primer for librarians: What your vendor forgot to tell you.* Lanham, MD: Scarecrow.

Pitts, Judy M. (Edited by Joy H. McGregor and Barbara Stripling) (1995). Mental models of information: The AASL/Highsmith Research Study Award. *School Library Media Quarterly.* 23(3): 177–84.

Poulter, Alan *et al.* (1999). *The library and information profession's guide to the World Wide Web.* London: The Library Association.

Rowley, Jennifer (1998). *The electronic library.* London: The Library Association.

Schneider, Karen (1997). *A practical guide to Internet filters.* Neal-Schuman Net-Guide Series. New York: Neal-Schuman.

Schrader, Alvin (1999). Internet censorship issues for teacher-librarians. *Teacher Librarian,* 26(5): May-June, 8–12.

Simpson, Carol (1998). The school librarian's role in the electronic age. ERIC Digest. Reprinted in *Emergency Librarian.* 25(5): May-June, 38–39.

Solomon, Paul (1994). Children, technology, and instruction: A case study of elementary school children using an online public access catalog (OPAC). *School Library Media Quarterly.* 23(1): Fall, 43–51.

Valauskas, Edward J., and Monica Ertel (1996). *The Internet for teachers and school library media specialists: Today's applications, tomorrow's prospects.* New York: Neal-Schuman.

Wilson, Elizabeth A. (1996). *The Internet road map for educators.* Arlington, VA: Educational Research Service.

Automated Library System Suppliers

The following list of suppliers of integrated library automation systems has been compiled from a variety of sources and verified where possible through communication with the suppliers. The inclusion of systems in this list should not be interpreted as a recommendation; no attempt has been made to evaluate the systems. Generally, further information is available on the Web sites of the suppliers; for this reason, the URL of the company has been included where known.

Alexandria
COMPanian Corporation
1831 Fort Union Boulevard
Salt Lake City, Utah 84121
USA
info@companioncorp.com
<http://www.companioncorp.com>

Alice, Annie, EMBLA, OASIS
Softlink Australia Pty. Limited
Softlink House
68 Commercial House
Shailer Park, Queensland 4128
Australia
info@softlink.com.au
<http://202.139.242.119/frmain.htm>

Softlink America Inc.
c/o Companion Corporation
1831 Fort Union Boulevard
Salt Lake City, Utah 84121
USA
info@companioncorp.com

Amlib Library Management System
Roger Armstrong
Suite 4, 18 Parry Street
Fremantle, WA 6150
Australia

Athena
Nichols Advanced Technologies
1100 Royal LePage Building
10130 — 103 Street
Edmonton, Alberta T4J 3N9
Canada
<http://www.nicholsinc.com/>

Best-Seller
Best-Seller Inc.
<http://www.bestseller.com/>

Book Mark Automated Library System
Dean Hodgson
PO Box 75
Ingle Farm, South Australia 5098
Australia
dhodgson@nexus.edu.au
<http://www.nexus.edu.au/bookmark/>

CHILD's Library System
Sunrise Software
805 Ormsby Close
Edmonton, Alberta T5T 4P3
Canada

Columbia Library System
CASPR Library Systems
sales@caspr.com
<http://www.caspr.com/home1.html>

Data Research Associates, Inc. (DRA)
1276 North Warson Road
PO Box 8495
St. Louis, Missouri 63132
USA
sales@DRA.COM
<http://www.dra.com/>

Eloquent Librarian
Eloquent Systems Inc.
25 – 1501 Lonsdale Street
North Vancouver, British Columbia V7M 2J2
Canada
info@eloquent-systems.com
<http://www.eloquentsystems.com/home.htm>

FILMS
Functional Solutions
Level 1, 434 St Kilda Road
Melbourne, Victoria 3004
Australia
info@librarysolutions.com.au
<http://www.librarysolutions.com.au>

Follett Circulation Plus/Catalog Plus
Follett Software Company
809 North Front Street
McHenry, Illinois 60050-5589
USA
info@fsc.follett.com
<http://www.fsc.follett.com/libraries/>

Gateway Library Management System
Gateway Software Corporation
PO Box 367
Fromberg, Montana 59029
USA
gateway@gscweb.com
<http://www.gscweb.com/>

Gaylord — Polaris, Galaxy
Gaylord Information Systems
<http://www.gaylord.com/>

Informativ
The Education Company
141-143 Burswood Road
Burswood, Western Australia 6100
Australia

Library 4 Universal
Kelowna Software (Braden Messenger)
#200 – 2000 Spall Road
Kelowna, British Columbia V1Y 9P6
Canada
sales@L4U.com
<http://www.L4U.com>

Library Pro
Chancery Software Limited
Suite 275
3001 Wayburne Drive
Burnaby, British Columbia V5G 4W1
Canada
info@chancery.com
<http://www.chancery.com/>

LibrarySoft
New Generation Technologies, Inc.
PO Box 340
Selma, Oregon 97538-0340
USA
quailrd@cdsnet.net
<http://www.librarysoft.com/>

Mac the Librarian
Richmond Software Corporation
500 Ashton Way Hall
Alpharetta, Georgia 30202
USA

MacSchool Library
Chancery Software Limited
<http://www.chancery.com/>

Mandarin
SIRS Inc.
PO Box 2348
Boca Raton, Florida 33427-2348
USA
mandarin@sirs.com
<http://www.sirs.com>

Master Library System
suzanne@booksys.com
<http://www.booksys.com/>

Metamarc
Microskil Pty Limited
461 Whitehorse Road
Balwyn, Victoria 3103
Australia
microskil@microskil.com.au
<http://www.microskil.com.
    au/~microskil/>

MicroCat
TKM Software Limited
839 18th Street, PO Box 1525
Brandon, Manitoba R7A 6N3
Canada
iman@access.tkm.mb.ca
<http://www.tkm.mb.ca/index.html>

Quinte Library System
Quinte Computer Services
141 William Street, PO Box 578
Belleville, Ontario K8N 5B2
Canada

Right On Programs —On-Line Catalog
    and Super Circulation Control
Right On Programs
755-M New York Avenue
Huntington, New York 11743
USA
CustomerService@RightOnPrograms.com
<http://www.rightonprograms.com/>

The School Library System (shareware)
Robert Pascas
rpascas@cam.org
<http://www.cam.org/~rpascas/>

SIRS Mandarin Inc.
PO Box 272348
Boca Raton, Florida 33427-2728
USA
custserve@sirs.com
<http://www.sirs.com/>

SIRSI — Unicorn
Sirsi Corporation
101 Washington Street SE
Huntsville, Alabama 35801-4827
USA
info@sirsi.com
<http://www.sirsi.com/>

Surpass Library Automation
Precision Computer Service, Inc.
519B Oothcalooga Street
Calhoun, Georgia 30701
USA
info@precisionservice.com
<http://www.precisionservice.com/>

VTLS
VTLS Inc.
1701 Kraft Drive
Blackburg, Virginia 24060
USA
<http://www.vtls.com/>

Winnebago
Winnebago Software Company
457 East South Street, PO Box 430
Caledonia, Minnesota 55921
USA
<http:www.winnebago.com>

Useful Print and Online Magazines

The following list of print and electronic journals, newsletters and magazines has been compiled from a variety of sources, and verified through searches of Ulrichs' International Periodicals Directory database on Dialog and through the relevant home pages on the World Wide Web. The list reflects the magazines and other serials that have been cited as sources of information in the various chapters of this book. Generally. Further information is available on the Web sites of the publishers; for this reason, the URL of the publisher or of the magazine itself has been included where known.

PRINT MAGAZINES

Access
Australian School Library Association
PO Box 450
Belconnen, Australian Capital Territory 2616
Australia

Boardwatch
13949 Colfax Avenue, Suite 250
Golden, Colorado 80401
USA
<http://boardwatch.inter.com/>

Byte
McGraw-Hill Inc.
One Phoenix Mill Lane
Peterborough, New Hampshire 03458
USA
<http://www.byte.com/>

Classroom Connect
1866 Colonial Village Lane
Lancaster, Pennsylvania 17601-6704
USA
<http://www.classroom.net/>

CMC (Computers in the Media Center) News
c/o Jim Deacon, Editor
515 Oak Street North
Cannon Falls, Minnesota 55009
USA

Computer Games
63 Millet Street
Richmond, Vermont 05477
USA
<http://www.cdmag.com/>

Computer Gaming World
ZD Inc.
One Park Avenue
New York, New York 10016
USA

Computers in Libraries
Information Today Inc.
143 Old Marlton Pike
Medford, New Jersey 08055-8750
<http://www.infotoday.com/>

Econtent (formerly Database)
Online Inc.
213 Danbury Road
Wilton, Connecticut 06897-4007
<http://www.ecmag.net/database/>

Electronic Gaming Monthly
ZD Inc.
PO Box 3338
Oak Brook, Illinois 60522-3338
USA

Electronic Learning
Scholastic Inc.
555 Broadway
New York, New York 10012
USA
<http://www.scholastic.com/>

The Electronic Library
Learned Information Inc.
Woodside
Hinksey Hill
Oxford OX1 5BE
England
<http://www.learned.co.uk/>

Feliciter
Canadian Library Association
200 Elgin Street, Suite 602
Ottawa, Ontario K2P 1L5
Canada
<http://www.cla.amlibs.ca/felcont.htm>

Information Searcher
Datasearch Group Inc.
14 Hadden Road
Scarsdale, New York 10583
USA

Information World Review
Learned Information Ltd.
Woodside
Hinksey Hill
Oxford OX1 5BE
England
<http://www.iwr.co.uk/>

Internet Magazine
Angel House
338 - 346 Goswell Road
London EC1V 7QP
England
<http://www.internet-magazine.com/>

Internet World
Mecklermedia Corporation
20 Ketchum Street
Westport, Connecticut 06880
USA
<http://www.iworld.com/>

Library HiTech
MCB University Press
60/62 Toller Lane
Bradford, West Yorkshire
England BD8 9B4
<http:/www.lib.msu.edu/hi-tech/>

MacWorld
301 Howard Street
San Francisco, California 94105
USA
<http://macworld.zdnet.com/>

.net
Future Publishing Ltd.
30 Monmouth Street
Bath BA1 2BW
England
<http://www.netmag.co.uk/>

Online
Online Inc.
303 Holly Creek Drive
Anderson, South Carolina 29621
USA
<http://www.onlineinc.com/onlinemag/>

Online Access
Chicago Fine Print
900 North Franklin, Suite 310
Chicago, Illinois 60610
USA

PC World
PC World Communications
PO Box 55029
Boulder, Colorado 80322-5029
USA
<http://www.pcworld.com/>

Scan
New South Wales Department of
    Education
Curriculum Support Directorate
Private Bag 3
Ryde, New South Wales 2112
Australia

School Libraries in Canada
Canadian School Library Association
Canadian Library Association
200 Elgin Street, Suite 602
Ottawa, Ontario K2P 1L5
Canada

School Library Journal
PO Box 57559
Boulder, Colorado 80321-9690
USA
<http://www.bookwire.com/slj>

Teacher Librarian (formerly
    Emergency Librarian)
Box 34069, Department 284
Seattle, Washington 98124-1069
USA
<http://www.rockland.com/>

VINE
<http://bubl.ac.uk/journals/lis/oz/vine/>

Windows Magazine
PO Box 420215
Palm Coast, Florida 32142
USA
<http://www.winmag.com/>

Yahoo! Internet Life
PO Box 53380
Boulder, Colorado 80332-3380
USA
<http://www.yil.com/>

ELECTRONIC MAGAZINES

D-lib
    <http://mirrored.ukoln.ac.uk/
        lis-journals/dlib/dlib/>

Edupage
    <http://www.educom.edu/web/pubs/>

Internet Trend Watch for Libraries
    <http://www.leonline.com/itw/>

**The Public-Access Computer
Systems Review**
    <http://info.lib.uh.edu/pacsrev.html>

School Library Media Research
    <http://www.ala.org/aasl/SLMR/
        index.html/>

The Scout Report
    <http://scout.cs.wisc.edu/scout/>

Index